IMAGES
of Rail

NEW JERSEY CENTRAL'S BLUE COMET

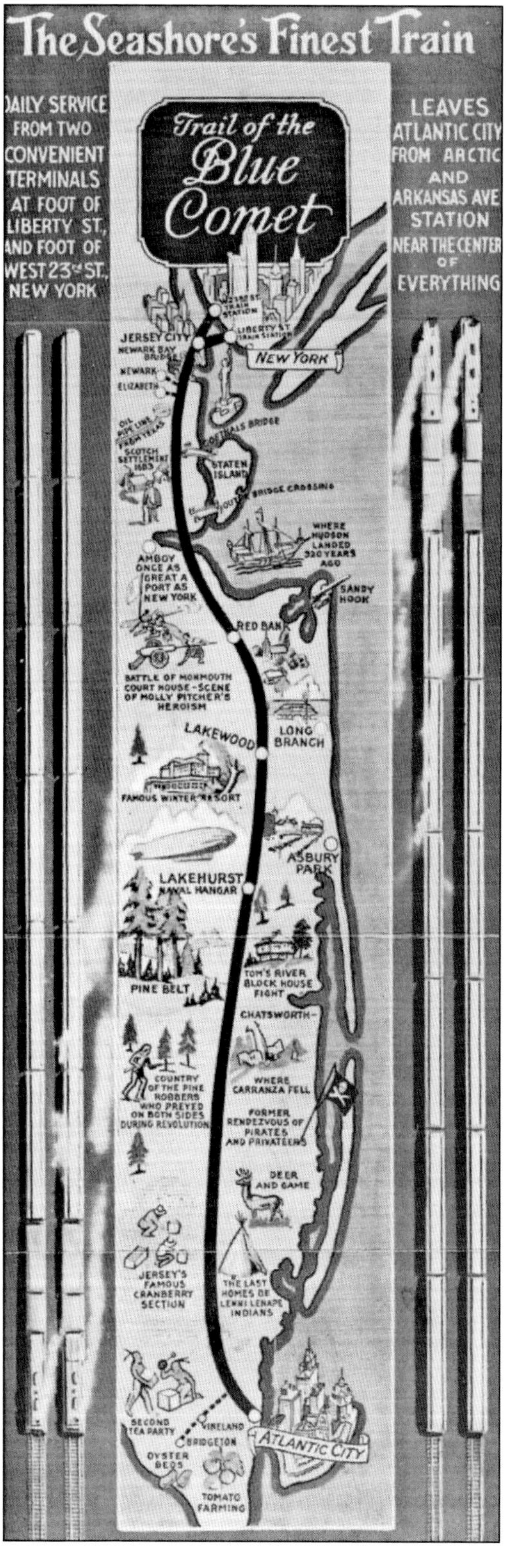

The Central Railroad Company of New Jersey, its corporate title, was known by several names throughout its history including Jersey Central Lines, Jersey Central Railroad, New Jersey Central, CNJ, and CRR of NJ. During the life of the Blue Comet, the company was referred to as the New Jersey Central (NJC), which will be used in this book. A notable exception is the nomenclature used by Lionel and other model train manufacturers for their Blue Comet train sets, which is, of course, within their own purview. This graphic representation of the route of the Blue Comet and historical aspects along the route originally appeared in an NJC brochure. Some points of interest are the Lakehurst Naval Air Station; Sandy Ridge, where Mexico's version of Charles Lindbergh, Emilio Carranza, was killed in an air crash; the cranberry bogs of the pinelands; the last habitat of the Lenni-Lenape Indians; and a favorite gathering place for pirates along New Jersey's southern coast. (Courtesy Joel Rosenbaum and Tom Gallo.)

On the Cover: NJC shop crews proudly pose in front of the innovation of speed and color they have just completed at the Elizabethport, New Jersey, shops. The four NJC officials directly responsible for the creation of the Blue Comet were Roy B. White, president of the Central Railroad; Howard E. Simpson, assistant general passenger agent; Frank H. Becherer, car superintendent; and John Lobano, creator of the advertising program. (Courtesy Joel Rosenbaum and Tom Gallo.)

IMAGES
of Rail

NEW JERSEY CENTRAL'S BLUE COMET

Anthony Puzzilla
Introduction by Mitchell Dakelman

ARCADIA
PUBLISHING

ISBN 978-1-4671-2654-0

Published by Arcadia Publishing
Charleston, South Carolina

Printed in the United States of America

Library of Congress Control Number: 2017931437

For all general information, please contact Arcadia Publishing:
Telephone 843-853-2070
Fax 843-853-0044
E-mail sales@arcadiapublishing.com
For customer service and orders:
Toll-Free 1-888-313-2665

Visit us on the Internet at www.arcadiapublishing.com

This book is dedicated to the late Joel Rosenbaum and Tom Gallo.
Their tireless help and assistance in the preparation
and review of this book made it all possible.

Contents

Acknowledgments

This book was inspired by my viewing of the documentary *De Luxe: The Tale of the Blue Comet* by Robert A. Emmons, who also provided me with his production images. I would like to thank Mitch Dakelman, first vice president and historian with the Jersey Central Railway Historical Society, who was kind enough to help me get started on this project, and wrote the introduction. Also, my sincere thanks go to Joel Rosenbaum and Tom Gallo for the use of the many photographs and graphics from their personal collections.

INTRODUCTION

In June 2015, I received a letter from Anthony Puzzilla of Maryland in regards to research material and photographs pertaining to the Blue Comet, a passenger train that was operated by the New Jersey Central Railroad between 1929 and 1941. Having just completed a book about the Western Maryland Railway, Tony was looking for a new project. As it turned out, I had some pictures of the locomotives and train to share, including several from the archives of the North Jersey Chapter, National Railway Historical Society (NRHS), of which I am the photograph curator.

During the course of the following months, Tony and I corresponded via emails and several phone calls. I gave him the contact information of Joel Rosenbaum and Tom Gallo, both Central Railroad of New Jersey historians and authors, including articles written for *Jersey Central News*, the monthly publication of the Jersey Central Railway Historical Society, also a chapter of the NRHS. Tony also asked me to write the book's introduction, for which I was honored, and to review his manuscript as portions were completed.

During Memorial Day weekend in 2016, Tony and his son visited New Jersey to search for further information about the train and to visit several sites where the train operated and where some vintage Blue Comet equipment is preserved. Tony's last stop in New Jersey was my home in Highland Park to meet me and to look through additional pictures and photograph some of my models of the train.

The Blue Comet may be remembered by many as a model train manufactured by the Lionel corporation during the 1930s. Both Standard and O-Gauge models from these initial runs are highly prized today. A model Blue Comet was also featured on an episode of HBO's *The Sopranos*.

The Blue Comet was conceived by railroad management during the late 1920s to offer a special experience for passengers traveling from New York, and intermediate stops, to Atlantic City, "America's Favorite Playground," and back. While a ferry ride was required for passengers from New York City to the railroad's Victorian-style passenger station at tidewater in Jersey City, the train ran entirely on New Jersey rails, passing over the open marshes and through the Pine Barrens of Southern New Jersey.

The train was painted in a two-tone blue-and-cream scheme to replicate the sea, sky, and sand seen along the New Jersey Shore south of Sandy Hook.

The Blue Comet played a very important role in the history of New Jersey, as well as in its rail heritage. The era in which the Blue Comet was born was characterized by an America striving for greatness, progress, and modernization, only to be struck down by the crippling and prolonged Depression. On September 27, 1941, the Blue Comet ended its brief reign after being an initial smashing success. Its demise was caused by the reemergence of prosperity and innovations in passenger travel characterized by modern highways and roads and efficient automobiles. Its untimely demise left only the cherished memories of those who rode it, worked on it, or preserved it in pictures, or those who were fortunate enough to own one of the prized Lionel train sets.

So now, let us turn the clock back and relive the era of the Blue Comet!

—Mitchell E. Dakelman
Historian, Jersey Central Railway Historical Society
July 15, 2016

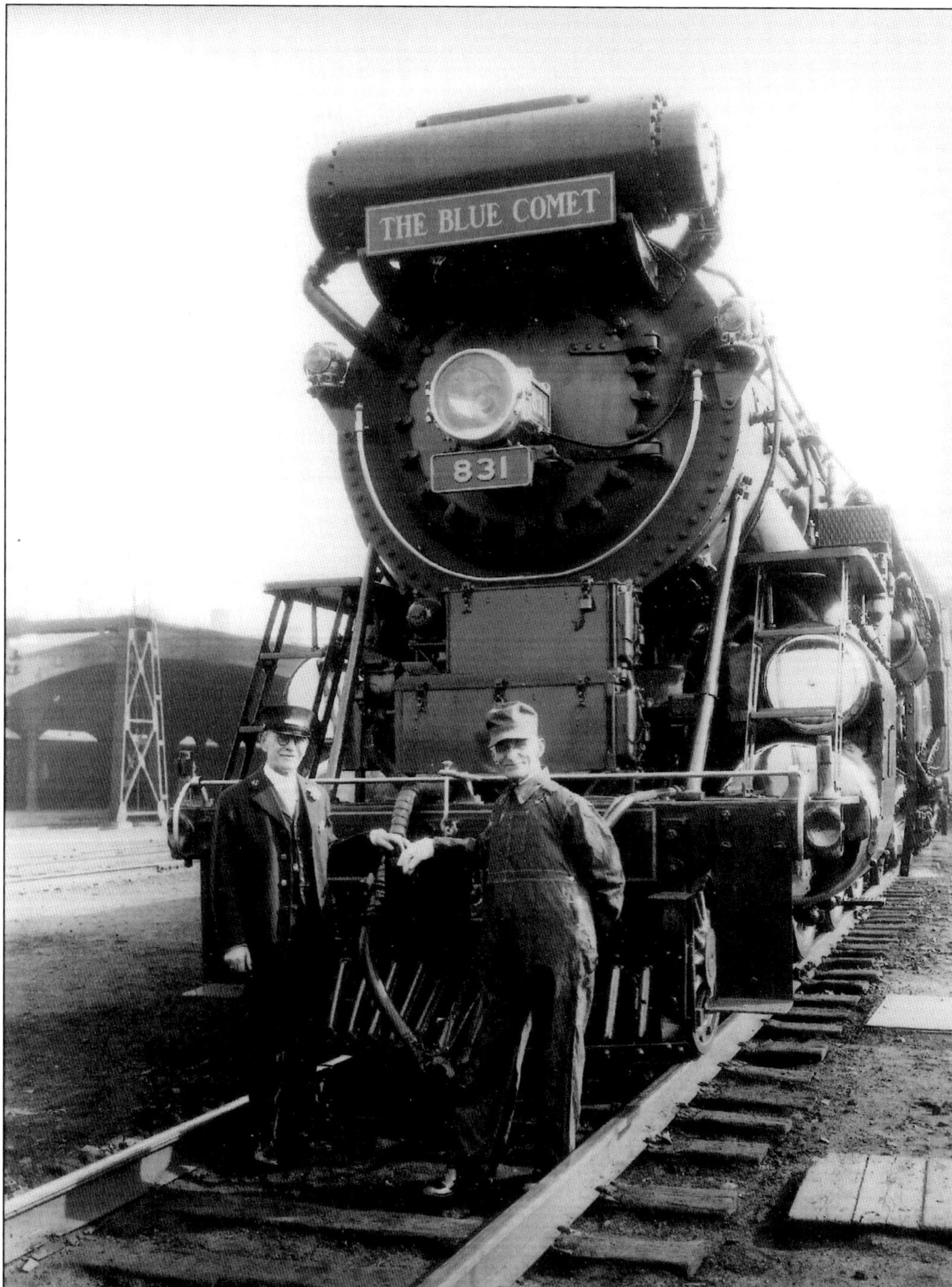

NJC engineer John V. Wait and conductor Joseph T. Ross pose for a publicity photo with the Blue Comet G-3 Pacific No. 831 at the Jersey City Terminal. Engineer Wait and conductor Ross were chosen to make the first revenue run on February 21, 1929. At the time of this photograph, Wait and Ross had 53 and 51 years of NJC service, respectively. (Courtesy Joel Rosenbaum and Tom Gallo.)

One

The Lure of Atlantic City, and Rail Service Prior to 1929

The development of Atlantic City as a major tourist attraction can be attributed to commencement of service to that city in 1854 by the Camden & Atlantic Railroad. By 1874, almost 500,000 passengers a year were coming to Atlantic City by rail. The community offered a wide range of attractions for all types and classes of people. This included its luxurious hotels and famous boardwalk and piers, which provided dance bands, movies, Hollywood stars, and water and circus acts. Of course, Atlantic City was also well known for its sandy beaches, which attracted families trying to escape the hot summers in the cities. Bringing vacationers, socialites, businessmen, and day-trippers to Atlantic City from New York City, Philadelphia, and suburban areas was a very lucrative endeavor for the railroads. The Pennsylvania Railroad provided a direct rail/ferry link from New York City to the West Jersey & Seashore Railroad (WJ&S) in Camden, New Jersey, through its Philadelphia Broad Street Station and Market Street Ferry Terminal. Beginning in 1891, the Pennsylvania Railroad provided express rail service to Atlantic City from New York City on its so-called "Nellie Bly" trains. The Pennsylvania Railroad also operated an all-parlor extra-fare train, the Atlantic City Limited, from New York's Pennsylvania Station to Atlantic City on Friday nights. On Sundays, the all-parlor extra-fare New York Limited departed Atlantic City for Manhattan. Two other railroads also vied for this lucrative tourist market. They were the Atlantic City Railroad (ACRR), which was owned by the Reading Railroad, and the WJ&S, which was owned by the Pennsylvania Railroad. Competition was extremely keen between these two railroads, reaching its peak in the late 1920s. Another railroad that provided service from its terminal in Jersey City was the NJC, using two named trains, the Atlantic City Express and the Playground Special.

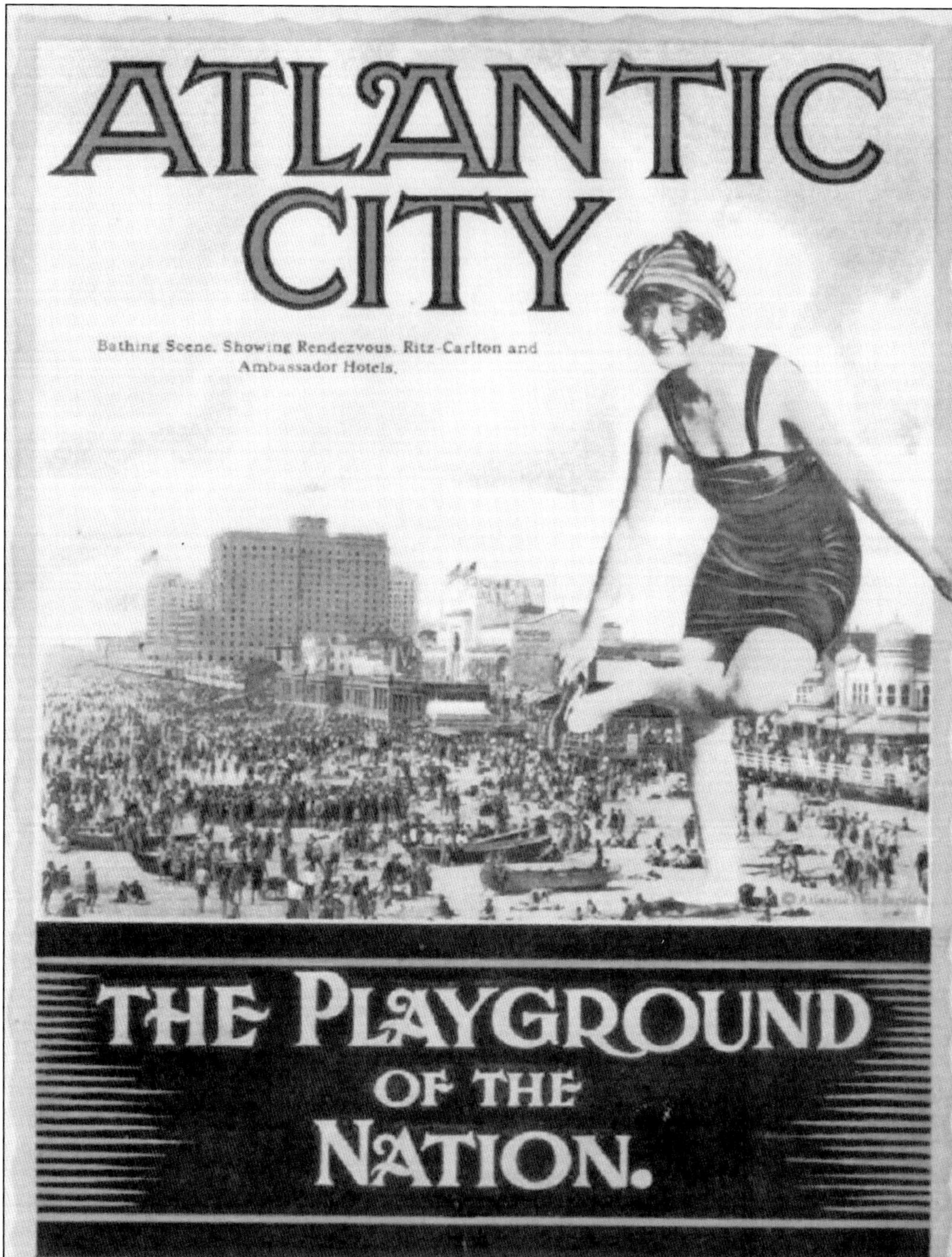

Atlantic City's heyday, or golden age, was the Roaring Twenties, when tourism was at its peak. This decade of Prohibition brought all sorts of shows, stunts, big bands, and pageants to the piers and boardwalk in Atlantic City. The city soon nicknamed itself America's Favorite Playground. (Author's collection.)

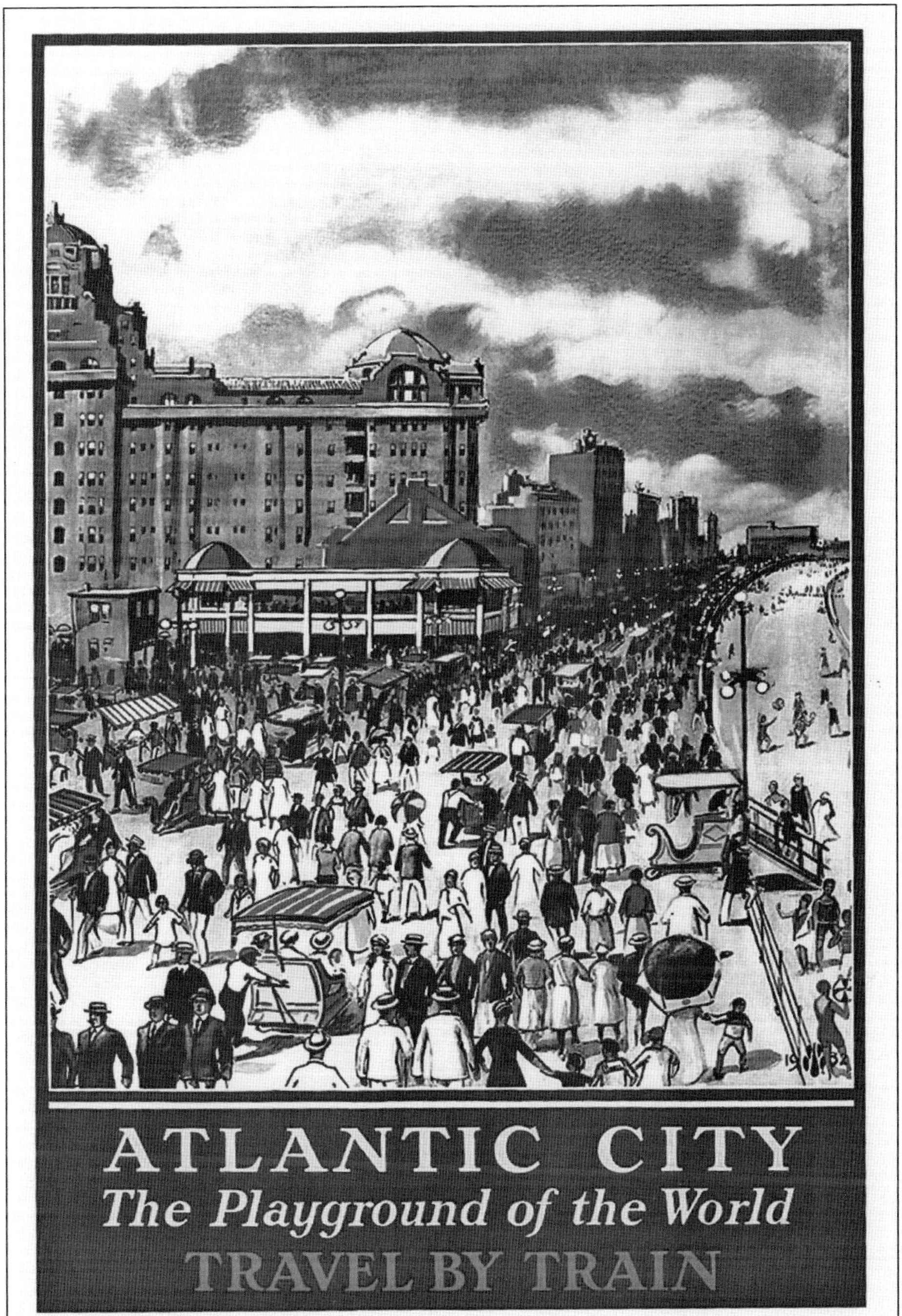

Prohibition, which lasted until 1933, was largely unenforced in Atlantic City, which further increased the already booming popularity of the city. Illegal alcohol was smuggled in and served in the backrooms of nightclubs and restaurants, where gambling was commonplace. With this influx of revenue, the city was easily able to attract notable headliners from around the world, and thus, by the end of Prohibition, the city had dubbed itself the "World's Playground." (Courtesy Library of Congress.)

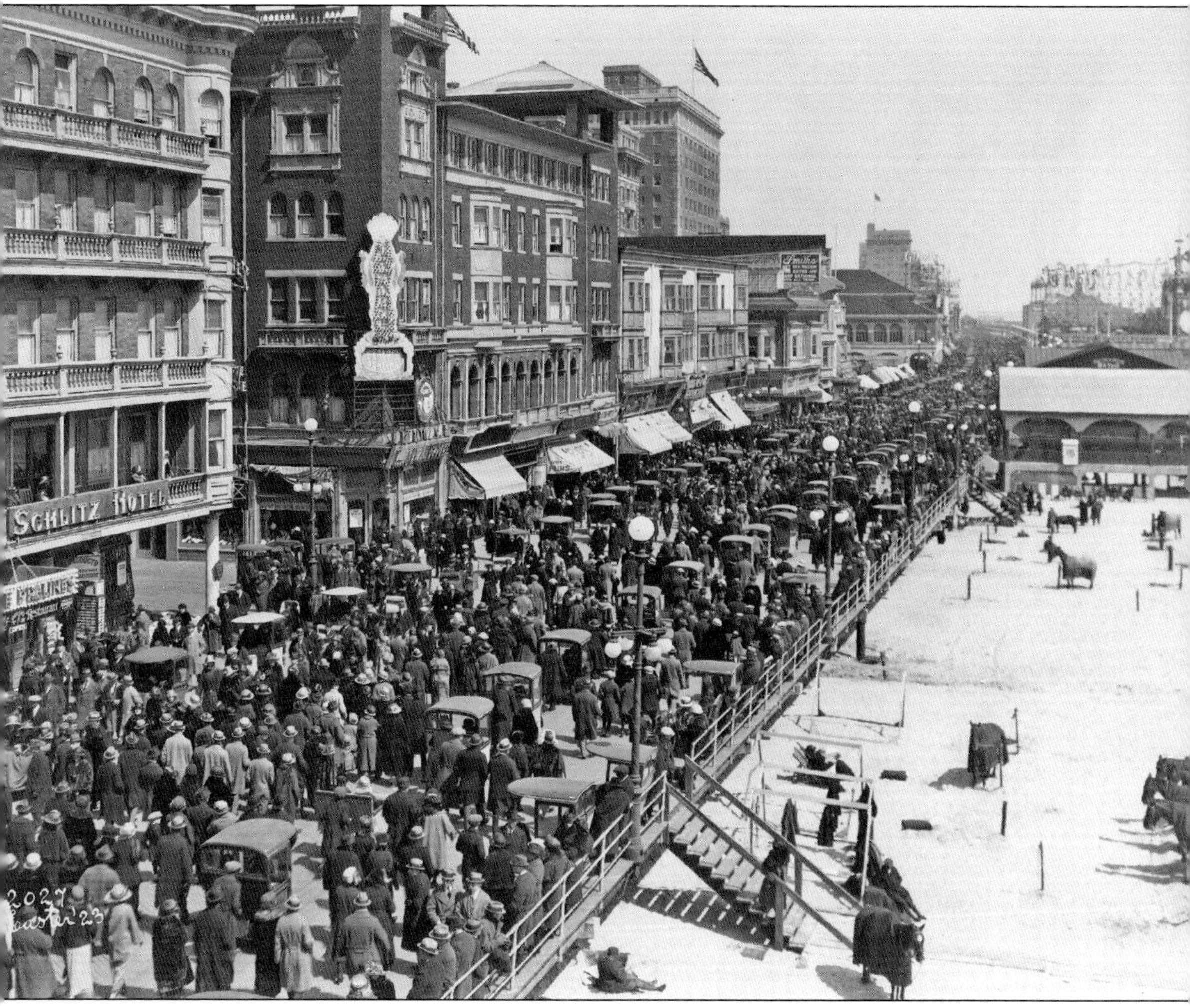

This photograph, taken from the Central Pier, shows throngs of visitors strolling on the Atlantic City Boardwalk on Easter Sunday in April 1923. Starting in 1876, the tradition of the annual Easter parade began. Hundreds of thousands of people packed the boardwalk every Easter Sunday to show off the latest fashions, especially hats. (Courtesy Robert A. Emmons.)

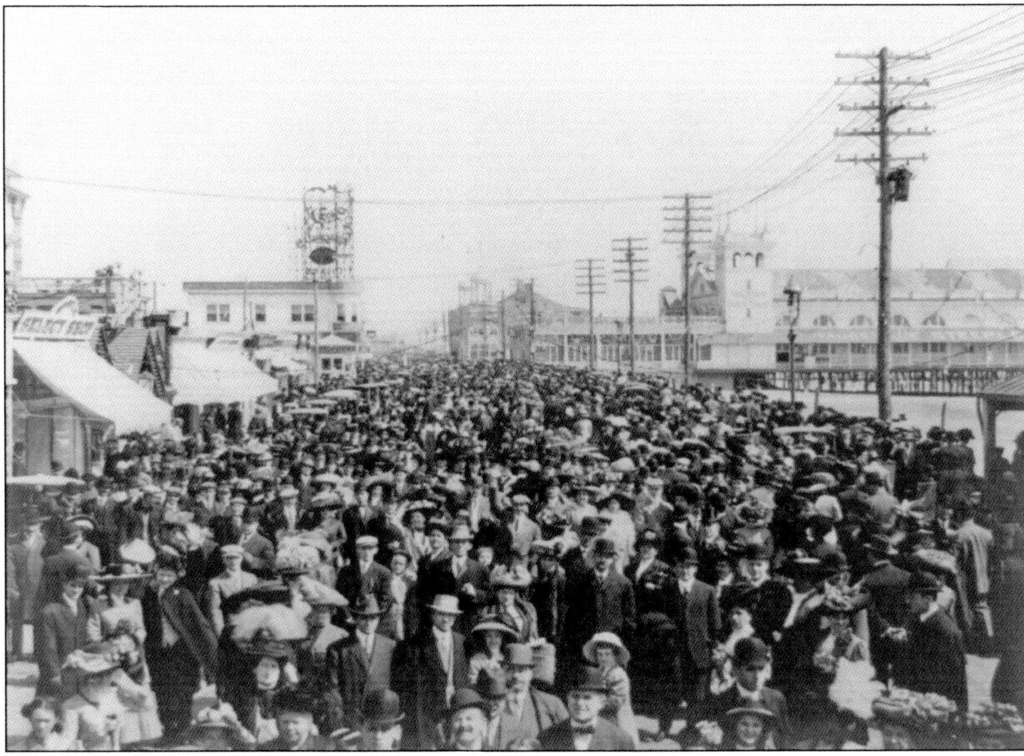

The original Atlantic City Boardwalk was built in 1870 along a portion of the beach in an effort to help hotel owners keep sand out of their lobbies. The historical length of the boardwalk was about seven miles. This 1910 photograph shows crowds of people strolling on the boardwalk amidst shops and stores. Note Central Pier on the right. (Courtesy Library of Congress.)

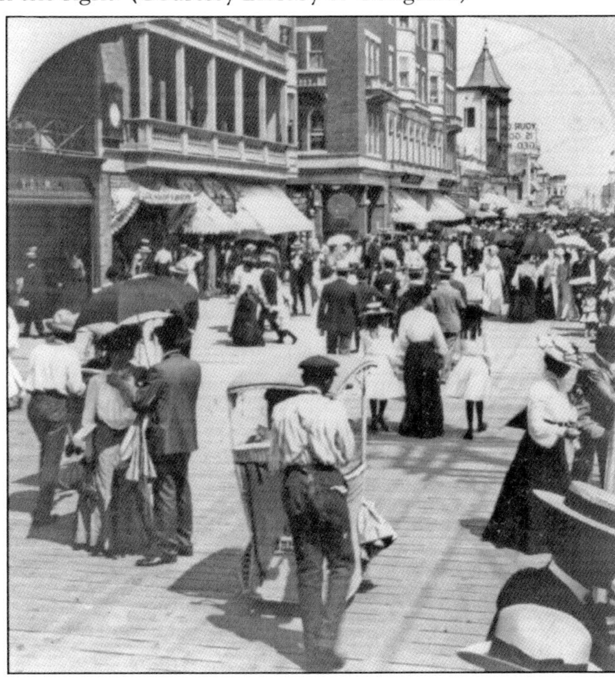

The rolling chair was developed by William Hayday in the late 1880s. While powered carts appeared in the 1960s, the original and most common were made of wicker. The rolling chair became a big hit on the boardwalk. (Courtesy Library of Congress.)

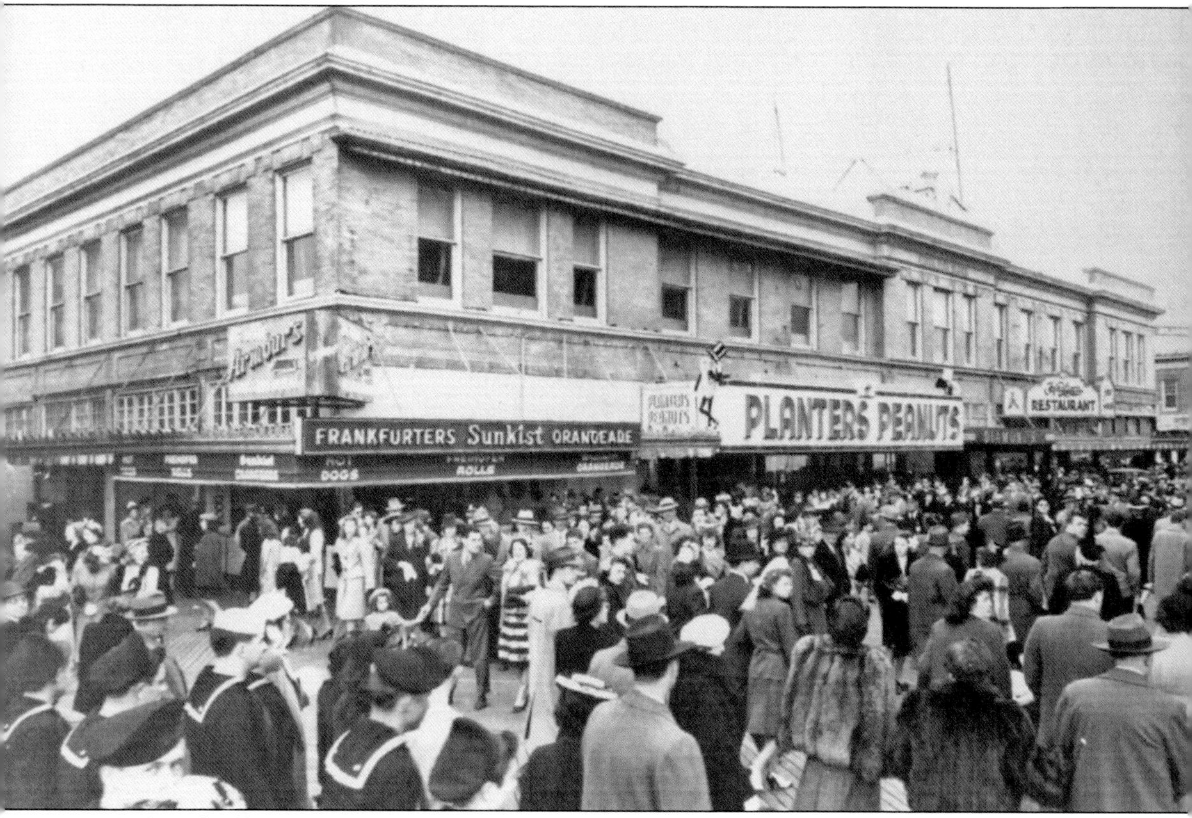

The boardwalk evolved into a major thoroughfare for commerce. This photograph shows the famed Planter's Peanuts store, which opened for business on the boardwalk in 1930, across from the Steel Pier. Mr. Peanut is seen raising his top hat on the store's sign. (Courtesy Robert A. Emmons.)

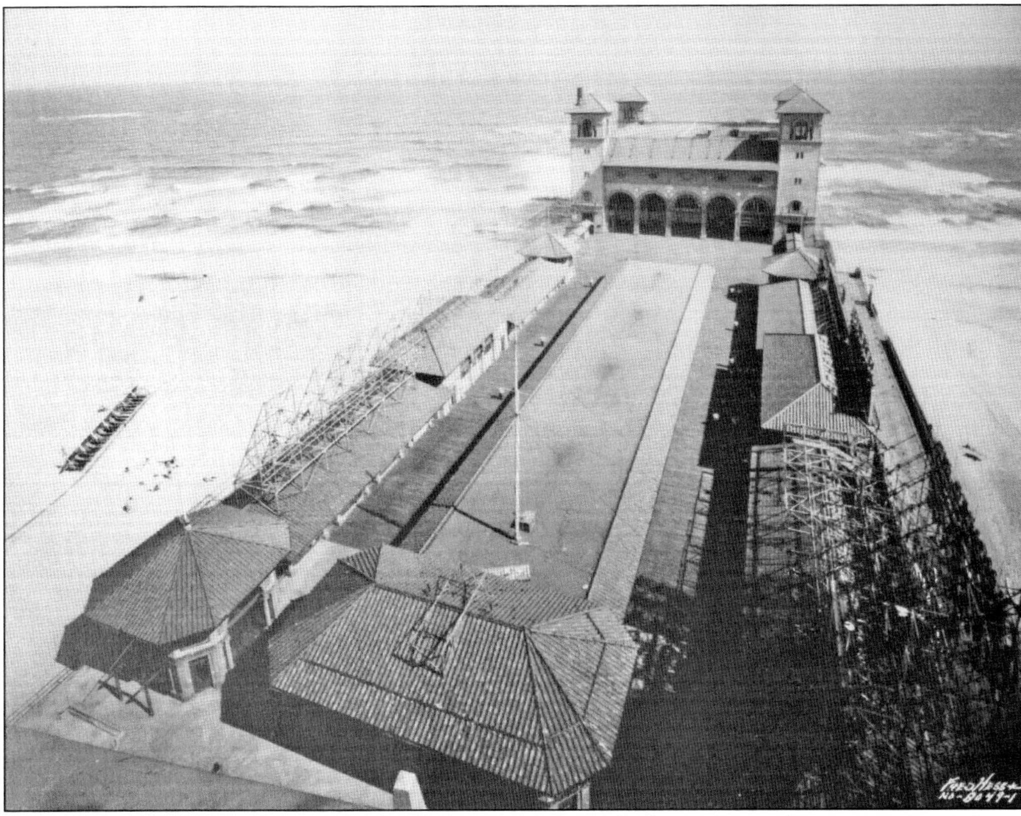

The 700-foot-long Garden Pier was built in 1913 at the end of New Jersey Avenue on the Atlantic City Boardwalk. The Spanish Renaissance architecture and the beautifully landscaped gardens gave it a formal appearance that attracted an upscale crowd and gave the pier its name. (Courtesy Robert A. Emmons.)

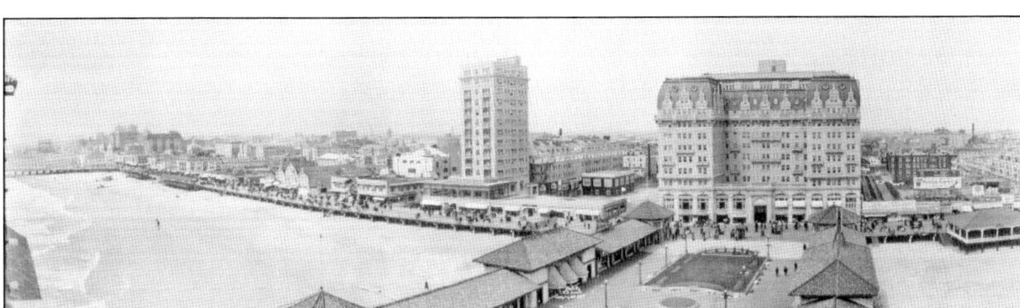

This ocean-side view of the Garden Pier was photographed in 1917. It shows the front of the Breakers Hotel, which was built the previous year. The hotel overlooked the boardwalk and the beach and was situated right across from the Garden Pier. The 450-room hotel catered to mainly Jewish clientele and was known as the "Aristocrat of Kosher hotels." (Courtesy Library of Congress.)

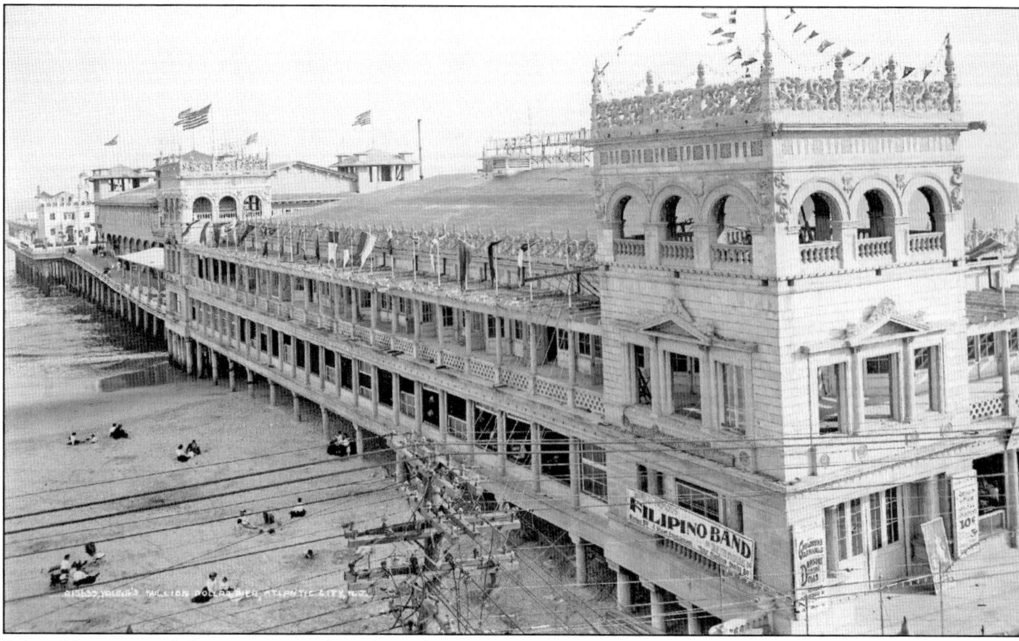

John Young and Stewart McShea bought the Applegate Pier in 1891 and named it Young and McShea's Pier. It was later called the "Ocean Pier." It was the first successful amusement pier in Atlantic City. The Ocean Pier burned down in 1902 and was replaced by a bigger and better pier that opened in 1910 named the Million Dollar Pier. This included the world's largest ballroom, named the Hippodrome, and a huge exhibit hall. The pier hosted amusement rides, movies, conventions, and exhibits of every description. (Courtesy Library of Congress.)

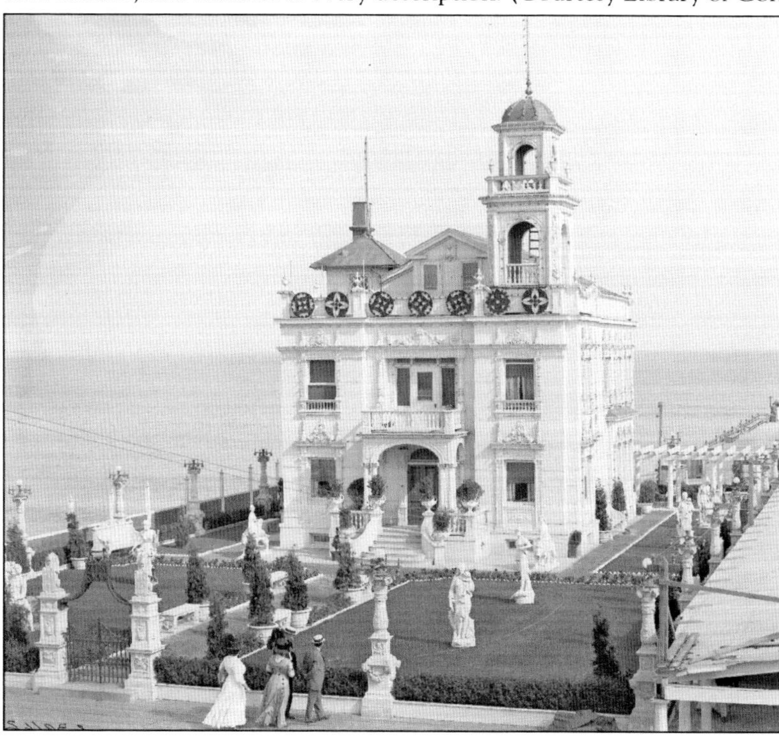

"Captain" John Young built his home out near the end of the Million Dollar Pier at the address 1 Atlantic Ocean. The home was made from marble, and the garden included statutes imported from Florence, Italy. Young loved to fish, and often fished off his pier with his friend Thomas Edison, who designed the lighting for his house and garden. (Courtesy Library of Congress.)

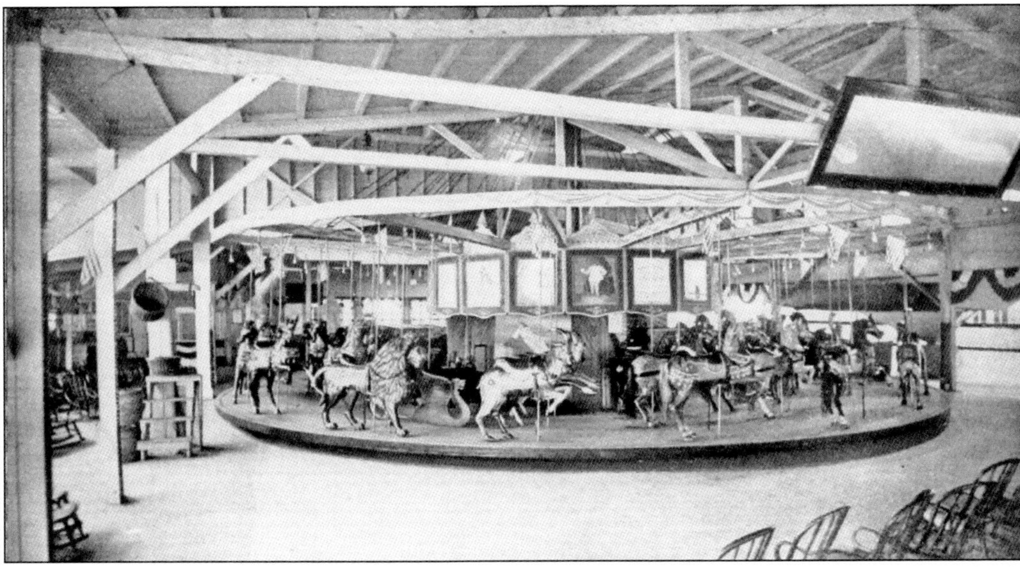

Young and McShea's merry-go-round was built by master German craftsman Gustav Dentzel. The beautiful hand-carved carousel operated on John Young's Million Dollar Pier for many years. The aggressive Young wanted to operate the carousel seven days a week, but his colleague McShea was a devout Christian. They came to a compromise, and the carousel organ played spiritual songs for the devout audience on Sundays while the carousel itself took a day off. This photograph of the carousel was taken in 1896. (Courtesy Library of Congress.)

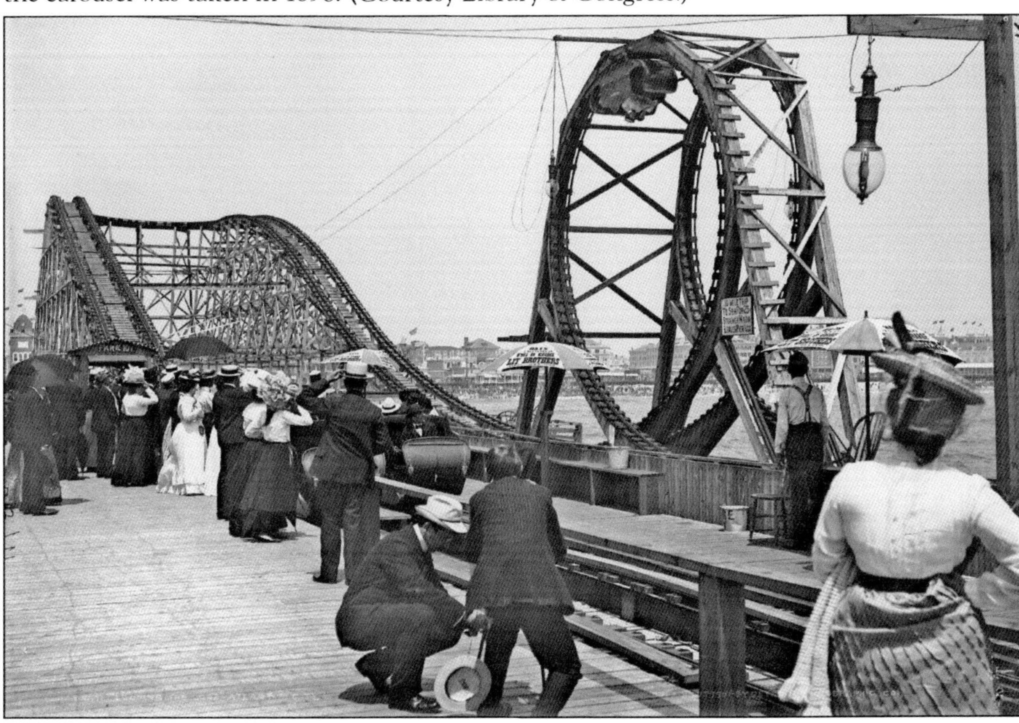

The Loop-the-Loop, also known as the Flip-Flap Railway, was a dual-tracked steel roller coaster that operated on John Young's Million Dollar Pier from 1901 until 1912. It was one of the earliest looping roller coasters in the United States. This photograph was taken in 1901. (Courtesy Library of Congress.)

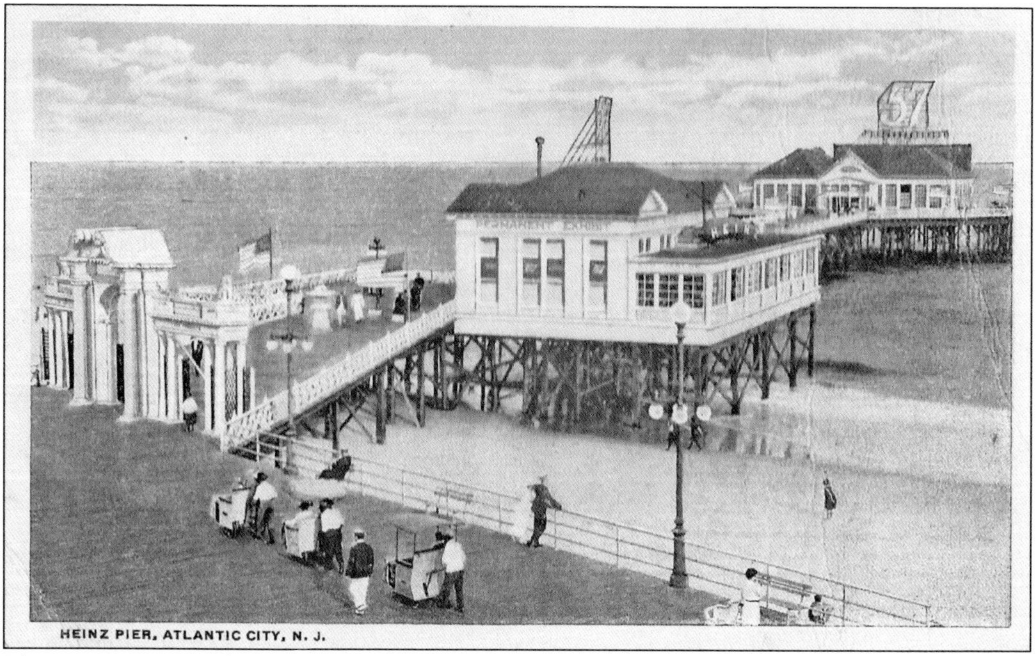

The Iron Pier opened in 1896 on Rhode Island Avenue and Boardwalk. Food manufacturer H.J. Heinz purchased the Iron Pier in 1898 and turned it into the Heinz Pier, calling it the "Crystal Palace by the Seas." Visitors to the Heinz Pier got to taste Heinz products, especially pickles, and were given a free Heinz pickle pin as a souvenir of their visit. (Author's collection.)

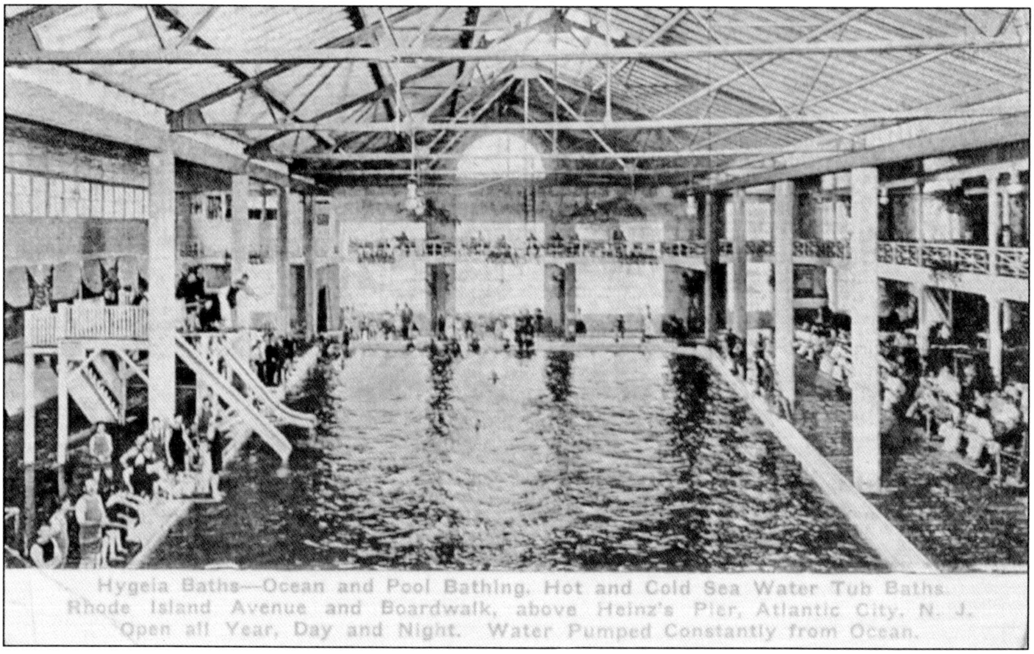

Situated on the Heinz Pier was the Hygeia Baths, which provided indoor all-weather ocean and pool bathing using both hot and cold seawater. It was open for business all year, day and night. Water was constantly pumped into the pool and baths from the ocean. (Author's collection.)

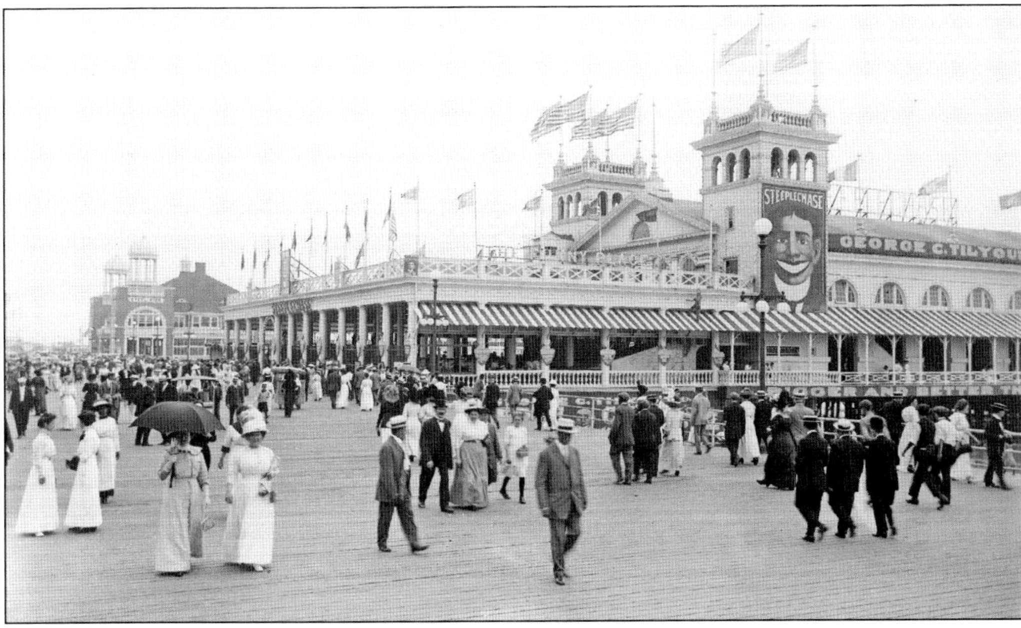

The Steeplechase Pier was originally called the Auditorium Pier. It was located between Pennsylvania and North Caroline Avenues, just south of the Steel Pier. In 1908, George C. Tilyou purchased the pier and renamed it the Steeplechase Pier. It quickly became known as "the Funny Place." Customers could enter through the mouth of a clown before getting dumped into a revolving barrel. An alternate entrance subjected female patrons to a skirt-lifting blast of air from below. The pier also rented out clown costumes to wear on rides like the Whip and Whirlpool. (Courtesy Library of Congress.)

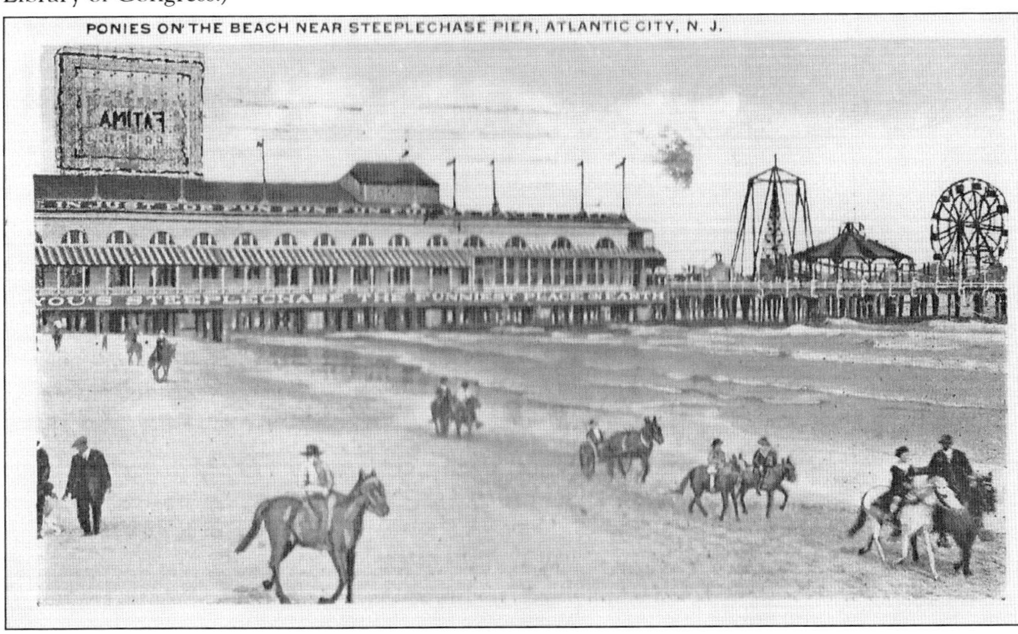

The Steeplechase Pier was complete with carousels, pony track, and Ferris wheels. It also featured a roller coaster and numerous other fun and exciting rides for children of all ages. John Philip Sousa and his 86-piece orchestra often played in the pier's auditorium. (Author's collection.)

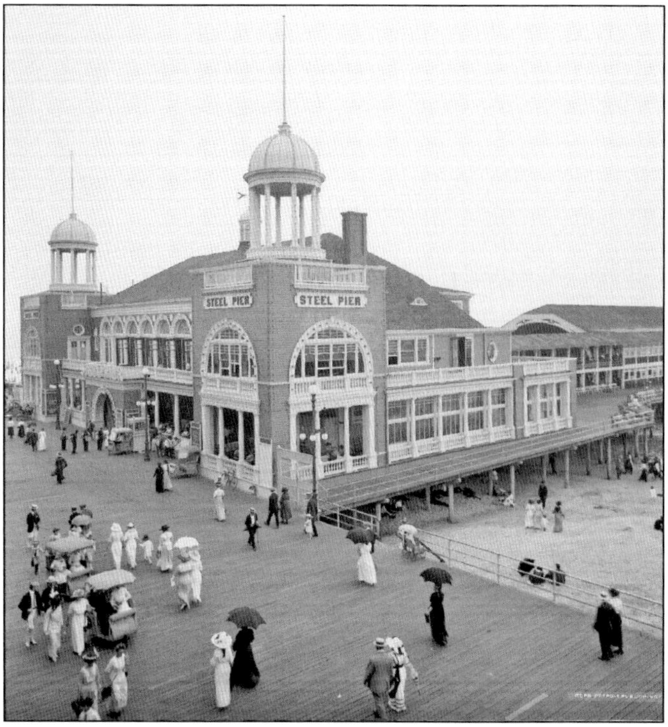

The Steel Pier opened in 1898 and became "the Showpiece of the Nation." This photograph was taken around 1915 from the boardwalk. The Steel Pier was the first amusement pier in Atlantic City to be built on iron pilings and steel girders. It was 1,760 feet long and extended 1,000 feet into the ocean. In 1925, businessman Frank Gravatt bought the pier and began its transformation into an entertainment and exhibition complex. It soon had an immense auditorium, theater, assembly hall, and a number of pavilions. The pier hosted dance bands, three movie theaters, exhibits, operas, children's shows, a water circus, stunts, and numerous other attractions. (Courtesy Library of Congress.)

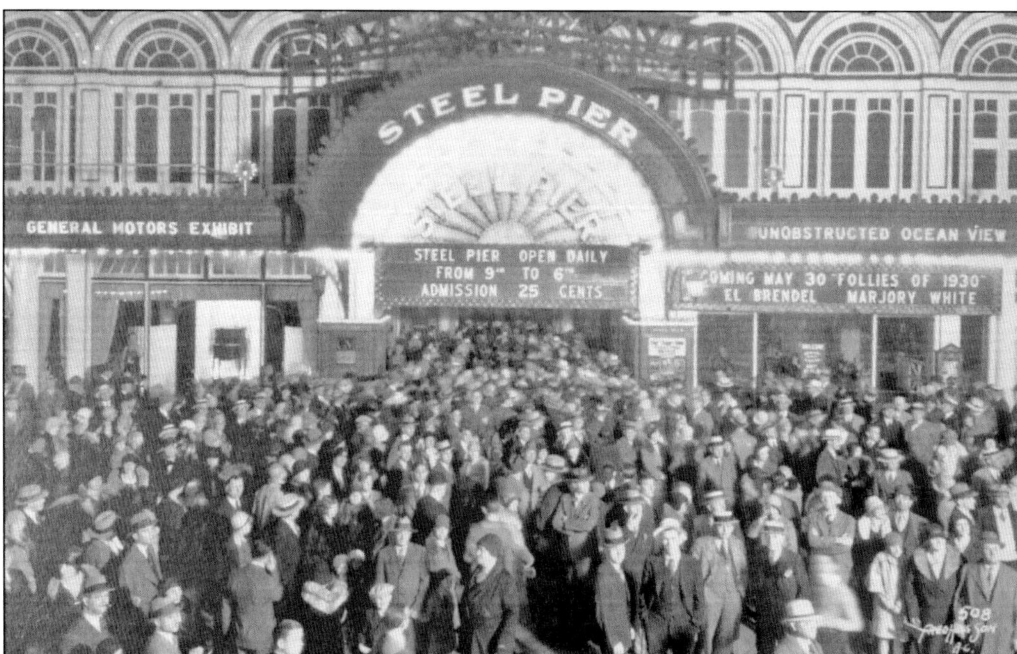

The reputation of the Steel Pier attracted hordes of visitors hoping for admittance, as this 1930 picture attests. For a quarter, these folks could see movies at either the Casino Hall Theatre (front boardwalk building), the Music Hall Theatre (center of pier), or the Ocean Hall Theater (behind Music Hall). In the early 1920s, a large exhibit hall was built and used by General Motors to present its shiny new car models to the public. (Courtesy Robert A. Emmons.)

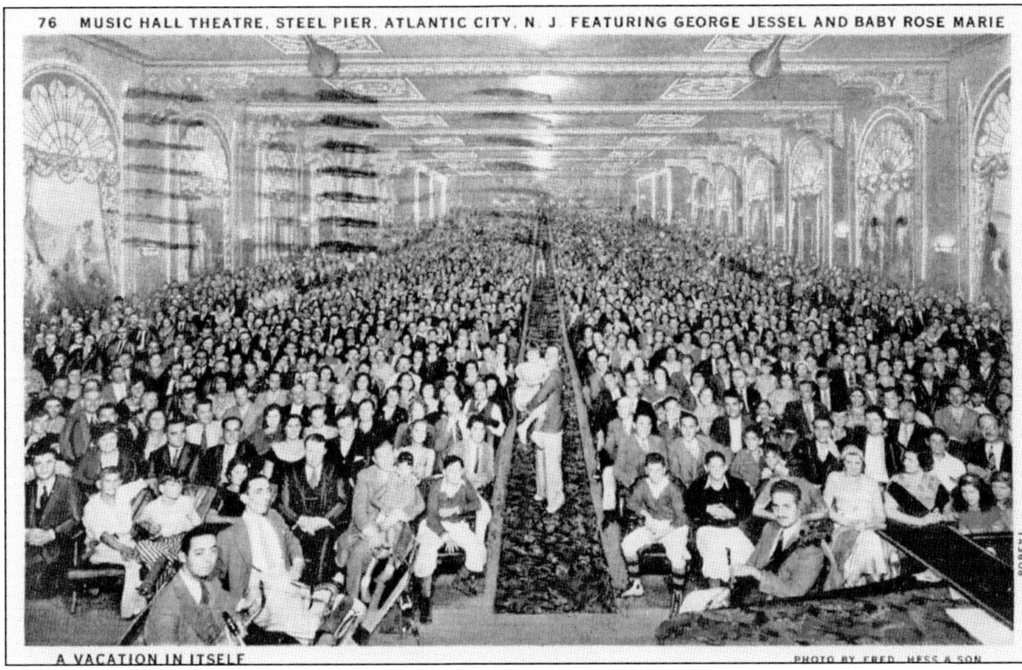

The Music Hall Theatre was in the middle of the Steel Pier and featured many notable entertainers over the years. For instance, in 1929, John Philip Sousa returned to the Music Hall to lead four concerts with his famous marching band. The theater also had two screens for showing movies. (Author's collection.)

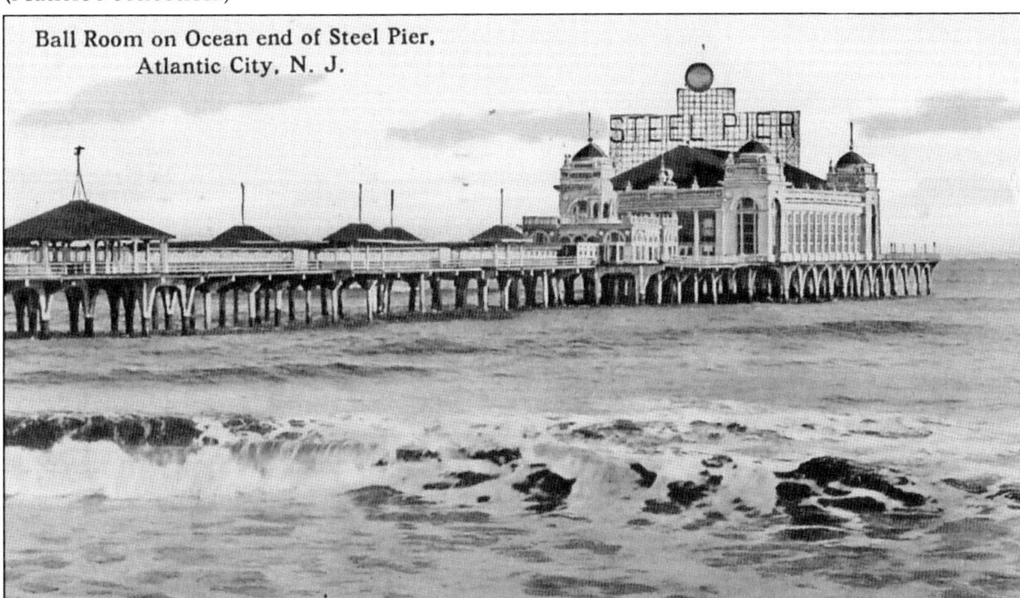

The Marine Ballroom, or simply the ballroom, stood at the end of Steel Pier. In 1926, the Ted Weems Orchestra was the first big-name band to play there. Famed Irish tenor John McCormack also performed that year. Tickets were only $2.50 per seat. In 1932, Rudy Vallée made his first of many appearances, bringing in record crowds. In 1939, the Harry James Band played for the Easter crowd; an unknown singer named Frank Sinatra made his Steel Pier debut with them. (Author's collection.)

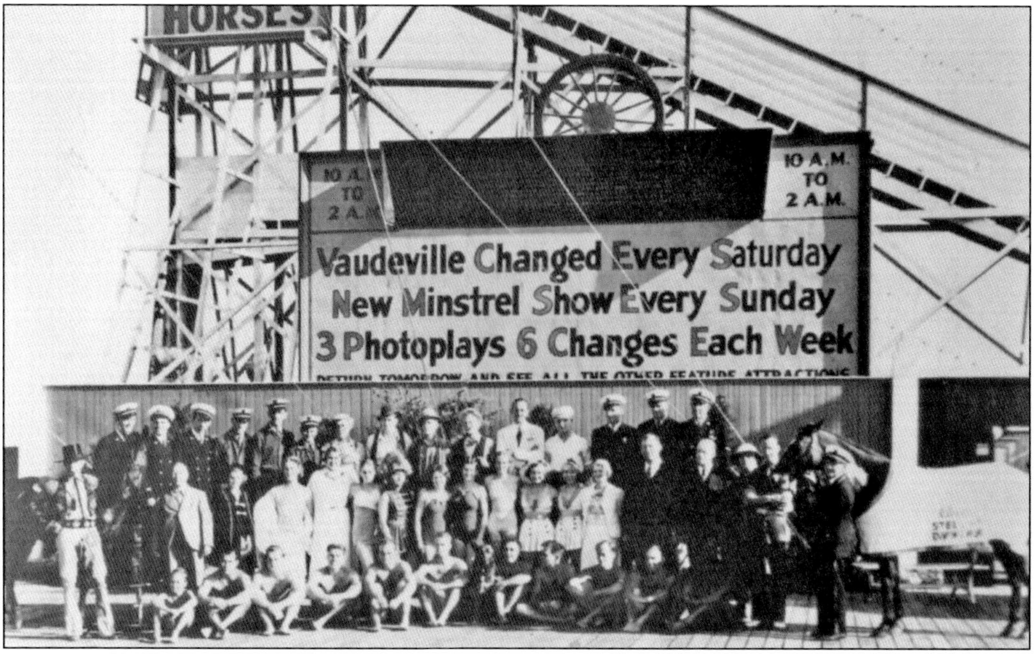

Extending beyond the Steel Pier was the world-famous Steel Pier Water Circus, which included the diving horse, the Submarine Diving Bell, the human cannonball, and high-wire performers, as well as acrobats. Many of Steel Pier's advertisements in the late 1920s stated, "Nowhere else can you see so much for so little money." In 1929, the diving horse made its debut, along with another first, the human cannonball. This group portrait shows many of the employees and performers in the Water Circus. (Courtesy Robert A. Emmons.)

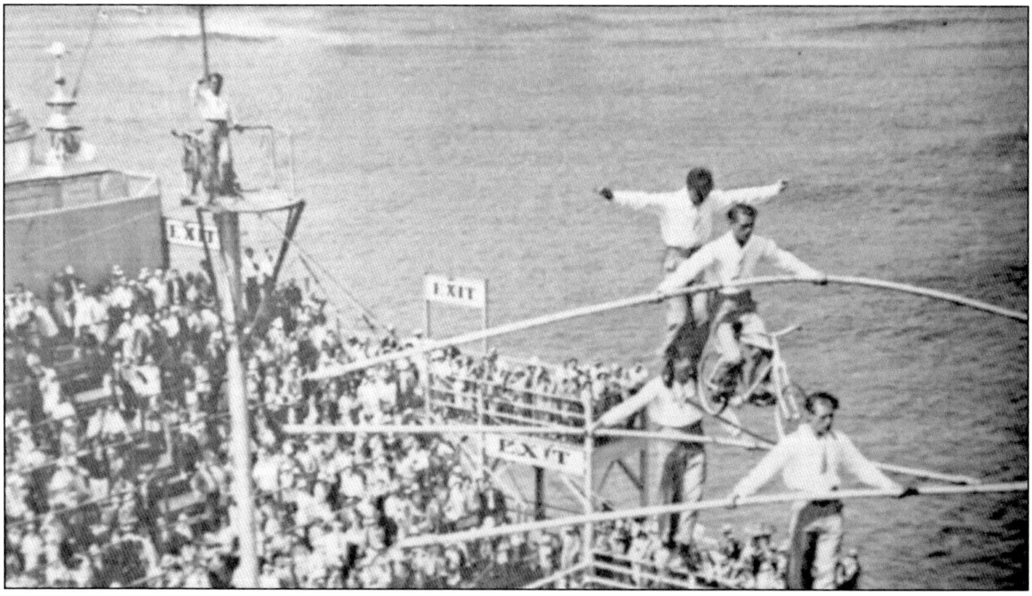

Another famous Steel Pier attraction was the daring tightrope aerialists who performed 100 feet above the ocean as part of the Water Circus attraction. It would have taken 18 consecutive hours to see all of the Steel Pier's attractions, which included the day's greatest artists of radio, stage, screen, and circus. (Courtesy Robert A. Emmons.)

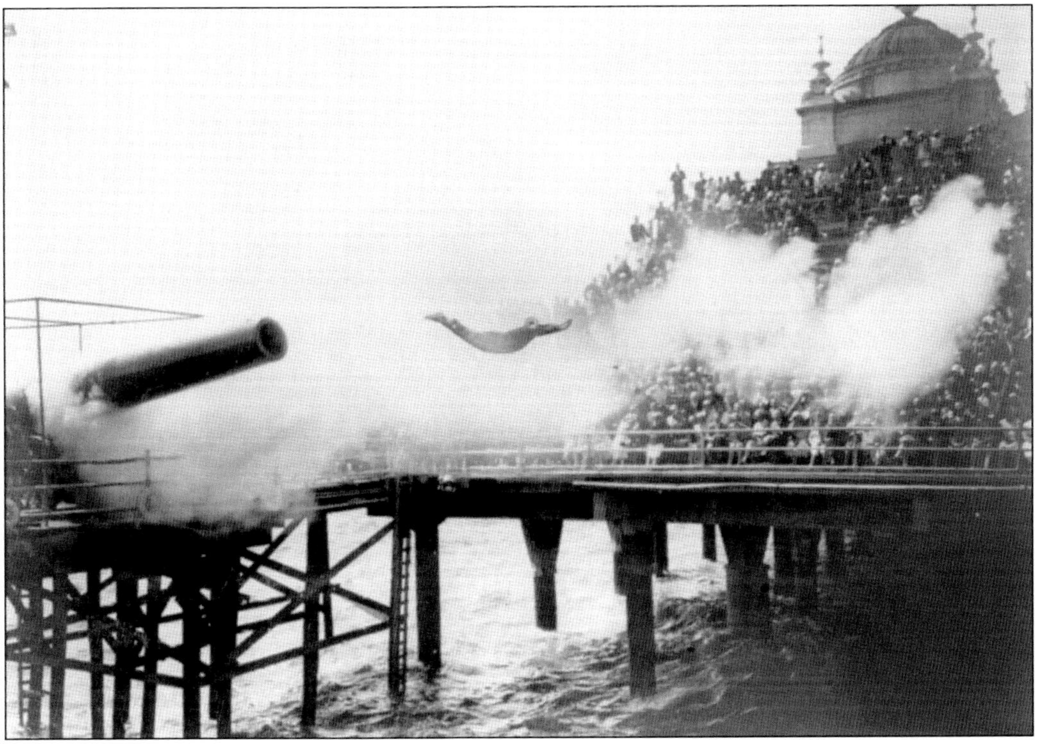

The Flying Zachines performed on the Steel Pier throughout the 1930s, blasting themselves from a cannon into suspended nets. This image was taken from a postcard, which read, "cannon used by human projectile." (Courtesy the Press of Atlantic City.)

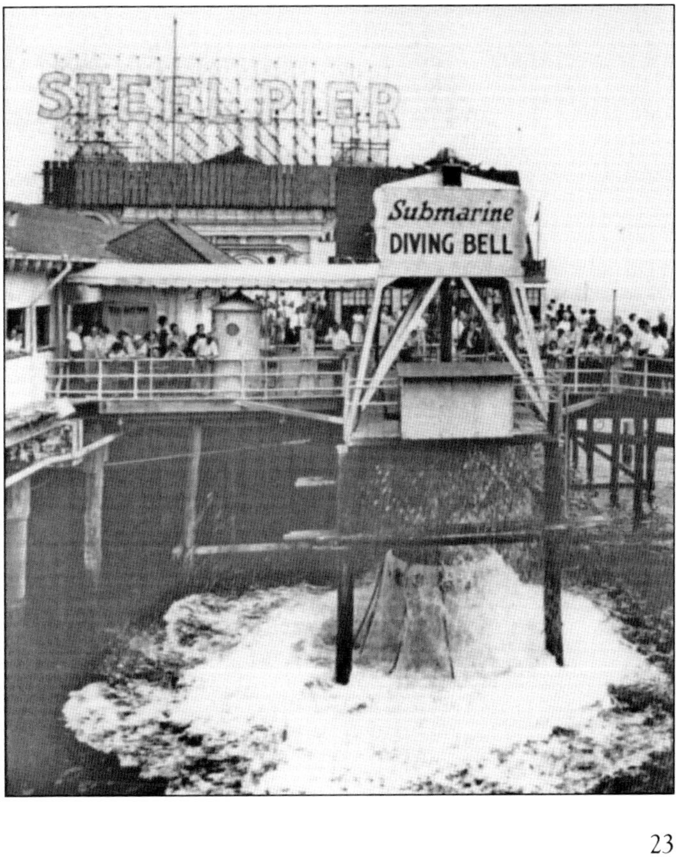

While most famous for its diving horse act, the Steel Pier was also known by many generations of vacationers and locals for another "diving" attraction—the Submarine Diving Bell. It opened in 1928 and, for only 25¢—or, in later days, $1—riders would plunge into the water off Steel Pier to observe the depths below for five minutes. Jim Craine ran the bell through the 1960s. (Courtesy Jim Craine.)

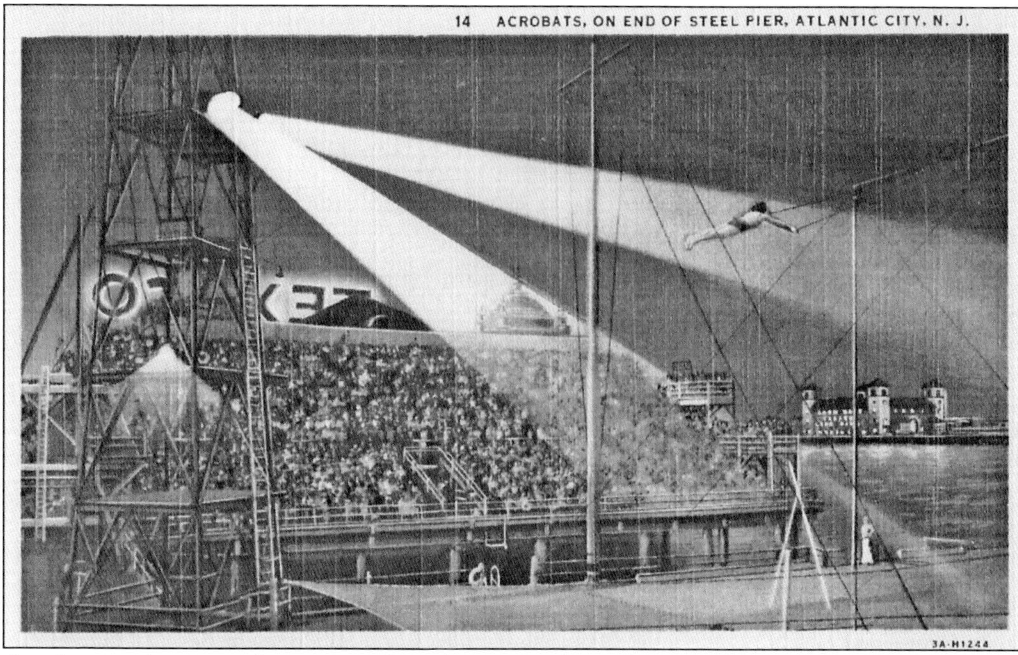

Acrobats made up another group of Steel Pier aerialists who performed high above the ocean. They were always a crowd favorite. The Steel Pier advertised the area as a "Stage for [a] Sensational Congress of International Daredevils." (Author's collection.)

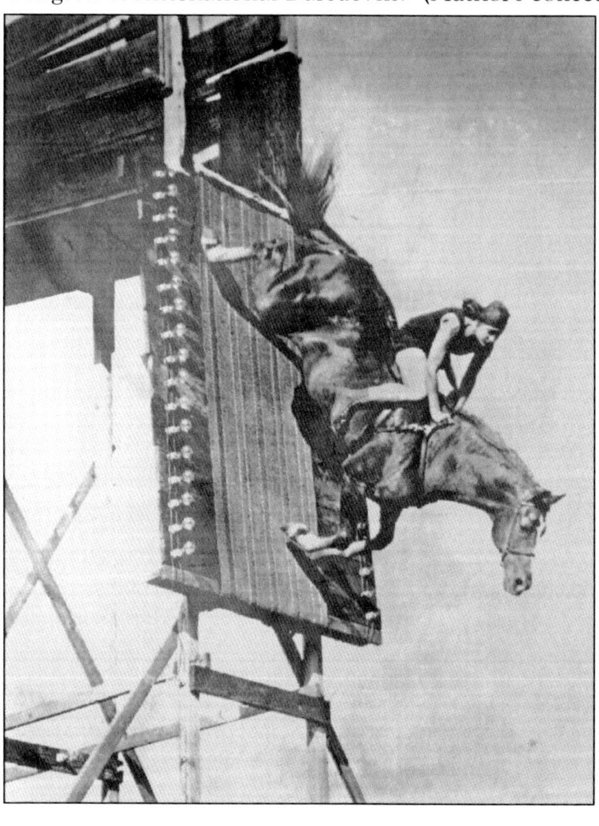

Starting in 1905 and ending in 1978, Atlantic City featured diving horses at the end of the Steel Pier. This was one of the best-known attractions on the entire Boardwalk. The horses were trained to dive from a 40-foot tower into a 12-foot-deep water tank with young ladies on their backs, two to four times a day. In 1924, Sonora Webster Carver joined the show. In 1931, she and her horse Red Lips lost their balance on the diving platform and fell into the tank out of control. Fortunately, Carver survived the fall but lost her sight because of the force of the impact, which detached both retinas. Amazingly, she continued performing as a diver until 1942 for a total of 18 years, 11 of them blind. (Courtesy Robert A. Emmons.)

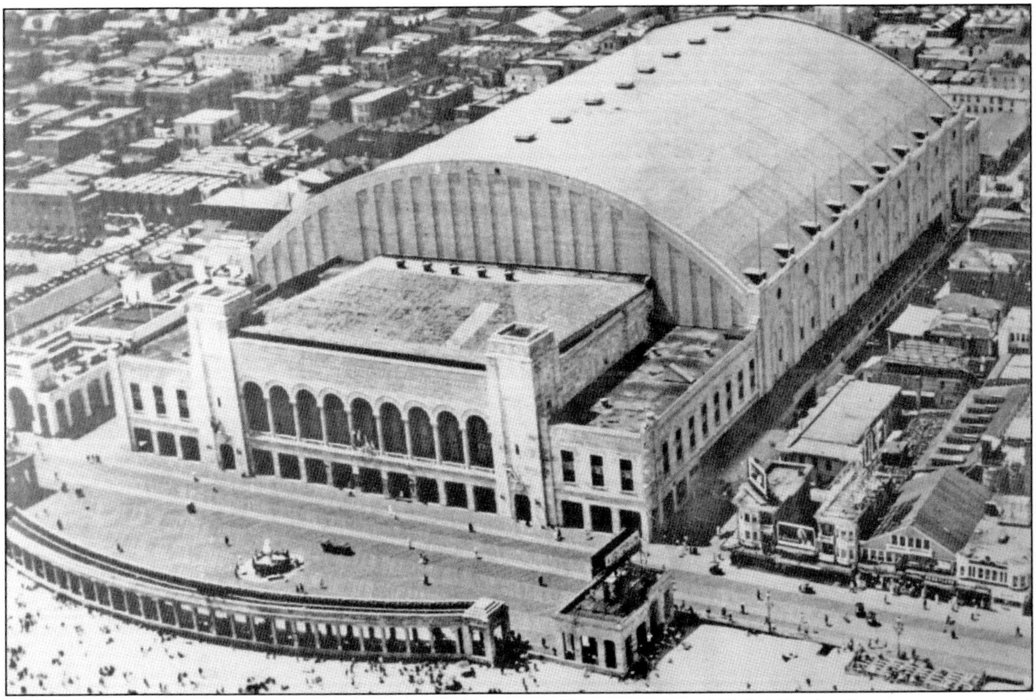

The historic Atlantic City Convention Hall originally opened in 1929. The hall was constructed without roof posts or pillars, and was considered an engineering marvel. It is located at 2301 Boardwalk and is now called Boardwalk Hall. It became the home of the Miss America Pageant beginning in 1940. (Courtesy Robert A. Emmons.)

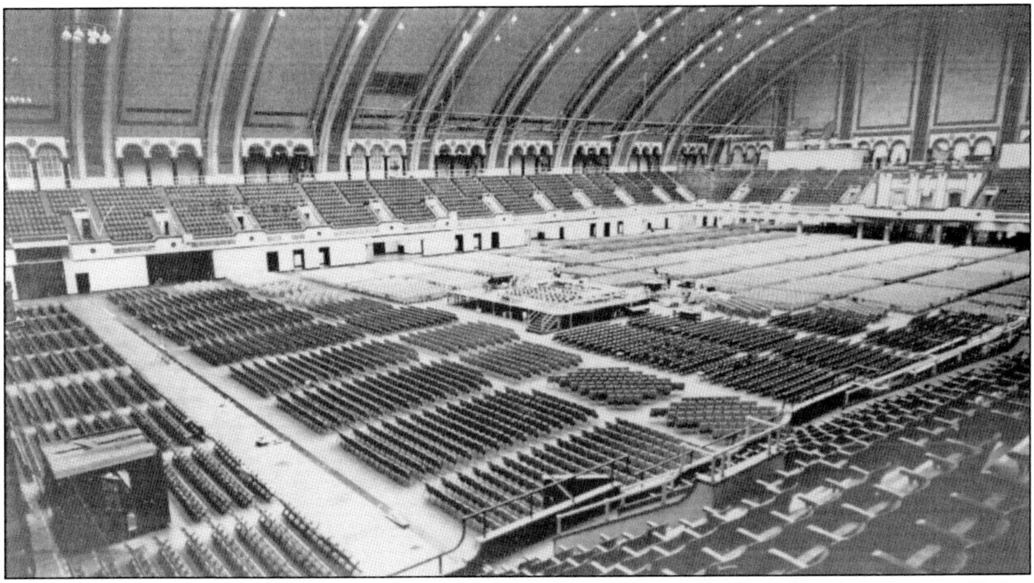

The interior of the Convention Hall measures 456 by 310 feet, and the barrel vault ceiling is 137 feet high. It has 268,000 square feet of exhibit space and 20 conference rooms. It also has what was at one time the world's largest stage, measuring 110 feet wide and 85 feet deep. It contains the world's largest musical instrument, a pipe organ of over 33,000 pipes, eight chambers, and the world's largest console. However, it is currently only 10 percent functional. (Courtesy Robert A. Emmons.)

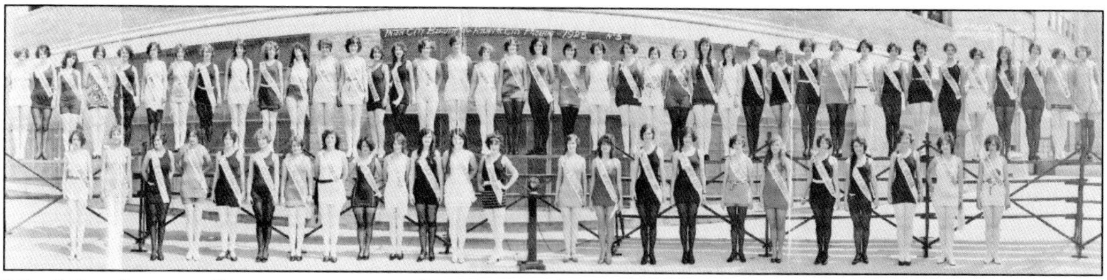

The Miss America Pageant originated on September 25, 1920, as the Fall Frolic, an event designed to bring business to the Boardwalk. It was so successful that the Businessmen's League immediately made plans to stage it again the following year as a beauty pageant, or "bather's revue." On September 8, 1921, over 100,000 people gathered at the Boardwalk to watch the contestants, mostly from the east coast. This photograph shows the contestants for Miss America 1925, the fifth pageant, when it was held at the Million Dollar Pier. The pageant continued over the next eight decades, except for 1928–1932 due to the Great Depression. From 1935 through 1938, Miss America was crowned on the Steel Pier. In 1940, the event officially became the Miss America Pageant and was held for the first time in Convention Hall. (Courtesy Robert A. Emmons.)

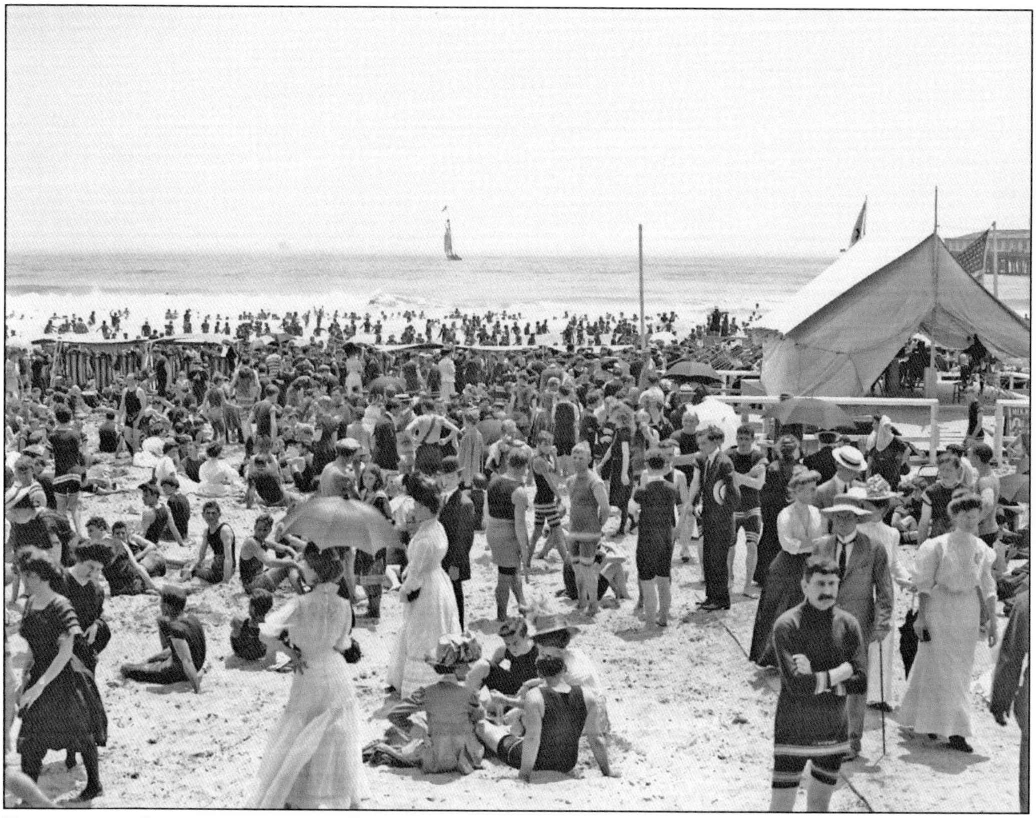

From its very beginning, visitors flocked to the beaches of Atlantic City during the warm summer months. It has more than four miles of gently sloping sandy beach, washed by the refreshing saltwater of the Atlantic Ocean. There were once strict dress codes for bathing for both men and women. Shaded canvas chairs, colorful canopies, and beach umbrellas became very popular to protect those on the beach from the blazing sun. On some weekends, the crowds on the beaches could reach into the tens of thousands. (Courtesy Library of Congress.)

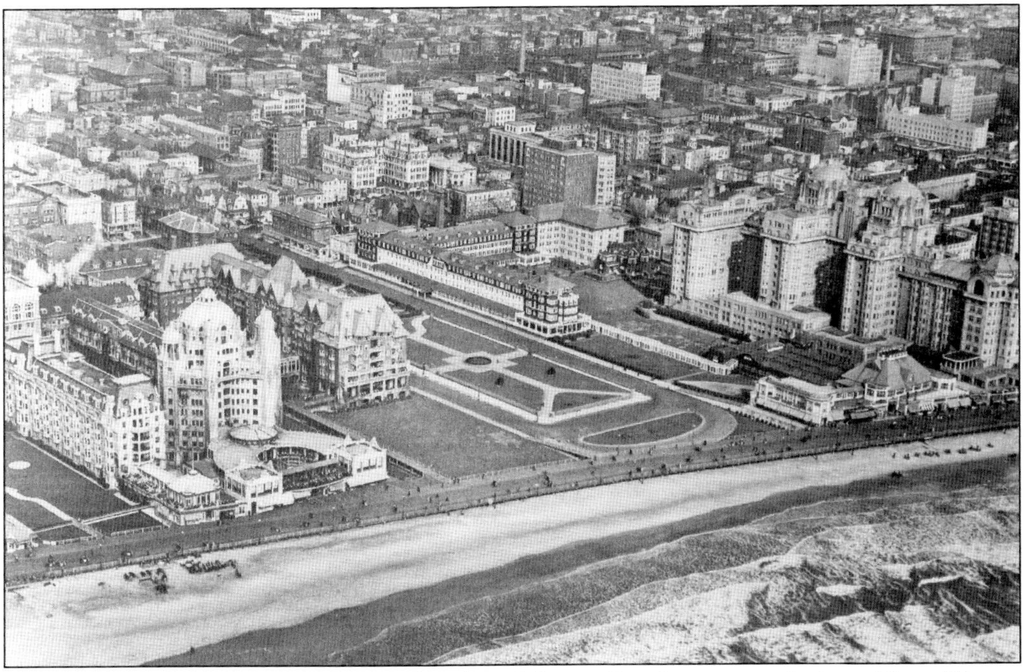

In 1918, there were approximately 1,200 hotels in Atlantic City; however, only about 30 could boast that they had a prestigious Boardwalk address. The city claimed to lead every resort in the world in the sheer number and splendor of its exquisite hotels. The intersection of Park Place and Boardwalk was photographed by Vistor Dallin in November 1928. From left to right are the luxury hotels Dennis, Blenheim, Marlborough, Brighton, and Traymore. (Courtesy Robert A. Emmons.)

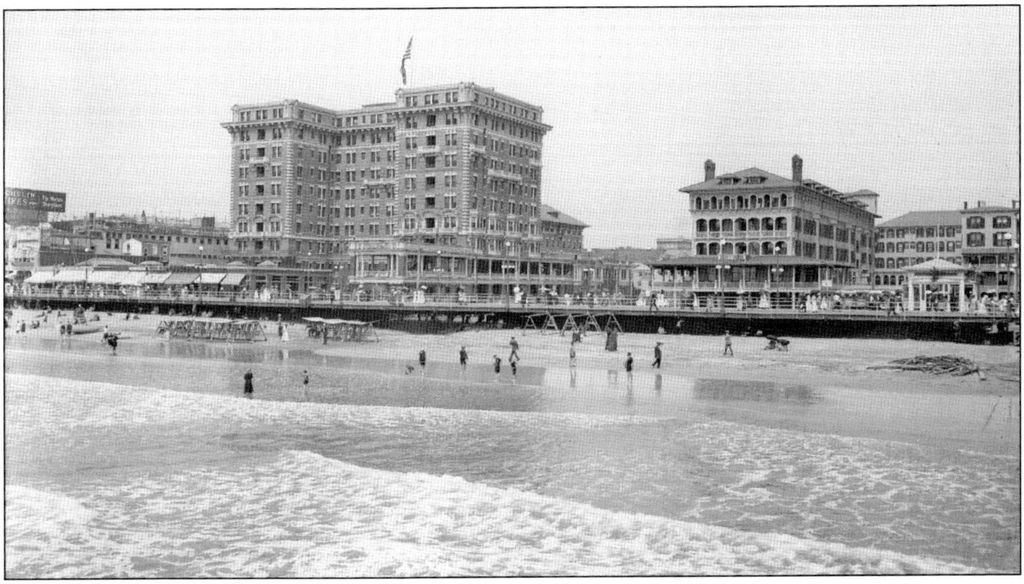

The Chalfonte–Haddon Hall Hotel was a unique Quaker-owned establishment, and therefore did not allow alcoholic beverages on the premises. The Chalfonte Hotel was built in 1868 and the Haddon Hall building was erected around 1893. The two properties were subsequently merged. The hotel had a year-round, all-weather saltwater pool and overlooked the boardwalk and the Atlantic Ocean. (Courtesy Library of Congress.)

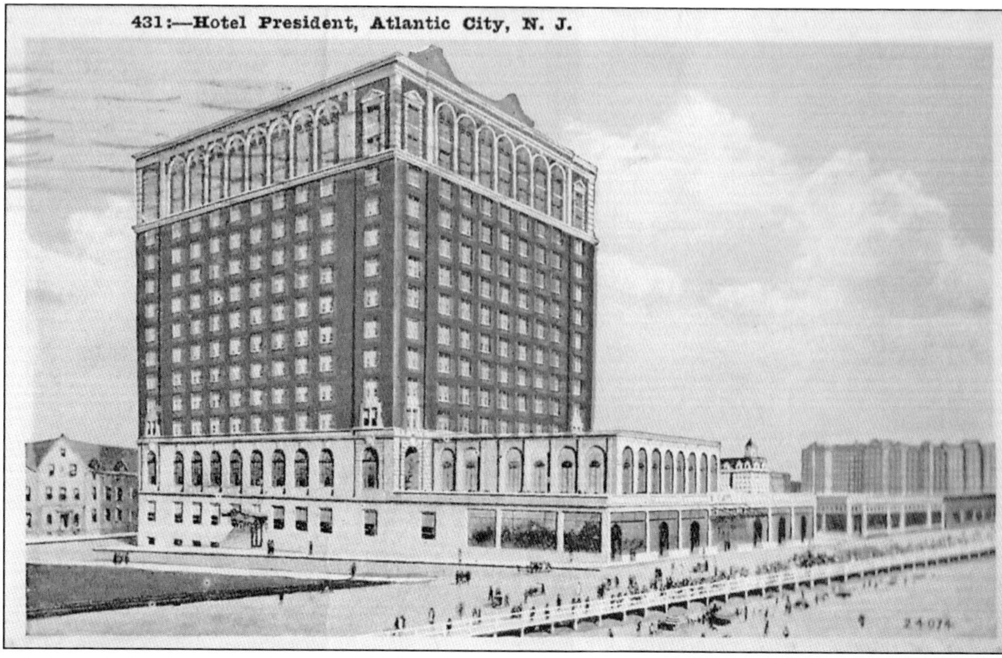

The Hotel President was built in 1926 at Boardwalk and Albany Avenue. It had 506 rooms with Turkish baths, plus beautiful lounges and ocean sundecks. The hotel featured the Around-the-World Room, which was a popular venue to see famous Broadway stars and nationally known bands preform. (Author's collection.)

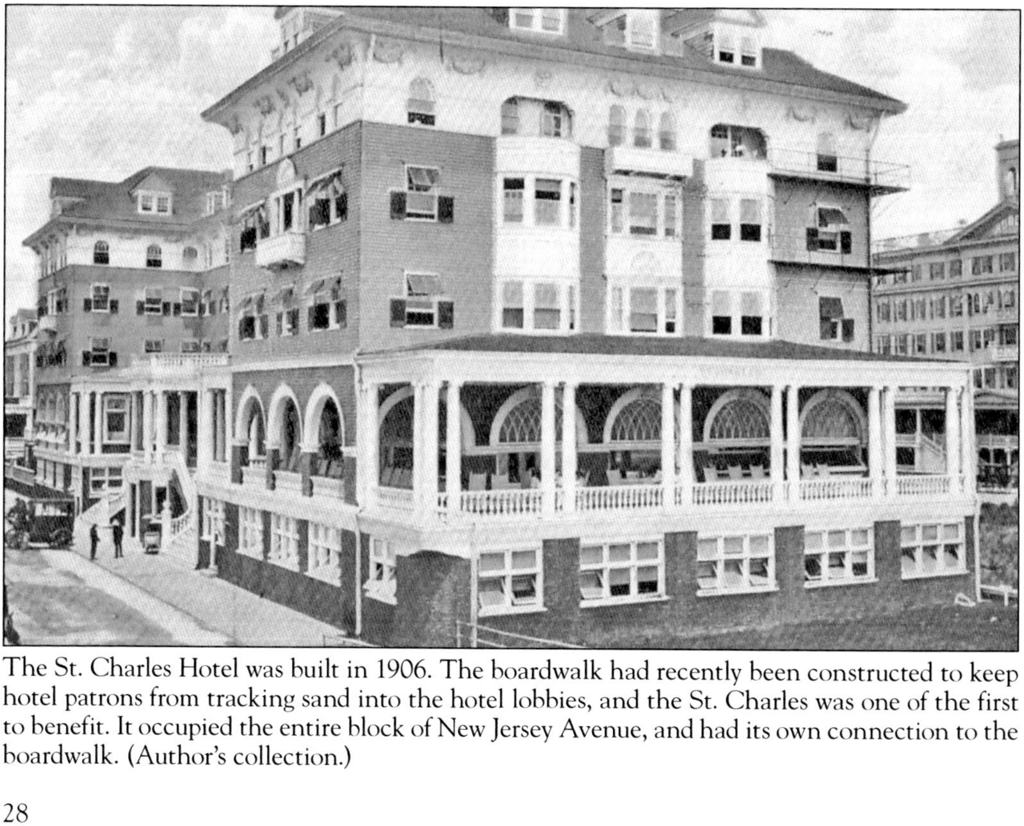

The St. Charles Hotel was built in 1906. The boardwalk had recently been constructed to keep hotel patrons from tracking sand into the hotel lobbies, and the St. Charles was one of the first to benefit. It occupied the entire block of New Jersey Avenue, and had its own connection to the boardwalk. (Author's collection.)

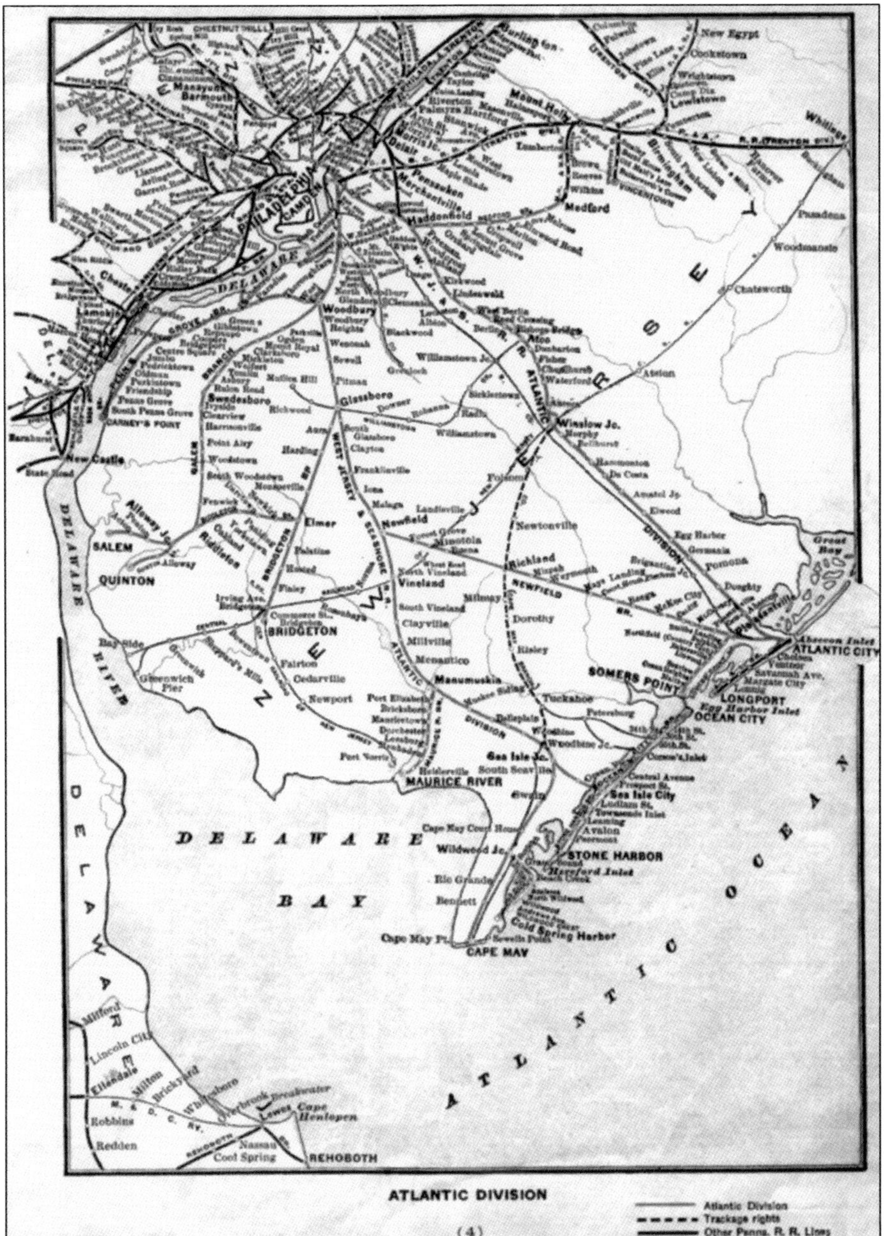

In the early 20th century, Atlantic City and the South Jersey seashore were major vacation destinations for both the wealthy and working-class residents of the Philadelphia area. Railroads provided inexpensive and fast service between the city and the seashore. There were two competing railroad companies connecting Camden and Philadelphia with the resorts of South Jersey's seashore. Due to their rivalry, the Atlantic City Railroad (ACRR), owned by the Reading Railroad, and the West Jersey & Seashore Railroad (WJ&S), owned by the Pennsylvania Railroad (PRR), had some of the fastest trains in the world, and express trains regularly raced one another so as to be the first to arrive at their destination, notably Atlantic City and to a lesser degree Cape May. In 1933, the ACRR and WJ&S were consolidated into the Pennsylvania-Reading Seashore Lines (PRSL). (Courtesy South Jersey Rails.)

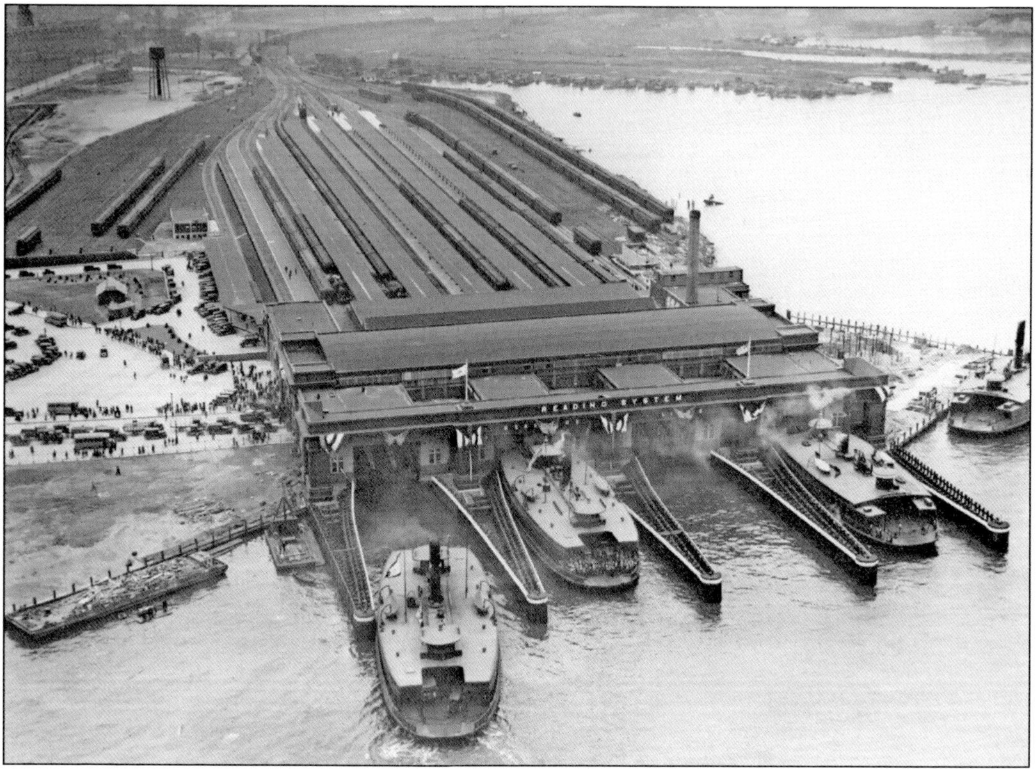

The photographs show the Atlantic City Railroad's Camden Terminal on its opening day on May 14, 1924. Passengers looking to travel to the Jersey Shore would catch ferries from Chestnut and South Street Station in Philadelphia to cross the Delaware River. (Both, courtesy railroad.net.)

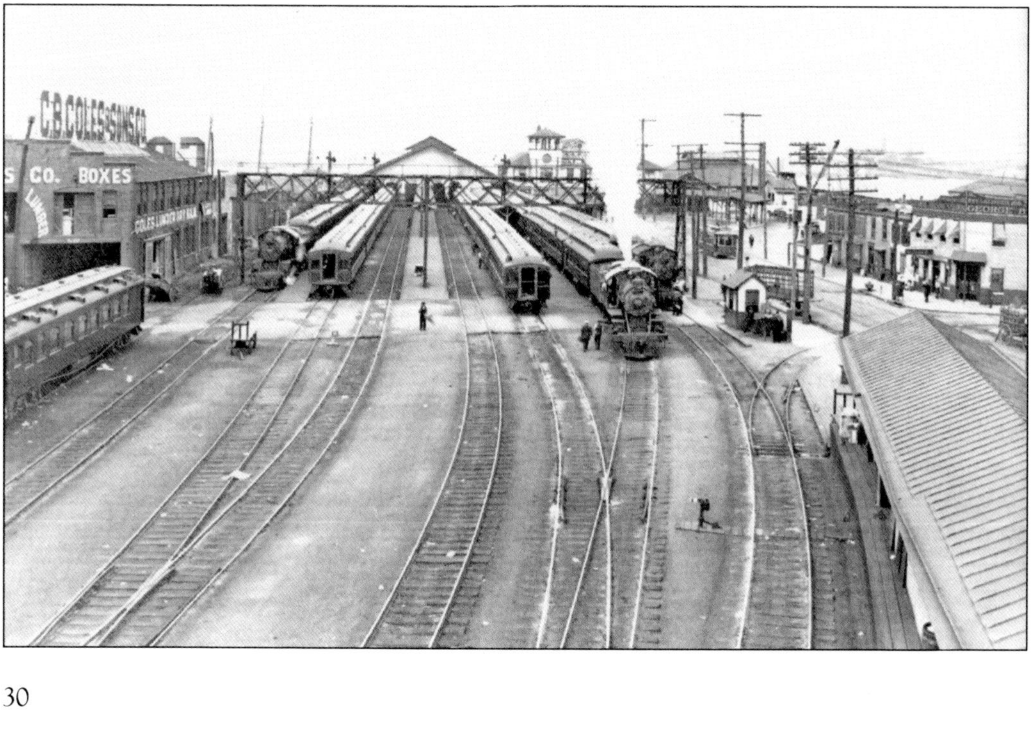

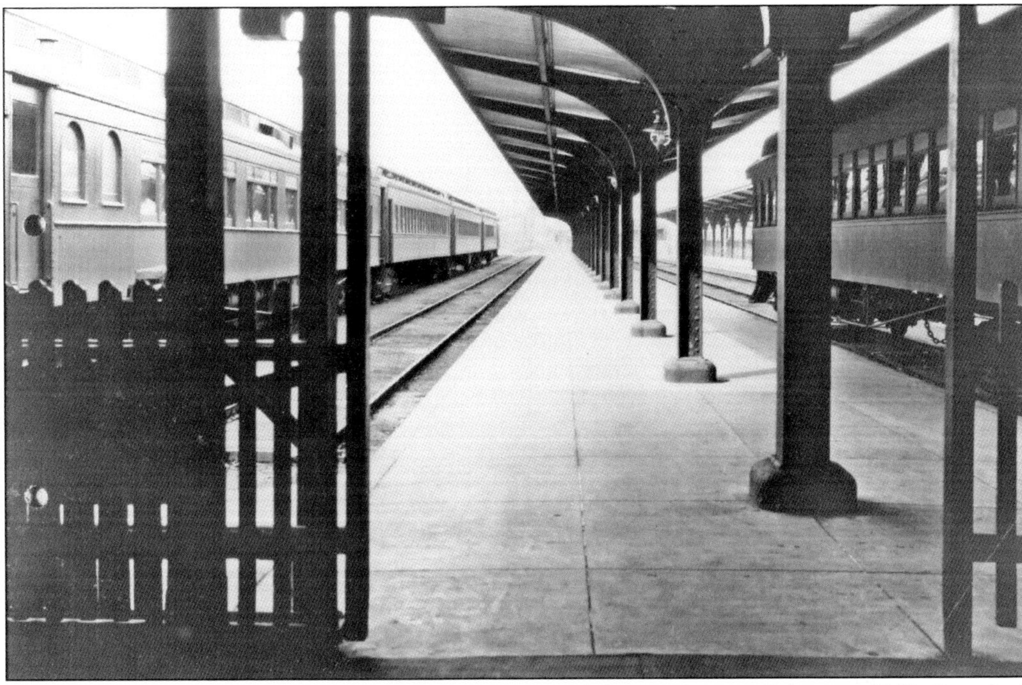

A Reading Railroad train sits inside the station in Atlantic City in February 1917. Camden's express train has a typical offseason consist of a steel combine, two steel coaches, and a wooden parlor car. (Courtesy West Jersey Chapter, National Railway Historical Society.)

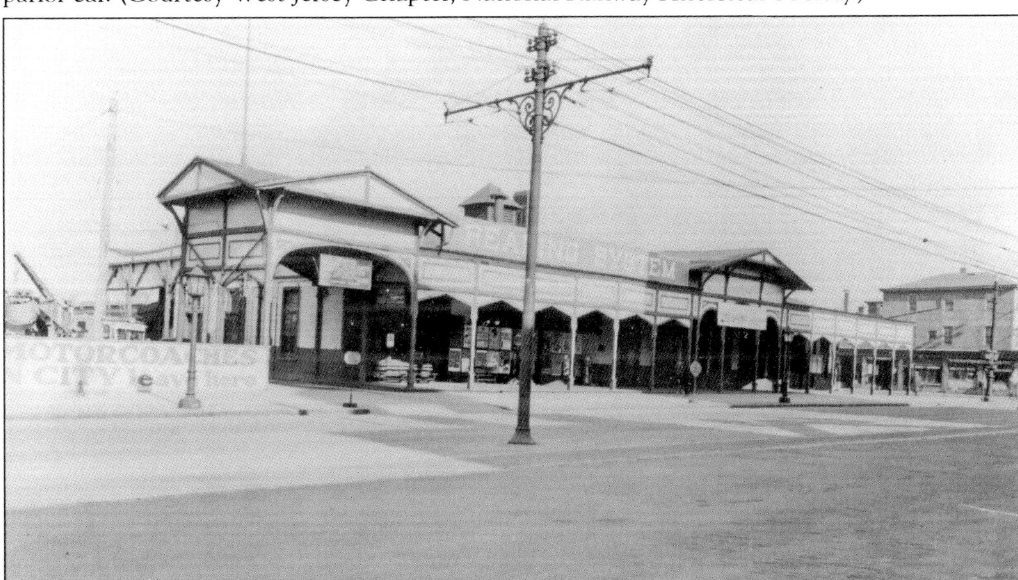

In January 1930, the 1890 Atlantic City station, jointly used by the Reading Railroad and the Philadelphia & Atlantic City Railway (P&AC), became known simply as the "Reading System" when the P&AC passenger and freight stations were removed from the facility. This is an official Reading company photograph taken on January 19, 1930. Since the Central New Jersey was taken over by the Reading Railroad in 1901, the CNJ was able to use this depot until it moved into the new Union Station in 1934. (Courtesy West Jersey Chapter, National Railway Historical Society.)

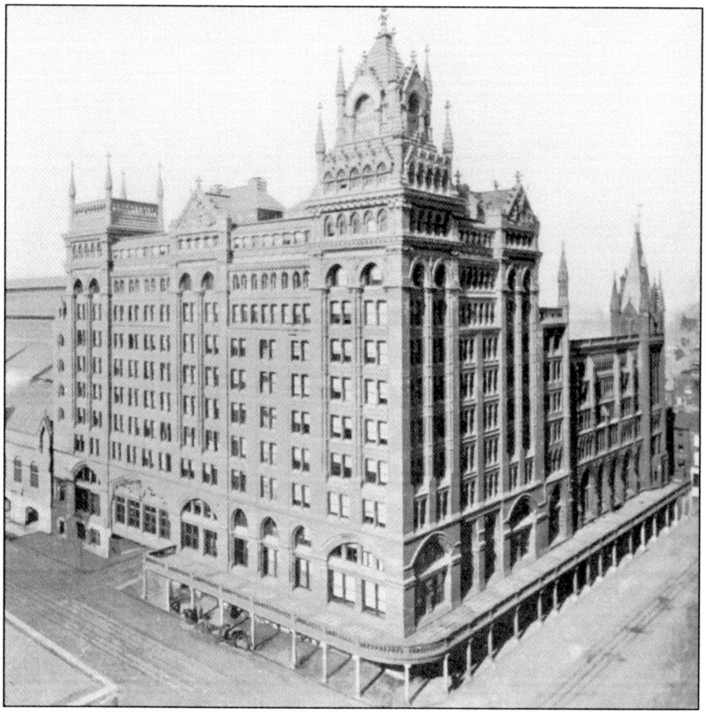

The Broad Street Station at Broad and Market Streets was the primary passenger terminal for the Pennsylvania Railroad in Philadelphia from 1881 to the 1950s. When completed in 1893, it was the largest passenger terminal in the world. Travelers riding the PRR from New York City and wishing to go to Atlantic City would disembark at Broad Street Station and take the Market Street trolley (Market-Frankford Elevated, or Market Street EL) to the Pennsylvania Railroad ferries at the foot of Market Street. (Author's collection.)

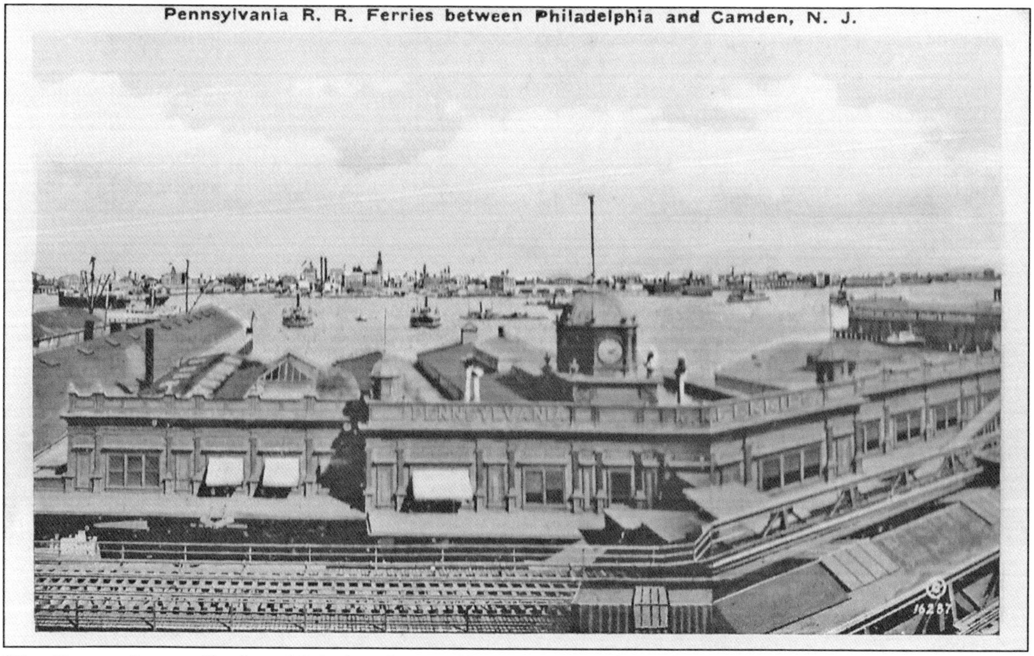

The Pennsylvania Railroad Market Street Ferry Terminal in Philadelphia was used by the PRR subsidiary Philadelphia & Camden Railroad Ferry Company to transport passengers across the Delaware River to waiting trains at the railroad's Federal Street Terminal in Camden. This facility was established in 1871, and the final terminal building was completed in March 1899. The Tuscan red ferries normally made the crossing in a few minutes. The ferryboat names in later years included the *Salem*, *Haddonfield*, *Millville*, and *Bridgeton*. (Author's collection.)

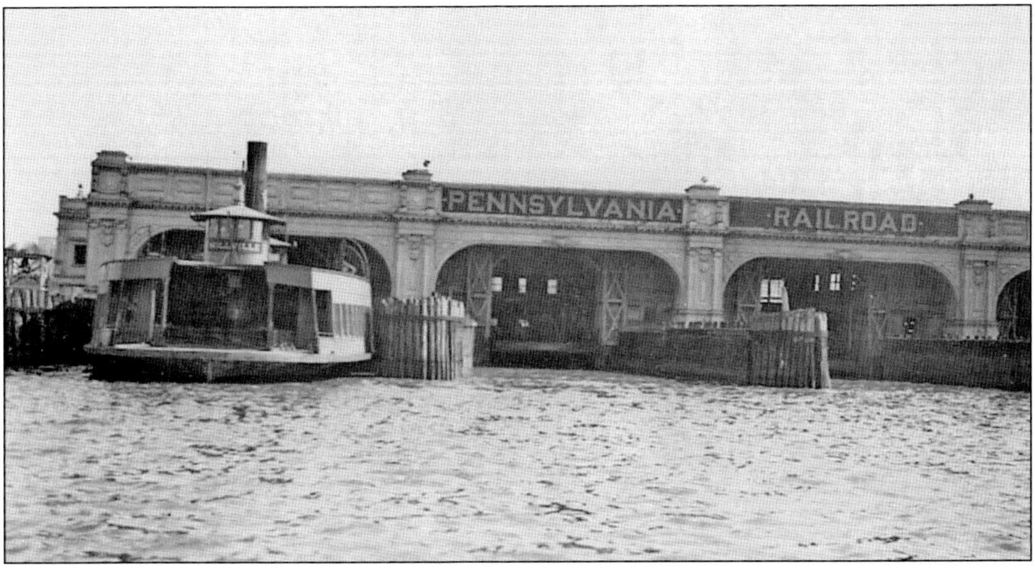

The Federal Street Terminal in Camden served the passenger rail traffic going to New Jersey's coast locations. The terminal served all PRR lines terminating at Camden, including the West Jersey & Seashore Railroad, the Camden & Amboy, the Camden & Burlington County Railway, and others. After the 1933 consolidation, this terminal served the former ACRR lines as well. The 60-by-175-foot steel masonry structure with its four ferry slips went into service on June 23, 1901, and provided the WJ&S rail service, on its main line, to Atlantic City via Winslow Junction. (Courtesy railroad.net.)

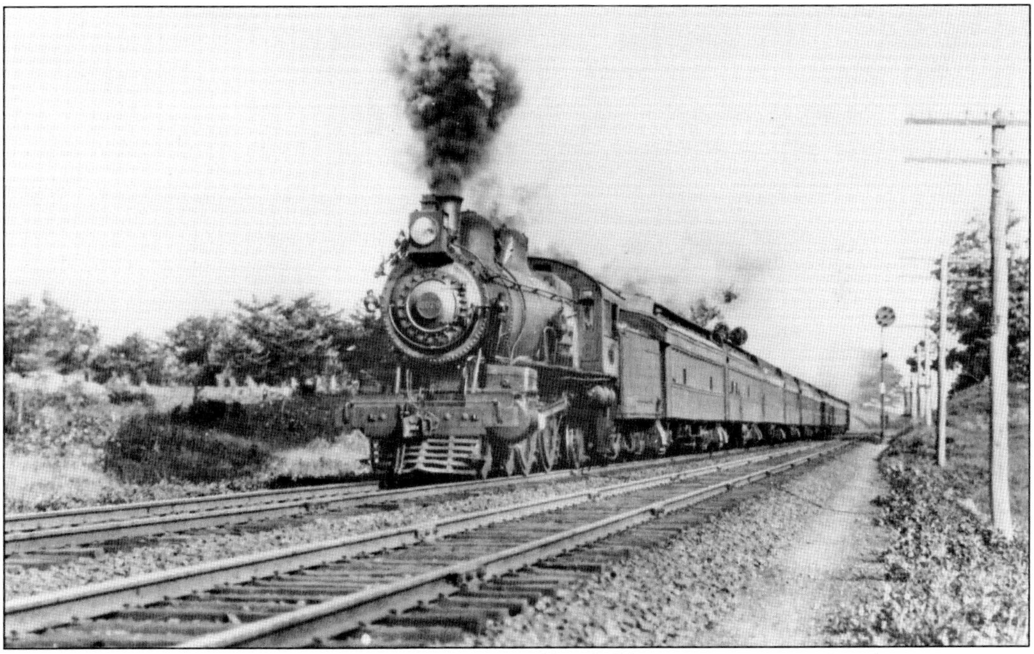

WJ&S locomotive E-2 6078 is seen departing Haddonfield, New Jersey, as it heads an excursion train bound for the New Jersey eastern shore in 1912. The train originated from the Pennsylvania Railroad–owned Federal Street Terminal in Camden. (Courtesy West Jersey Chapter, National Railway Historical Society.)

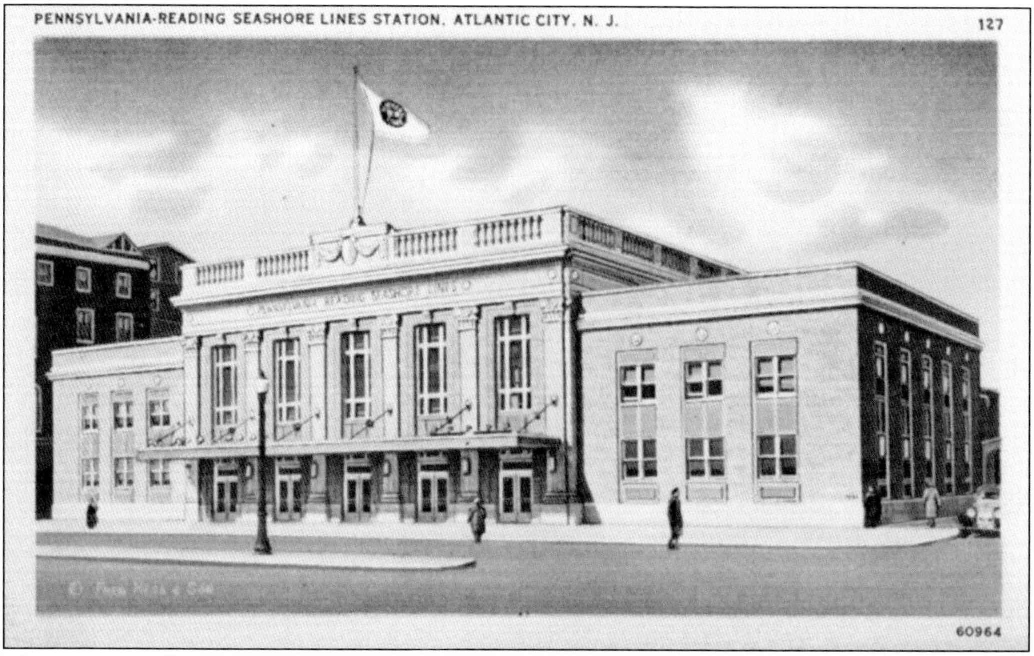

This was initially the Atlantic City terminal of the Camden & Atlantic Railroad (C&A) and was located near the intersection of Atlantic and Southern Avenues in 1876. The Pennsylvania Railroad's WJ&S was the last of the major railroads to enter Atlantic City and, subsequently, had the worst terminal location. In an effort to improve its location, the PRR purchased from its owners a majority of the stock of the Camden & Atlantic Railroad. The PRR then used the C&A's terminal as the main terminal in Atlantic City until the new Pennsylvania-Reading Seashore Union Station was built in 1934. (Courtesy Historical Society of Riverton, NJ.)

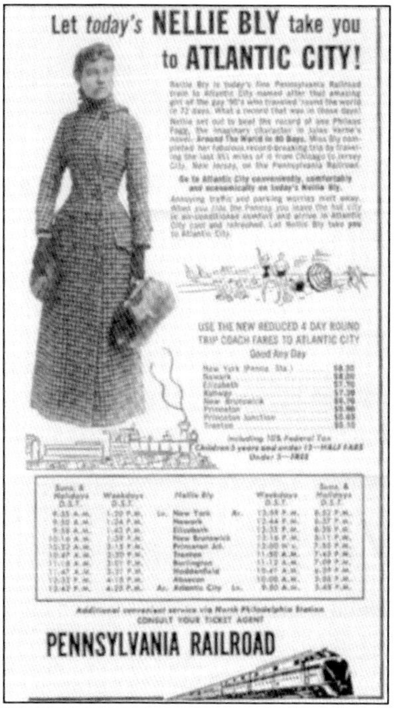

Nellie Bly, the pen name of Elizabeth Cochrane Seaman, was a journalist, investigative reporter, industrialist, and champion for women's suffrage and equality who lived from 1864 to 1922. Her greatest achievement, however, was circling the world in 72 days in 1889–1890, beating the achievement of the fictional character Phileas Fogg in Jules Verne's popular novel *Around the World in 80 Days*. To honor her adventure, and take advantage of it for marketing purposes, the Pennsylvania Railroad named its fastest round-trip trains between New York and Atlantic City after her. The Nellie Bly trains operated from 1891 to 1961 via Trenton, New Jersey. (Courtesy corvallistoday.com.)

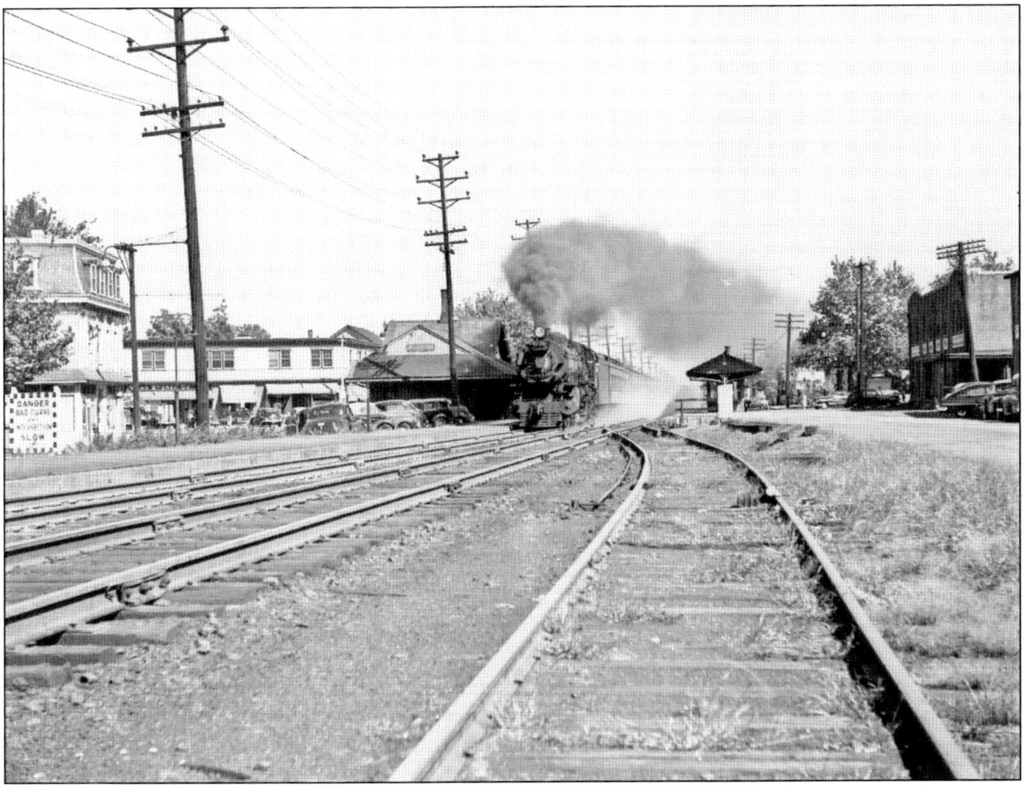

This photograph was taken in the late 1940s of the Nellie Bly as it highballed through Riverton, New Jersey. (Courtesy Historical Society of Riverton, NJ.)

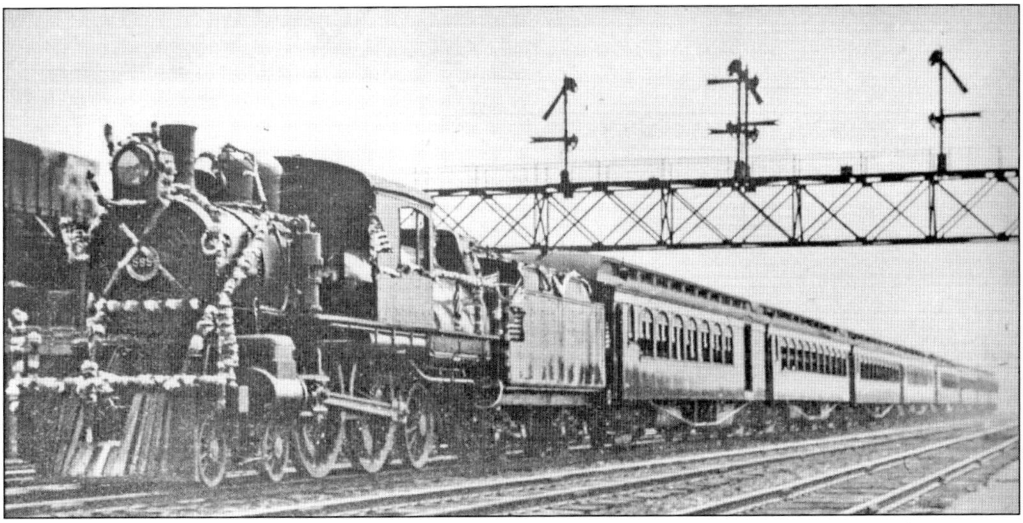

Locomotive No. 585 is appropriately decorated for its morning Jersey City run to Atlantic City on the Fourth of July in 1912. The Atlantic City Express No. 307 appears to include a vestibuled combine, vestibuled coach, two Pullman parlor cars, and a café-diner car. This particular train was one of a series of such trains, Nos. 307–318, which entered service on June 15, 1901, leaving New York at 9:40 a.m. and Atlantic City at 2:15 p.m. The Atlantic City trains featured the best motive power and equipment the NJC could muster. (Courtesy Robert A. Emmons.)

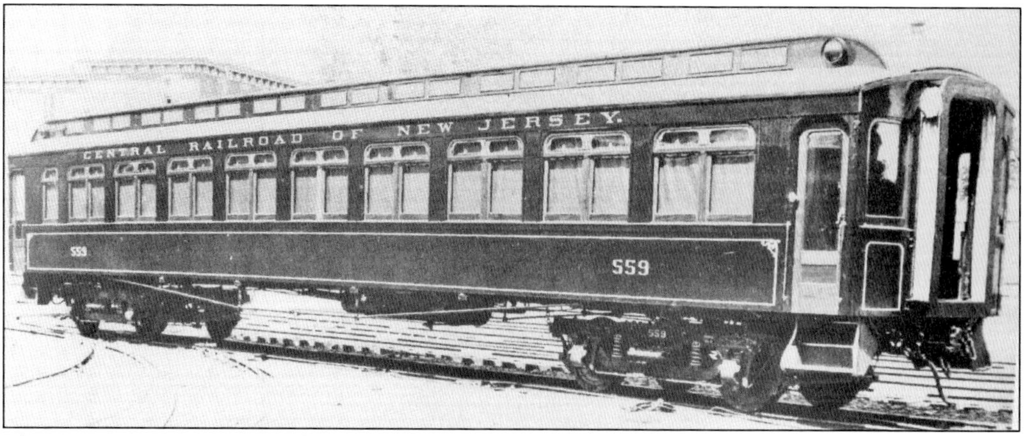

The American Car & Foundry produced one of the NJC's first deluxe vestibule coaches in 1899. No. 559 was renumbered No. 103 in 1905 and retired from revenue service in May 1931. This particular coach probably found service in the NJC's Atlantic City Express and Playground Special. (Courtesy Robert A. Emmons.)

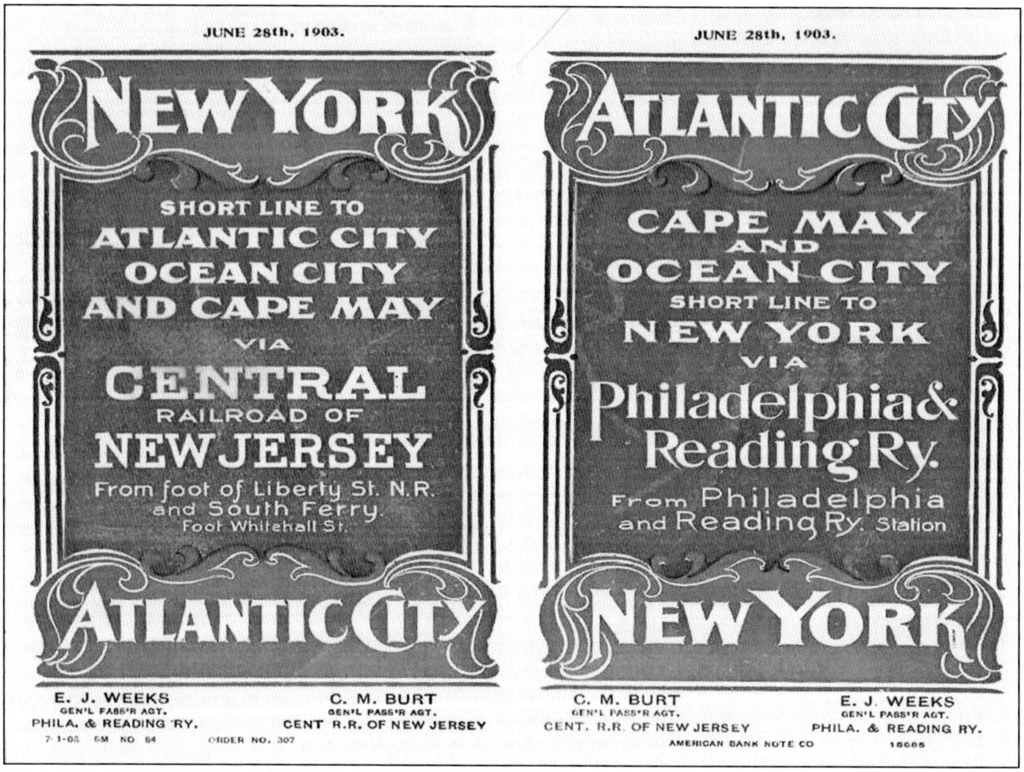

These are the front and back covers of a timetable brochure dated June 28, 1903, for the NJC Short Line to Atlantic City, Ocean City, and Cape May and return. The service originated from the Liberty Street and South Ferry Terminals in Lower Manhattan. The return trip originated in Cape May and utilized the Philadelphia & Reading Railway Station in Atlantic City. This service is assumed to have been in conjunction with the NJC Atlantic City Express and Playground Special. (Author's collection.)

The interior of this brochure advertises vestibule coaches and Pullman parlor cars along with schedules and a system map. The schedule shows that the NJC provided two daily weekday trips to Atlantic City, one leaving Jersey City at 9:51 a.m. and the other at 3:52 p.m. The return trip left Atlantic City, via Cape May, at 8:30 a.m. and 2:15 p.m. The system map indicates the use of Reading Railway tracks between Winslow Junction and Cape May. (Author's collection.)

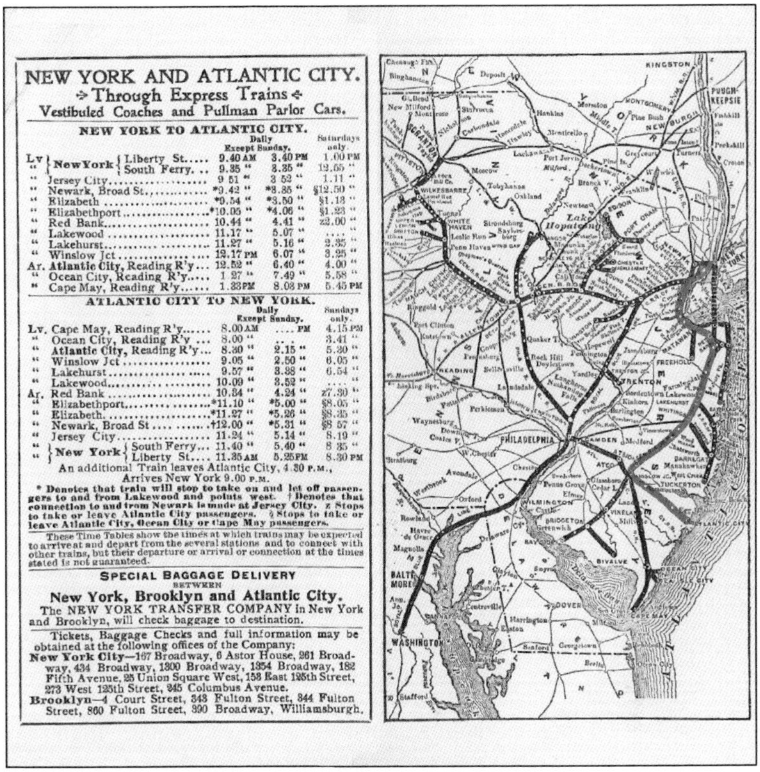

NEW YORK AND ATLANTIC CITY.

Through Express Trains

Vestibuled Coaches and Pullman Parlor Cars.

NEW YORK TO ATLANTIC CITY.

		Daily Except Sunday.		Saturdays only.
Lv.	New York { Liberty St.	9.40 AM	3.40 PM	1.00 PM
"	New York { South Ferry.	9.35 "	3.35 "	12.55 "
"	Jersey City	9 51 "	3 52 "	1.11 "
"	Newark, Broad St.	*9.42 "	*3.35 "	§12.50 "
"	Elizabeth	*9.54 "	*3.50 "	§1.13 "
"	Elizabethport	*10.05 "	*4.06 "	§1.23 "
"	Red Bank	10.44 "	4.41 "	z2.00 "
"	Lakewood	11.17 "	5.07 "	.... "
"	Lakehurst	11.27 "	5.16 "	2.35 "
"	Winslow Jct	12.17 PM	6.07 "	3.25 "
Ar.	**Atlantic City**, Reading R'y	12.52 "	6.40 "	4.00 "
"	Ocean City, Reading R'y	1 27 "	7.49 "	5.58 "
"	Cape May, Reading R'y	1.33 PM	8.03 PM	5.45 PM

ATLANTIC CITY TO NEW YORK.

		Daily Except Sunday.		Sundays only.
Lv.	Cape May, Reading R'y	8.00 AM	.... PM	4.15 PM
"	Ocean City, Reading R'y	8.00 "	...	3.41 "
"	**Atlantic City**, Reading R'y	8.30 "	2.15 "	5.30 "
"	Winslow Jct	9.05 "	2.50 "	6.05 "
"	Lakehurst	9.57 "	3.38 "	6.54 "
"	Lakewood	10.09 "	3.52 "	.... "
Ar.	Red Bank	10.34 "	4.24 "	z7.30 "
"	Elizabethport	*11.10 "	*5.00 "	§8.05 "
"	Elizabeth	*11.27 "	*5.26 "	§8.35 "
"	Newark, Broad St	†12.00 "	*5.31 "	§8 57 "
"	Jersey City	11.24 "	5.14 "	8.19 "
"	New York { South Ferry	11.40 "	5.40 "	8 35 "
"	New York { Liberty St.	11.35 AM	5.25 PM	8.30 PM

An additional Train leaves Atlantic City, 4.30 P.M., Arrives New York 9.00 P.M.

*** Denotes that train will stop to take on and let off passengers to and from Lakewood and points west. † Denotes that connection to and from Newark is made at Jersey City. z Stops to take or leave Atlantic City passengers. § Stops to take or leave Atlantic City, Ocean City or Cape May passengers.**

These Time Tables show the times at which trains may be expected to arrive at and depart from the several stations and to connect with other trains, but their departure or arrival or connection at the times stated is not guaranteed.

SPECIAL BAGGAGE DELIVERY
BETWEEN
New York, Brooklyn and Atlantic City.
The NEW YORK TRANSFER COMPANY in New York and Brooklyn, will check baggage to destination.

Tickets, Baggage Checks and full information may be obtained at the following offices of the Company:
New York City—167 Broadway, 6 Astor House, 261 Broadway, 434 Broadway, 1300 Broadway, 1354 Broadway, 182 Fifth Avenue, 25 Union Square West, 153 East 125th Street, 273 West 125th Street, 245 Columbus Avenue.
Brooklyn—4 Court Street, 343 Fulton Street, 344 Fulton Street, 860 Fulton Street, 390 Broadway, Williamsburgh.

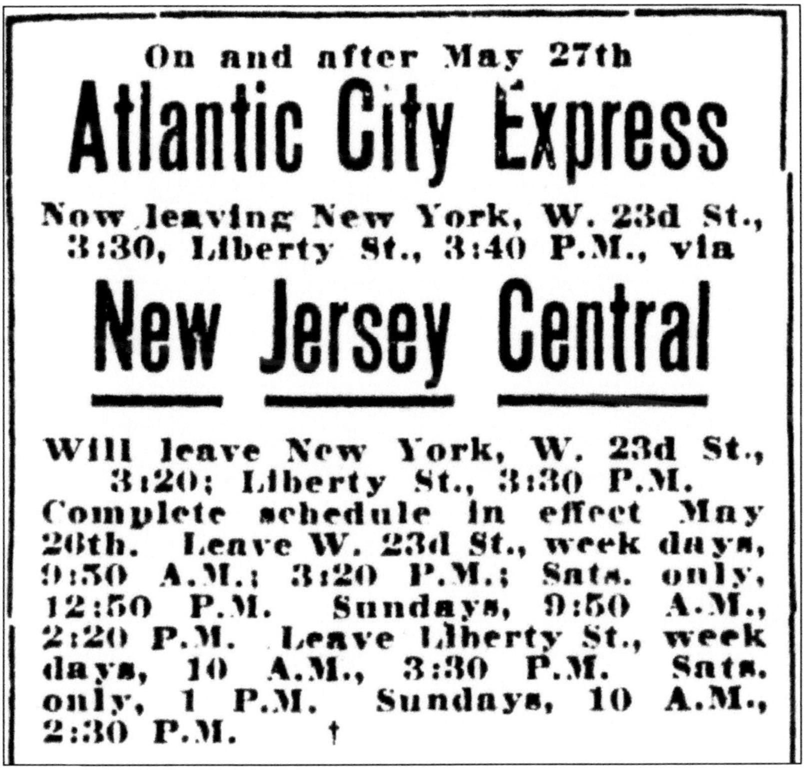

On and after May 27th

Atlantic City Express

Now leaving New York, W. 23d St., 3:30, Liberty St., 3:40 P.M., via

New Jersey Central

Will leave New York, W. 23d St., 3:20; Liberty St., 3:30 P.M. Complete schedule in effect May 26th. Leave W. 23d St., week days, 9:50 A.M.; 3:20 P.M.; Sats. only, 12:50 P.M. Sundays, 9:50 A.M., 2:20 P.M. Leave Liberty St., week days, 10 A.M., 3:30 P.M. Sats. only, 1 P.M. Sundays, 10 A.M., 2:30 P.M. †

This Atlantic City Express advertisement appeared in the *Brooklyn Daily Eagle* on May 25, 1912. The ad gives departure information from the two NJC terminals on West Twenty-Third Street and Liberty Street during the week and on weekends beginning after May 27, 1912. (Courtesy Joel Rosenbaum and Tom Gallo.)

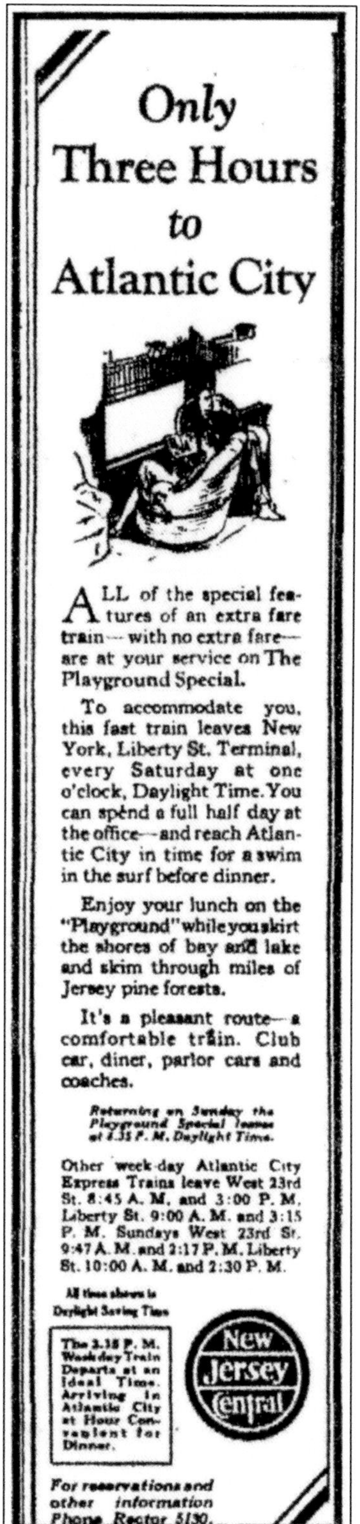

The Playground Special advertisement at left appeared in the *Brooklyn Daily Eagle* on August 25, 1926. The ad brags that it was "Only Three Hours to Atlantic City" from New York. The NJC trip originated at the Liberty Street ferry terminal every Saturday leaving at 1:00 p.m., and provided train service from the Jersey Street Terminal to Atlantic City in approximately three hours. "You can spend a full half day at the office—and reach Atlantic City in time for a swim in the surf before dinner." This ad was geared toward New York City office workers daydreaming of lying on the warm sandy beaches of Atlantic City on a Saturday afternoon. (Courtesy Joel Rosenbaum and Tom Gallo.)

The Playground Special advertisement at right appeared in the *Brooklyn Daily Eagle* on September 1, 1926. The ad discusses the Saturday departure of the Playground Special from the NJC's Liberty Street Terminal. It promises a nice, clean train and a tasty lunch as passengers enjoy views of the Jersey pine forests. (Courtesy Joel Rosenbaum and Tom Gallo.)

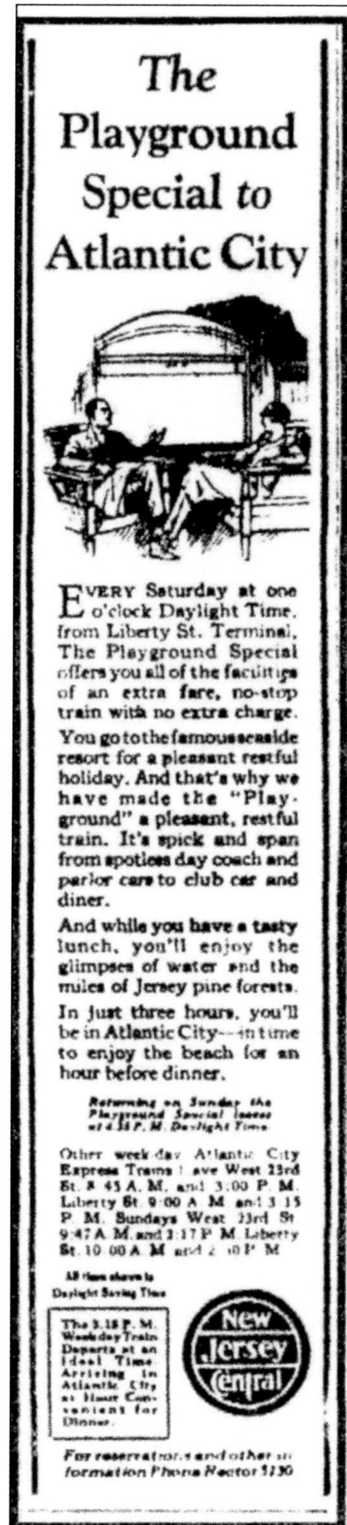

Two

THE RISE AND FALL OF THE BLUE COMET, 1929–1941

The Blue Comet, often referred to as the "Seashore's Finest Train," was the brainchild of the NJC's president R.B. White in 1928. Inspired by the Playground Special, he envisioned a train that would whisk all classes of passengers from Jersey City to Atlantic City in about three hours in luxury accommodations at regular coach fare, unlike the PRR's Atlantic City Limited and New York Limited services. There were three factors behind the creation of the Blue Comet. It was to eliminate passenger service south of Winslow Junction and replace rail service with bus connections, to better compete with the PRR for Atlantic City passengers, and to eliminate a costly Pullman parlor car lease. The Blue Comet train would operate on the NJC's home rails from Jersey City to the north end of the Raritan River drawbridge in Perth Amboy. From there, it would travel over the New York & Long Branch, jointly owned by the NJC and PRR, to Red Bank, New Jersey, then on to the NJC's Southern Division to Winslow Junction, where it would travel over the Atlantic City Railroad's tracks to Atlantic City. Initially, two brand-new Baldwin G-3 Pacific locomotives, Nos. 831 and 832, were assigned to the train. A third G-3, No. 833, would be added later. Initially, NJC refurnished 13 cars for the two round trips. Two coaches and an observation car were added later. A typical Blue Comet train would consist of a baggage car, combine-smoker, coaches, diner, and an observation car. The colors chosen for the Blue Comet cars were Packard blue, which represented the sky; Jersey cream, for the sandy coastal beaches; and royal blue, for the sea. The locomotives were painted a combination of Packard blue and royal blue as well. Prior to being placed into regular revenue service, the NJC staged large publicity exhibitions where the trains made special appearances. Before the first revenue run on February 14, 1929, the NJC published special Blue Comet promotional brochures and saturated the newspapers with all kinds of advertising. Initially, the Blue Comet was a success. The train carried 56,746 passengers in 1930, its first full year of operation; however, as the economic effects of the Depression deepened, ridership and revenues began to decline. On April 30, 1933, the Blue Comet was reduced from two round trips daily to one. The reduction in service resulted in only 17,351 passengers being carried in 1933. The creation of the Pennsylvania-Reading Seashore Lines in 1933 adversely affected Blue Comet ticket sales at the Atlantic City terminal, as well as the loss of rail service as the PRR gained a controlling interest of the track from Winslow Junction to Atlantic City. In addition, the Pennsylvania Railroad, with its convenient mid-city New York rail terminal, was able to provide more direct and frequent rail service to Atlantic City. The major derailment of the Blue Comet on August 19, 1939, only expedited the demise of the service. The Blue Comet made its final run on September 27, 1941, as the end of the Depression brought back prosperity, an expansion in New Jersey's public highway system, and a boom in the private ownership of automobiles. The Blue Comet service to Atlantic City became a thing of the past.

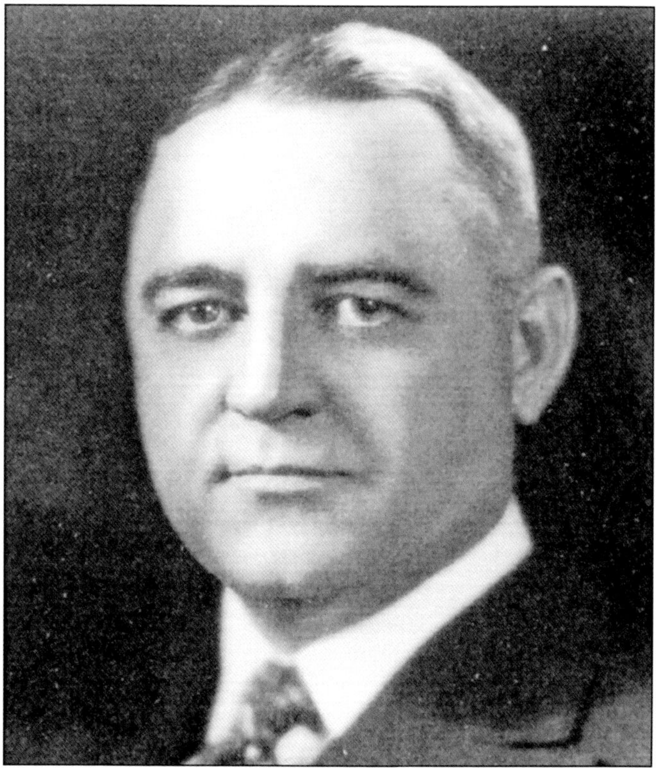

Roy Barton White was the ninth President of the NJC, from 1926 to 1933. He was the visionary responsible for spearheading the development of the Blue Comet. White kept the Blue Comet secret and limited information regarding it to a very few close business associates. He personally selected the colors and planned the appropriate features. In remarks made to the *Jersey Central News* in June 1929, White stated that the Blue Comet "was to be more than a mechanical train. It was to have personality and character—it was to be an innovation of speed and color, in tune with the modern trend—a creation of art, a symphony in blue." (Courtesy Robert A. Emmons.)

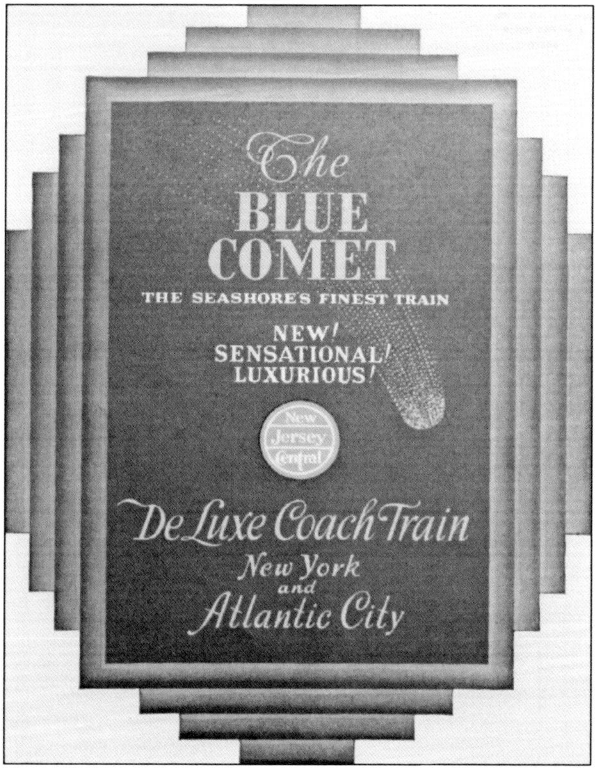

This Art Deco–style cover of a color brochure, published by the NJC, shows the imaginative flare of the advertising department of the company, under the direction of John Lobano. (Courtesy Robert A. Emmons.)

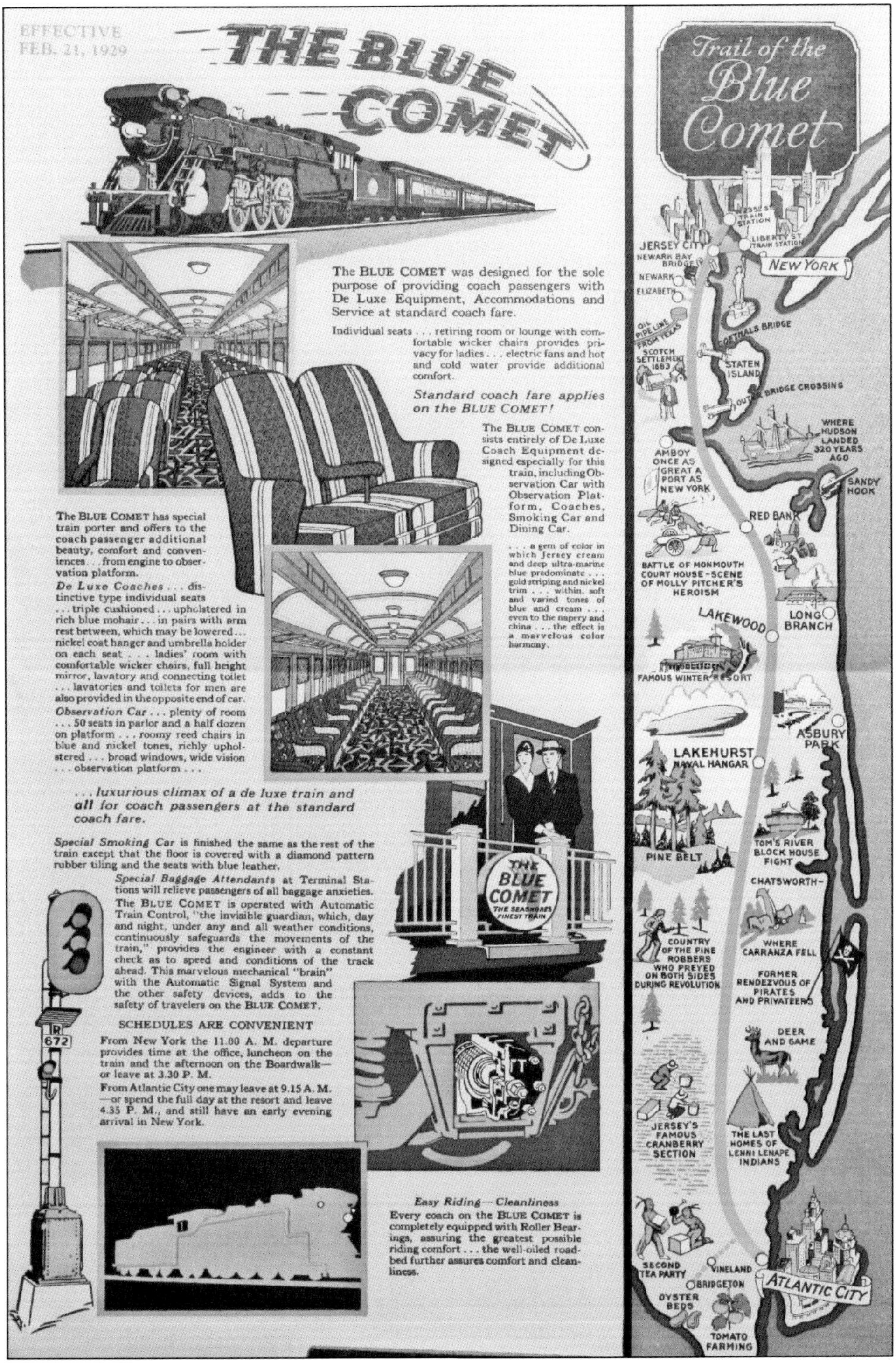

The interior of the brochure provided illustrative information regarding all aspects of the Blue Comet, including descriptions of its consist, its luxurious and comfortable coaches, its attentive personnel, and its easy riding and cleanliness. Note the route map. (Courtesy Robert A. Emmons.)

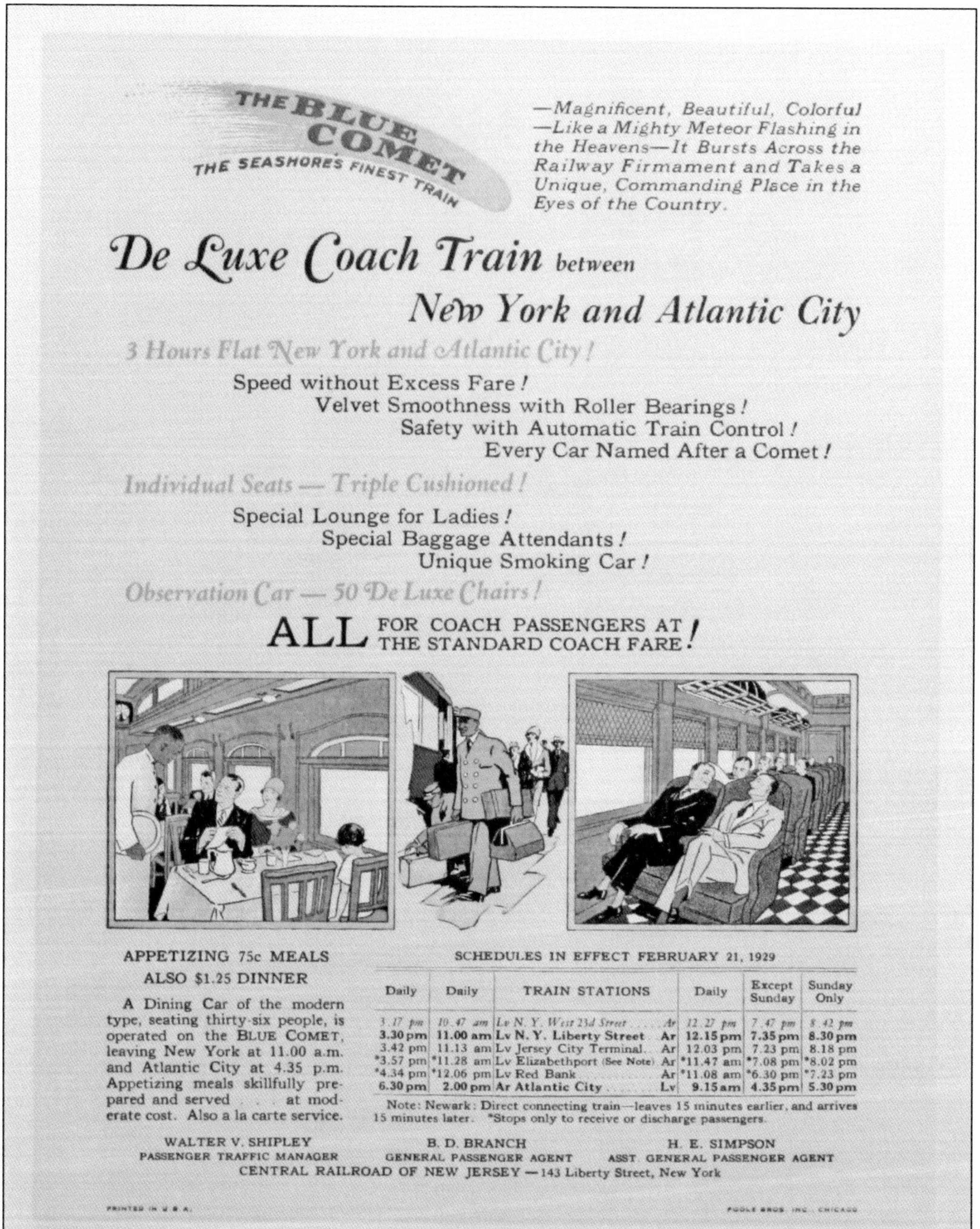

THE BLUE COMET
THE SEASHORE'S FINEST TRAIN

—Magnificent, Beautiful, Colorful —Like a Mighty Meteor Flashing in the Heavens—It Bursts Across the Railway Firmament and Takes a Unique, Commanding Place in the Eyes of the Country.

De Luxe Coach Train between *New York and Atlantic City*

3 Hours Flat New York and Atlantic City!

Speed without Excess Fare!
Velvet Smoothness with Roller Bearings!
Safety with Automatic Train Control!
Every Car Named After a Comet!

Individual Seats — Triple Cushioned!

Special Lounge for Ladies!
Special Baggage Attendants!
Unique Smoking Car!

Observation Car — 50 De Luxe Chairs!

ALL FOR COACH PASSENGERS AT THE STANDARD COACH FARE!

APPETIZING 75c MEALS
ALSO $1.25 DINNER

A Dining Car of the modern type, seating thirty-six people, is operated on the BLUE COMET, leaving New York at 11.00 a.m. and Atlantic City at 4.35 p.m. Appetizing meals skillfully prepared and served . . . at moderate cost. Also a la carte service.

SCHEDULES IN EFFECT FEBRUARY 21, 1929

Daily	Daily	TRAIN STATIONS		Daily	Except Sunday	Sunday Only
3.17 pm	*10.47 am*	*Lv N. Y. West 23d Street*	*Ar*	*12.27 pm*	*7.47 pm*	*8.42 pm*
3.30 pm	**11.00 am**	**Lv N. Y. Liberty Street**	**Ar**	**12.15 pm**	**7.35 pm**	**8.30 pm**
3.42 pm	11.13 am	Lv Jersey City Terminal	Ar	12.03 pm	7.23 pm	8.18 pm
*3.57 pm	*11.28 am	Lv Elizabethport (See Note)	Ar	*11.47 am	*7.08 pm	*8.02 pm
*4.34 pm	*12.06 pm	Lv Red Bank	Ar	*11.08 am	*6.30 pm	*7.23 pm
6.30 pm	**2.00 pm**	**Ar Atlantic City**	**Lv**	**9.15 am**	**4.35 pm**	**5.30 pm**

Note: Newark: Direct connecting train—leaves 15 minutes earlier, and arrives 15 minutes later. *Stops only to receive or discharge passengers.

WALTER V. SHIPLEY, PASSENGER TRAFFIC MANAGER
B. D. BRANCH, GENERAL PASSENGER AGENT
H. E. SIMPSON, ASST. GENERAL PASSENGER AGENT
CENTRAL RAILROAD OF NEW JERSEY — 143 Liberty Street, New York

The back cover of the brochure continues the superlative narrative. In addition, a table shows the schedule in effect as of February 21, 1929, the inaugural date for Blue Comet service. (Courtesy Robert A. Emmons.)

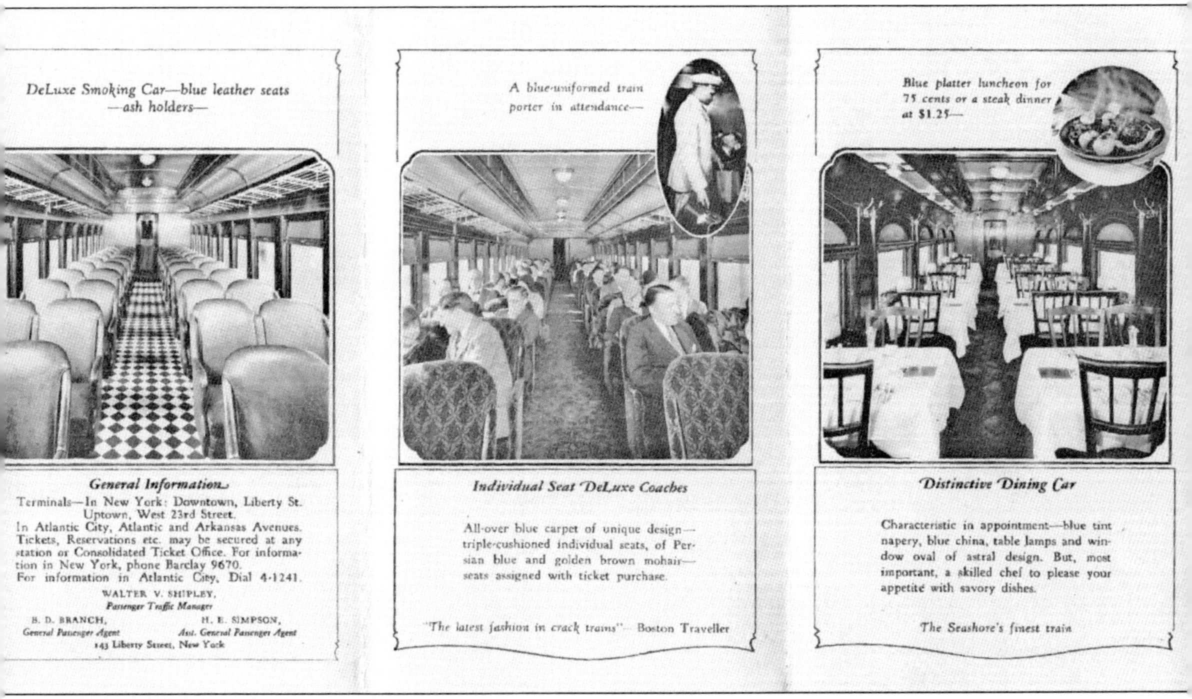

This NJC publicity flyer provided illustrations and descriptions of the different Blue Comet cars. Additional information appeared in the March 2, 1929, issue of *Railway Age* magazine. (Courtesy Ben Kranefeld.)

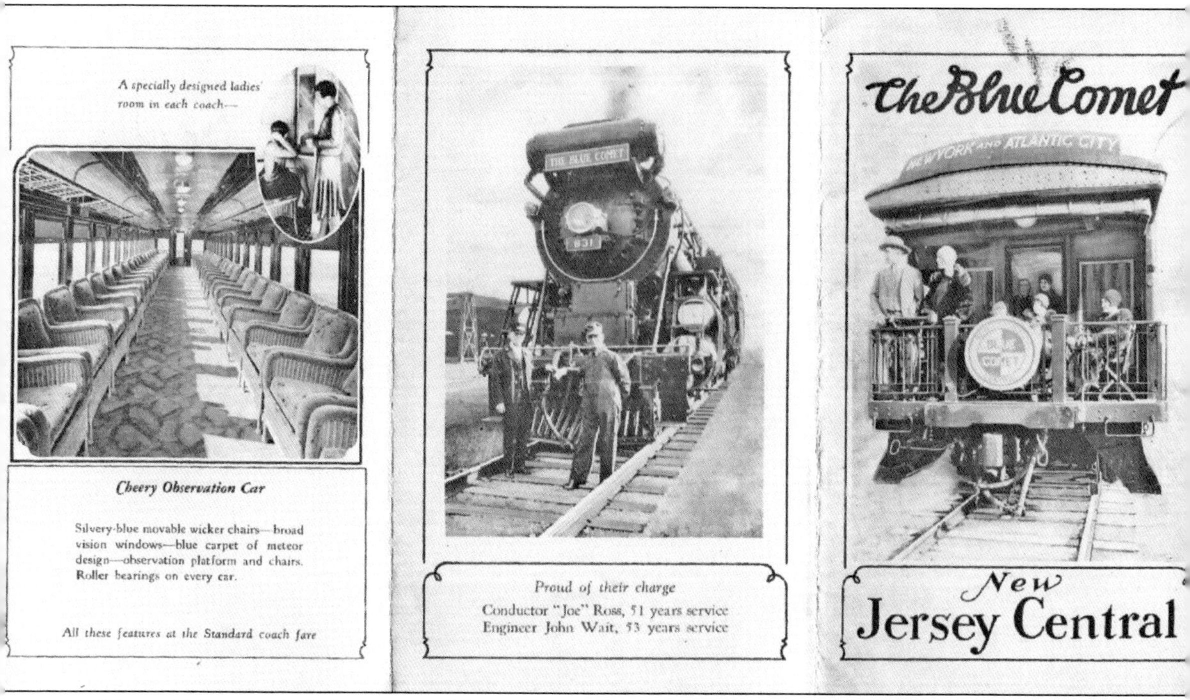

The middle panel of the same publicity flyer is shown, showing both the interior and exterior of a typical observation car in the Blue Comet service. (Courtesy Ben Kranefeld.)

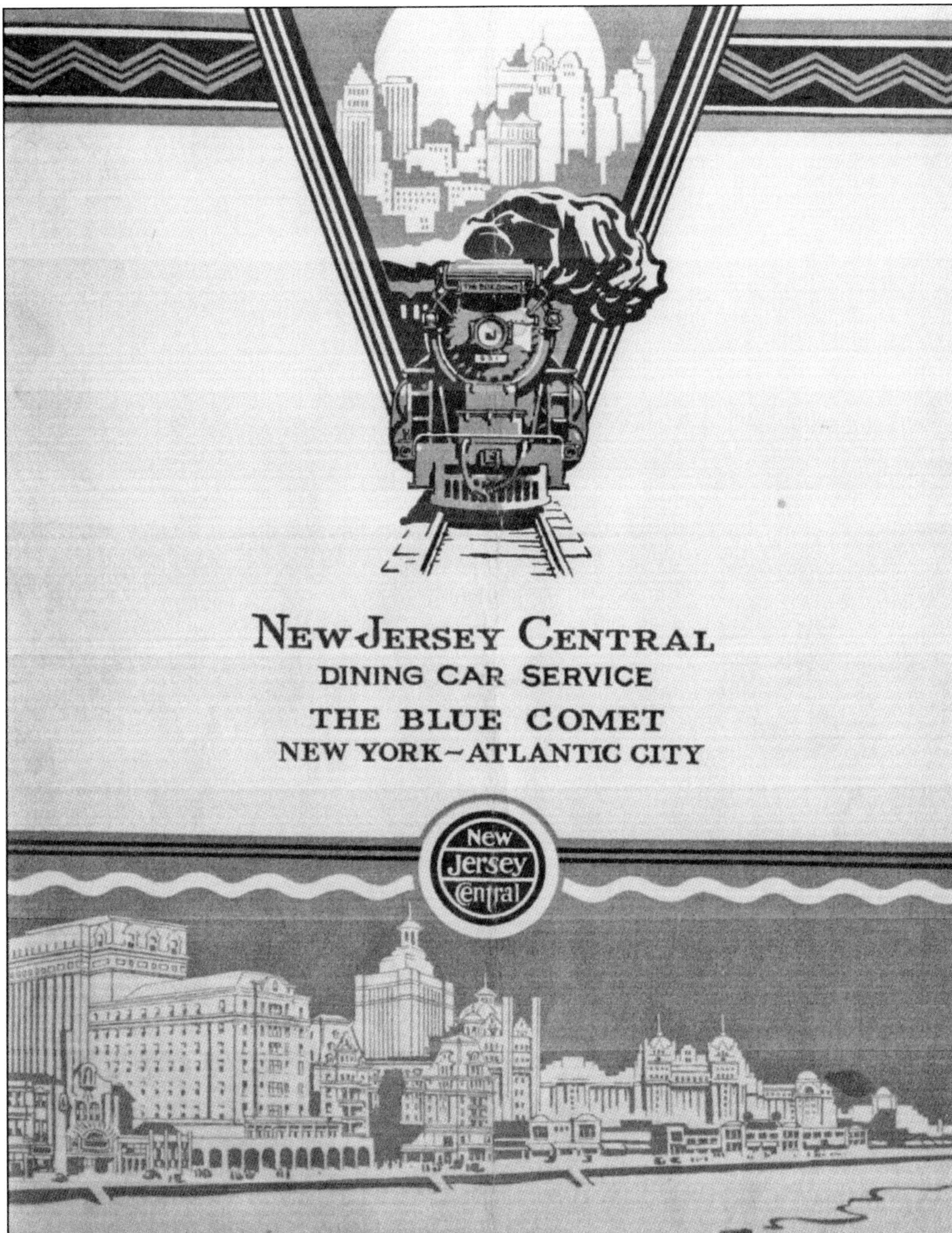

The Blue Comet's food menu shows the continuance of the Art Deco influence on NJC's operations. On the upper portion of the menu, a G-3 Pacific locomotive is seen with a view of the New York City skyline in the background, and a scene of the Atlantic City skyline is shown at the bottom, with its famous boardwalk and luxurious hotels. (Courtesy Robert A. Emmons.)

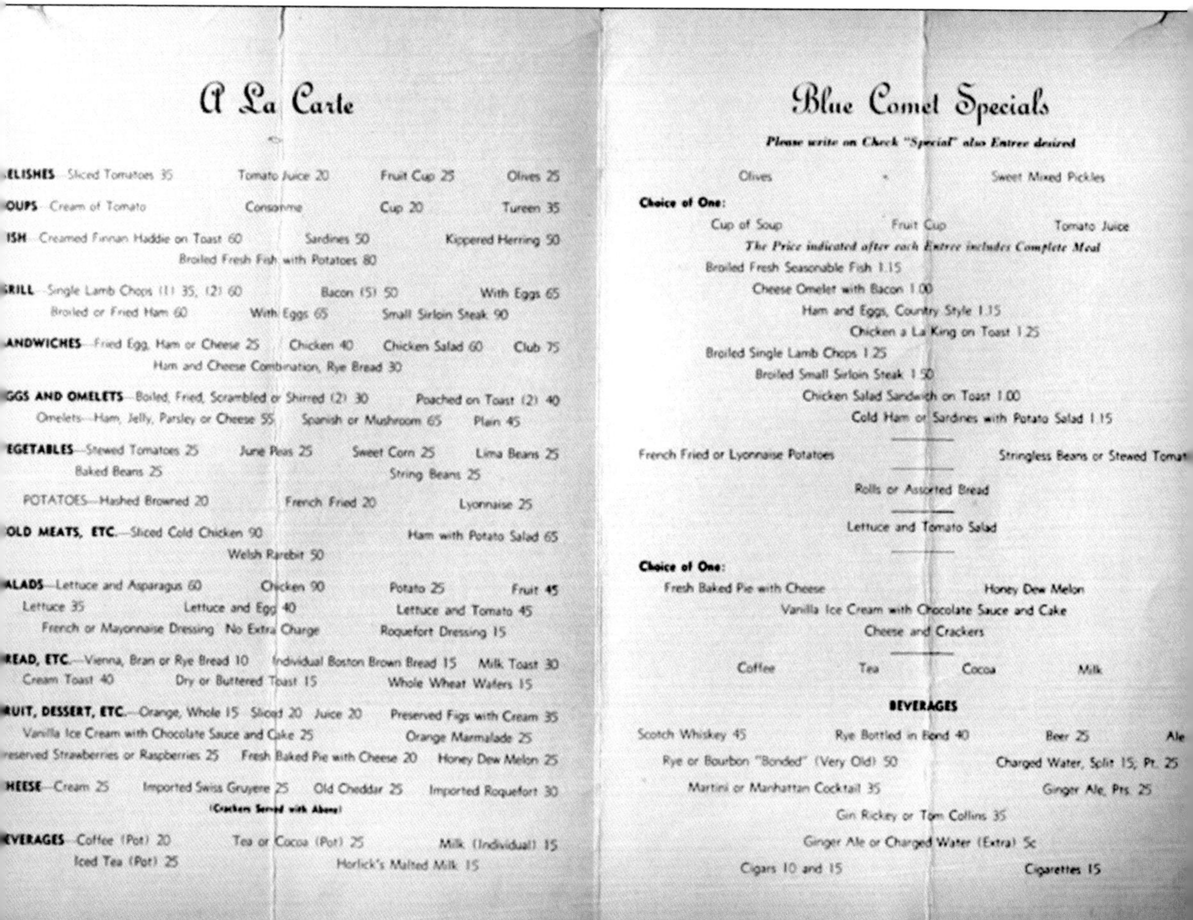

A La Carte

ELISHES—Sliced Tomatoes 35 Tomato Juice 20 Fruit Cup 25 Olives 25

OUPS—Cream of Tomato Consomme Cup 20 Tureen 35

ISH—Creamed Finnan Haddie on Toast 60 Sardines 50 Kippered Herring 50
Broiled Fresh Fish with Potatoes 80

RILL—Single Lamb Chops (1) 35; (2) 60 Bacon (5) 50 With Eggs 65
Broiled or Fried Ham 60 With Eggs 65 Small Sirloin Steak 90

ANDWICHES—Fried Egg, Ham or Cheese 25 Chicken 40 Chicken Salad 60 Club 75
Ham and Cheese Combination, Rye Bread 30

GGS AND OMELETS—Boiled, Fried, Scrambled or Shirred (2) 30 Poached on Toast (2) 40
Omelets—Ham, Jelly, Parsley or Cheese 55 Spanish or Mushroom 65 Plain 45

EGETABLES—Stewed Tomatoes 25 June Peas 25 Sweet Corn 25 Lima Beans 25
Baked Beans 25 String Beans 25

POTATOES—Hashed Browned 20 French Fried 20 Lyonnaise 25

OLD MEATS, ETC.—Sliced Cold Chicken 90 Ham with Potato Salad 65
Welsh Rarebit 50

ALADS—Lettuce and Asparagus 60 Chicken 90 Potato 25 Fruit 45
Lettuce 35 Lettuce and Egg 40 Lettuce and Tomato 45
French or Mayonnaise Dressing No Extra Charge Roquefort Dressing 15

READ, ETC.—Vienna, Bran or Rye Bread 10 Individual Boston Brown Bread 15 Milk Toast 30
Cream Toast 40 Dry or Buttered Toast 15 Whole Wheat Wafers 15

RUIT, DESSERT, ETC.—Orange, Whole 15 Sliced 20 Juice 20 Preserved Figs with Cream 35
Vanilla Ice Cream with Chocolate Sauce and Cake 25 Orange Marmalade 25
reserved Strawberries or Raspberries 25 Fresh Baked Pie with Cheese 20 Honey Dew Melon 25

HEESE—Cream 25 Imported Swiss Gruyere 25 Old Cheddar 25 Imported Roquefort 30
(Crackers Served with Above)

EVERAGES—Coffee (Pot) 20 Tea or Cocoa (Pot) 25 Milk (Individual) 15
Iced Tea (Pot) 25 Horlick's Malted Milk 15

Blue Comet Specials

Please write on Check "Special" also Entree desired

Olives Sweet Mixed Pickles

Choice of One:
Cup of Soup Fruit Cup Tomato Juice

The Price indicated after each Entree includes Complete Meal

Broiled Fresh Seasonable Fish 1.15
Cheese Omelet with Bacon 1.00
Ham and Eggs, Country Style 1.15
Chicken a La King on Toast 1.25
Broiled Single Lamb Chops 1.25
Broiled Small Sirloin Steak 1.50
Chicken Salad Sandwich on Toast 1.00
Cold Ham or Sardines with Potato Salad 1.15

French Fried or Lyonnaise Potatoes Stringless Beans or Stewed Tomat

Rolls or Assorted Bread

Lettuce and Tomato Salad

Choice of One:
Fresh Baked Pie with Cheese Honey Dew Melon
Vanilla Ice Cream with Chocolate Sauce and Cake
Cheese and Crackers

Coffee Tea Cocoa Milk

BEVERAGES

Scotch Whiskey 45 Rye Bottled in Bond 40 Beer 25 Ale
Rye or Bourbon "Bonded" (Very Old) 50 Charged Water, Split 15; Pt. 25
Martini or Manhattan Cocktail 35 Ginger Ale, Pts. 25
Gin Rickey or Tom Collins 35
Ginger Ale or Charged Water (Extra) 5c
Cigars 10 and 15 Cigarettes 15

The Blue Comet a la carte menu offers plenty of selections no matter the preferences and tastes of the train's passengers. There were certainly enough choices for either a light snack or a more substantial meal. The specials menu offered a broiled small sirloin steak with French fried or lyonnaise potatoes, stringless beans, and fresh baked pie with cheese for $1.50. The variety of the dinner selections and sheer pleasure of watching the scenery pass by made the journey as exciting and memorable as the destination. (Courtesy Joel Rosenbaum and Tom Gallo.)

The Blue Comet certainly provided a wide variety of ephemera for the passengers of the time. This Blue Comet ticket to Atlantic City is good for passage in coach. There is no date stamped on the ticket itself, but since it mentions that "return reservations may be secured . . . at Station Ticket Office, Arkansas and Arctic Avenue," it would have to be after the opening of the Pennsylvania-Reading Seashore Lines Union Terminal in October 1934, which was at that location. (Courtesy Robert A. Emmons.)

A Blue Comet paper cup was made available on board to patrons. It is nicely decorated with the Blue Comet design. A Blue Comet matchbook was available in the combines, which also served as the smoking cars (Courtesy Robert A. Emmons.)

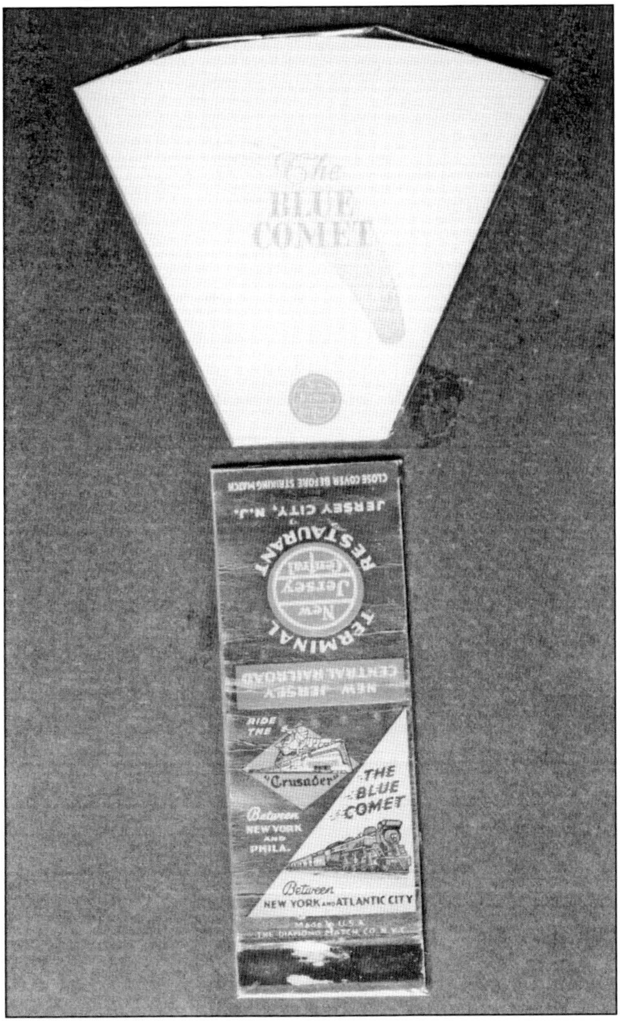

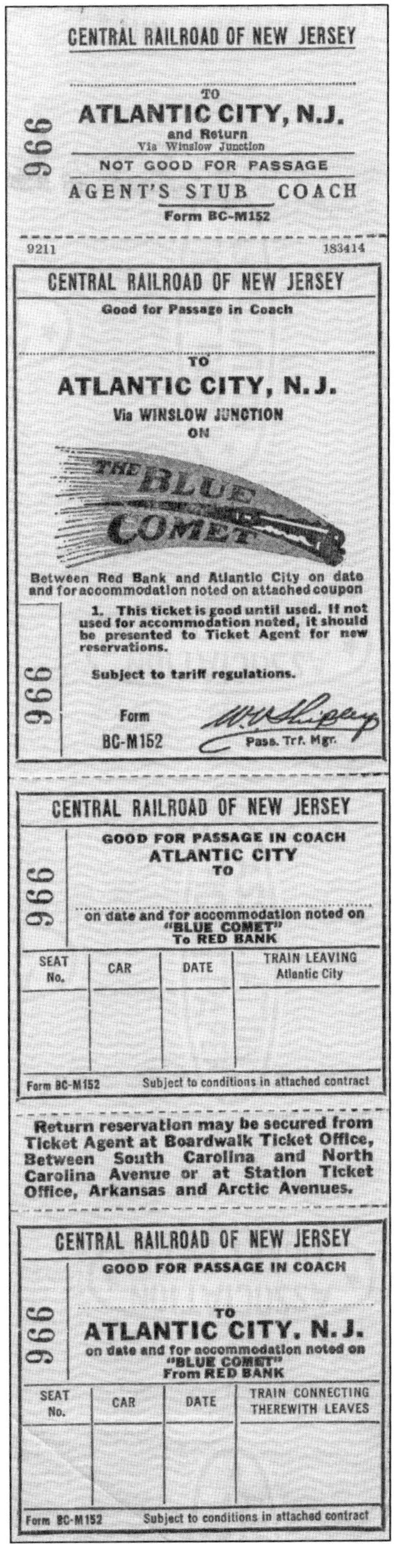
CENTRAL RAILROAD OF NEW JERSEY

TO

ATLANTIC CITY, N.J.

and Return

Via Winslow Junction

966

NOT GOOD FOR PASSAGE

AGENT'S STUB COACH

Form BC-M152

9211 183414

CENTRAL RAILROAD OF NEW JERSEY

Good for Passage in Coach

TO

ATLANTIC CITY, N.J.

Via WINSLOW JUNCTION

ON

THE BLUE COMET

Between Red Bank and Atlantic City on date and for accommodation noted on attached coupon

1. This ticket is good until used. If not used for accommodation noted, it should be presented to Ticket Agent for new reservations.

Subject to tariff regulations.

966

Form BC-M152

W. C. Shipley, Pass. Trf. Mgr.

CENTRAL RAILROAD OF NEW JERSEY

966

GOOD FOR PASSAGE IN COACH

ATLANTIC CITY

TO

on date and for accommodation noted on "BLUE COMET" To RED BANK

SEAT No.	CAR	DATE	TRAIN LEAVING Atlantic City

Form BC-M152 Subject to conditions in attached contract

Return reservation may be secured from Ticket Agent at Boardwalk Ticket Office, Between South Carolina and North Carolina Avenue or at Station Ticket Office, Arkansas and Arctic Avenues.

CENTRAL RAILROAD OF NEW JERSEY

966

GOOD FOR PASSAGE IN COACH

TO

ATLANTIC CITY, N.J.

on date and for accommodation noted on "BLUE COMET" From RED BANK

SEAT No.	CAR	DATE	TRAIN CONNECTING THEREWITH LEAVES

Form BC-M152 Subject to conditions in attached contract

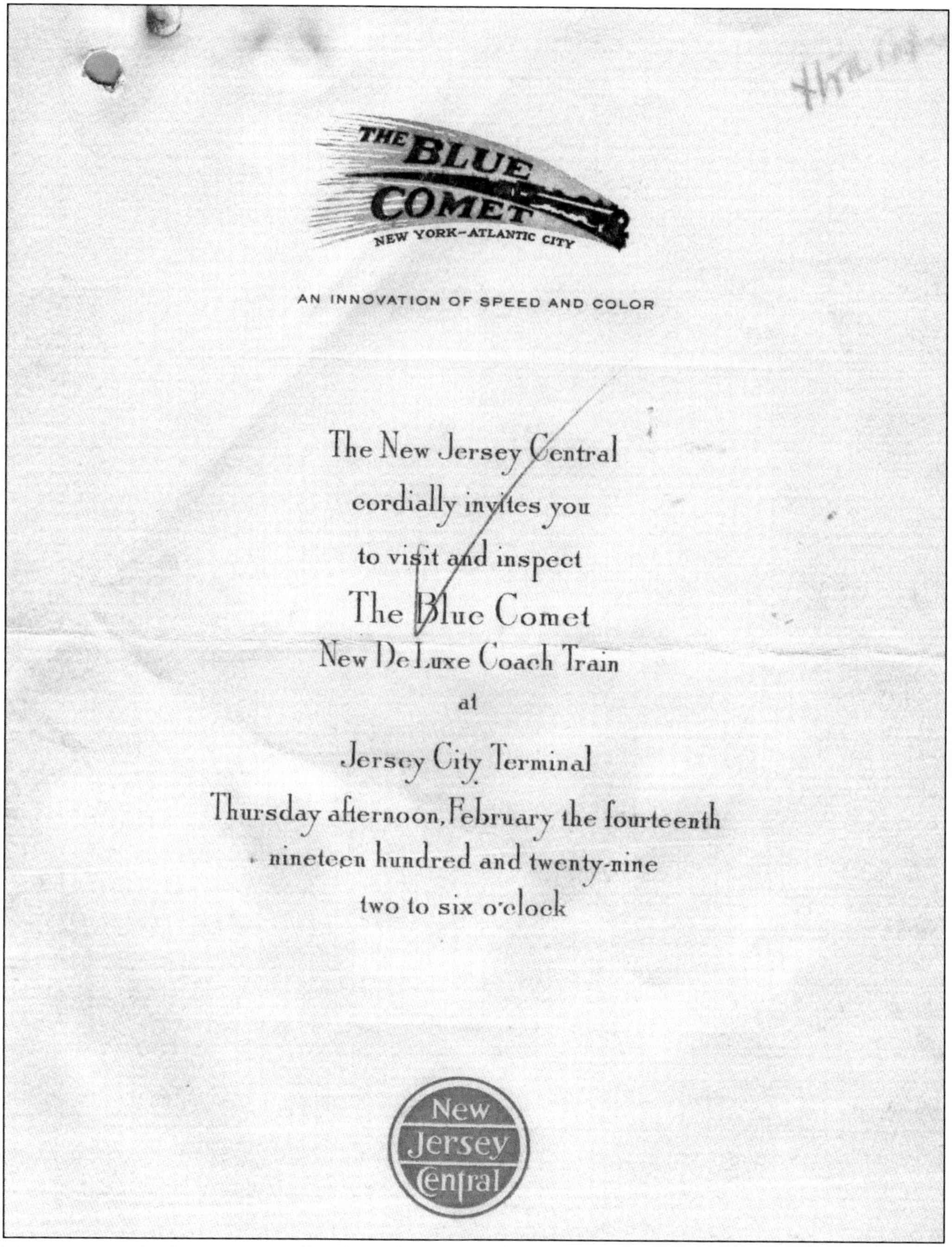

THE BLUE COMET
NEW YORK–ATLANTIC CITY

AN INNOVATION OF SPEED AND COLOR

The New Jersey Central
cordially invites you
to visit and inspect
The Blue Comet
New De Luxe Coach Train
at
Jersey City Terminal
Thursday afternoon, February the fourteenth
nineteen hundred and twenty-nine
two to six o'clock

New Jersey Central

To promote the luxurious and unique features of its soon-to-be inaugurated Blue Comet, on Thursday, February 21, 1929, the NJC arranged to put the train on public exhibition at three separate locations. Special invitation cards were printed for each location. At the top of each card appeared the Blue Comet logo and the words "an innovation of speed and color." At the NJC Jersey City terminal, a train set was displayed on Thursday, February 14, 1929, from 2:00 p.m. to 6:00 p.m. All this was due in part to a clever ad campaign via radio and newspaper that spurred public interest in the new train service. (Courtesy Robert A. Emmons.)

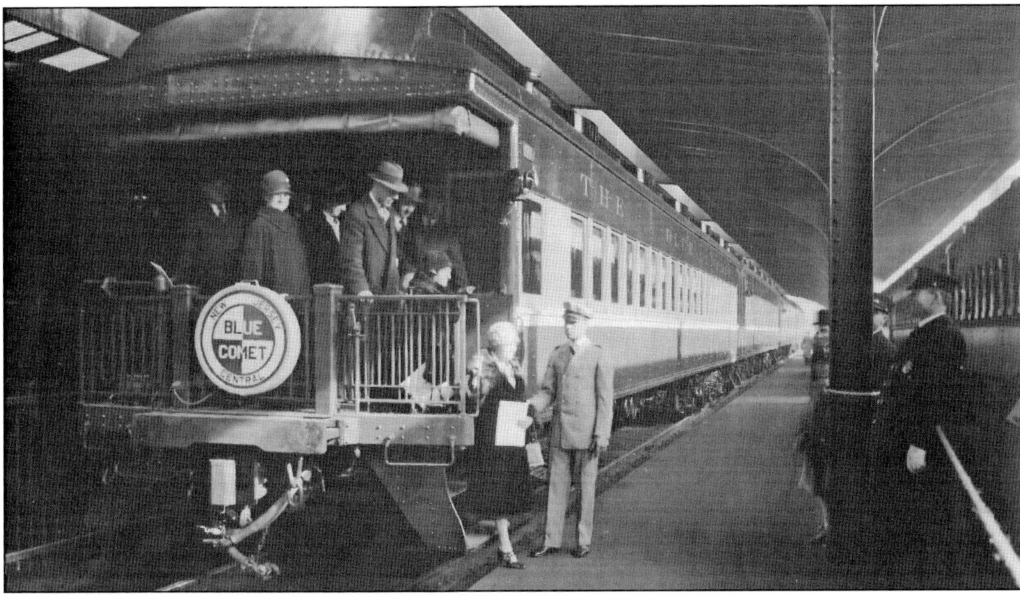

This publicity photograph, taken at the Jersey City terminal on February 14, 1929, shows a group of visitors exiting a Blue Comet observation car during a tour. The porter dressed in the Blue Comet French-blue uniform is probably James S. McKennan. The special blue porters' uniforms were made at the well-known Sigmund Eisner factory in Red Bank. (Courtesy Joel Rosenbaum and Tom Gallo.)

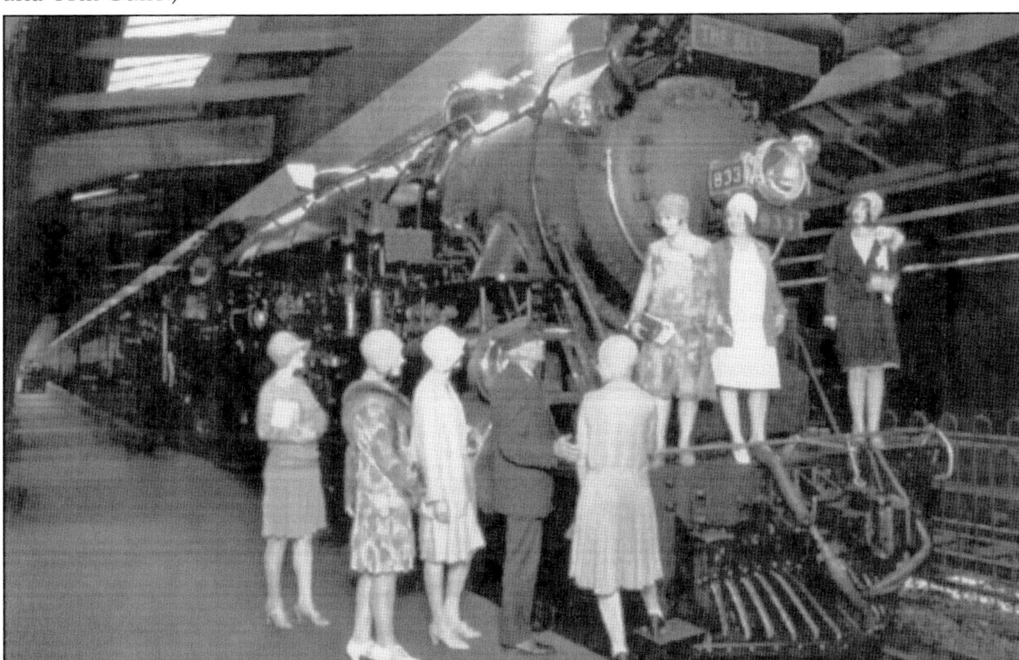

As the train conductor looks on, flapper girls are seen gracing the Blue Comet train, headed by Locomotive No. 833, at one of the passenger platforms at the NJC terminal in Jersey City. This was a publicity picture introducing the new Blue Comet service to Atlantic City. (Courtesy Tuckerton Railroad.)

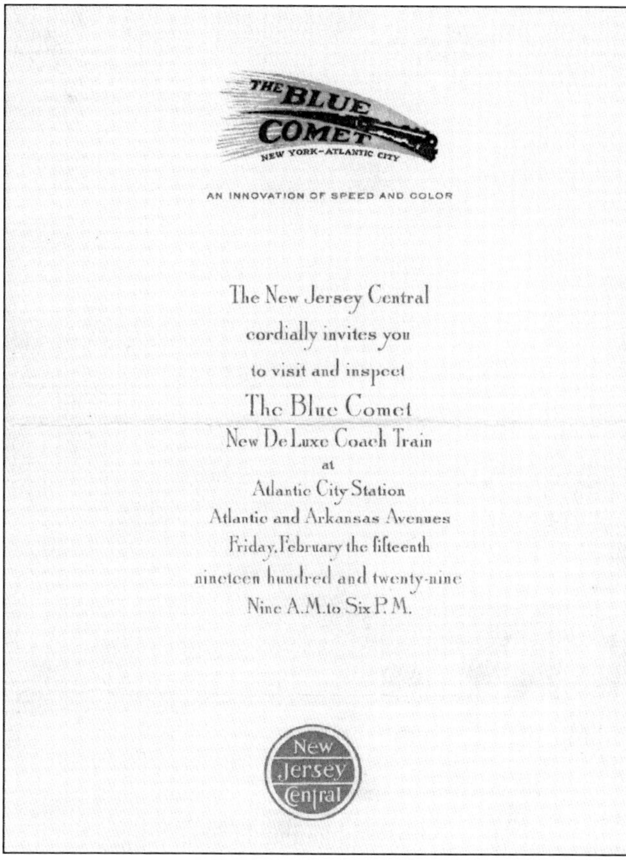

THE BLUE COMET
NEW YORK–ATLANTIC CITY

AN INNOVATION OF SPEED AND COLOR

The New Jersey Central
cordially invites you
to visit and inspect
The Blue Comet
New DeLuxe Coach Train
at
Atlantic City Station
Atlantic and Arkansas Avenues
Friday, February the fifteenth
nineteen hundred and twenty-nine
Nine A.M. to Six P.M.

New Jersey Central

A set of Blue Comet equipment was also put on exhibition at the Reading-owned Atlantic City Railroad station at Atlantic and Arkansas Avenues. This exhibition was on Friday, February 15, 1929, from 9:00 a.m. to 6:00 p.m. The following day, a set of Blue Comet equipment was exhibited at the NJC Broad Street Newark Station from 12:30 p.m. to 6:00 p.m. (Courtesy Joel Rosenbaum and Tom Gallo.)

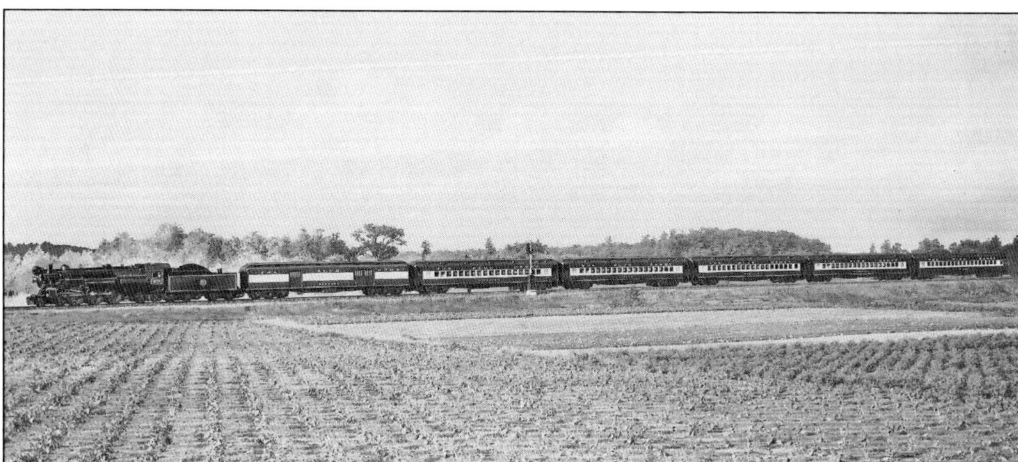

In addition to these static exhibitions, at Jersey City, Atlantic City, and Newark, a pre-inaugural publicity run was made along the main line from Atlantic City to Jersey City. Along the way, the NJC took a host of publicity pictures of its new train and distributed them to newspapers prior to the beginning of revenue service. This particular photograph was used by the NJC in its ticket counter displays; revenue service began on February 21, 1929. The cream-color band running horizontally through each car created the image of a comet streaking through space. (Author's collection.)

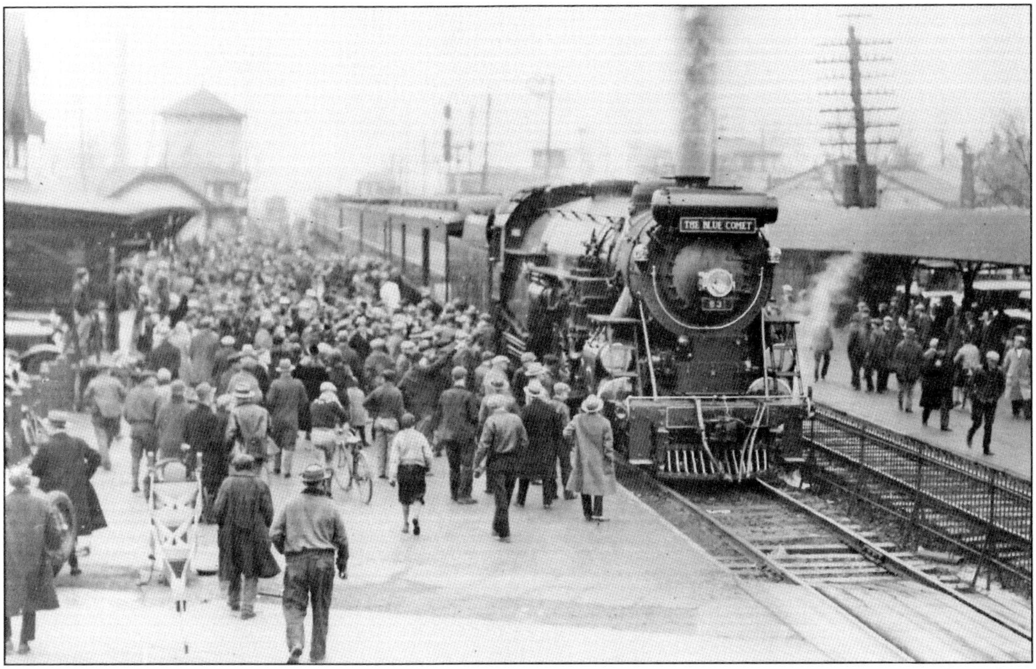

The Blue Comet is seen on its publicity run at Red Bank on Sunday, February 17, 1929, four days before the start of its revenue service. The festivities at Red Bank were covered in detail by the *Red Bank Register* on Wednesday, February 20, 1929, in the article "The Comet's New Trail." The article noted: "The third largest gathering ever at the Red Bank railroad depot was there Sunday morning to greet the Central railroad's "Blue Comet" which is to be the seashore's finest train." The article also said that nearly 3,000 people turned out on the platform to see the train. (Courtesy Joel Rosenbaum and Tom Gallo.)

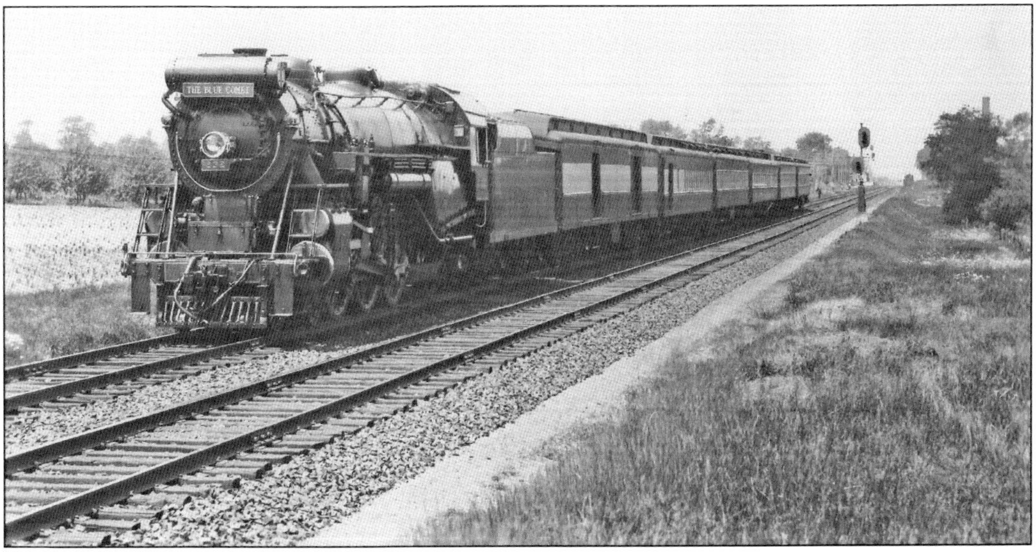

Another of the many publicity pictures of the Blue Comet prior to its inauguration, this one was taken at Hazlet, New Jersey, on the New York & Long Branch Railroad. A complete set of equipment is on hand, headed by the G-3 Pacific No. 832 locomotive. (Courtesy Joel Rosenbaum and Tom Gallo.)

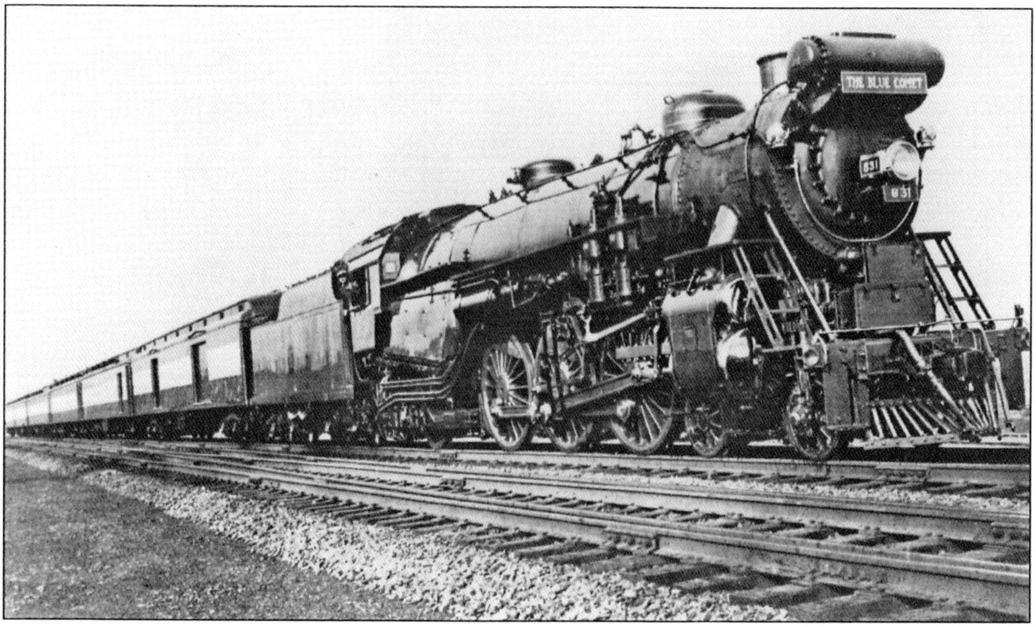

The Blue Comet is staged for still another NJC publicity photograph. The locomotive No. 831 is heading up this set of equipment. This same photograph was used in advertisements for seats used on the Blue Comet, roller bearings, and a colorized pocket calendar. This photograph can be seen hanging at the Clinton Diner. (Courtesy Joel Rosenbaum and Tom Gallo.)

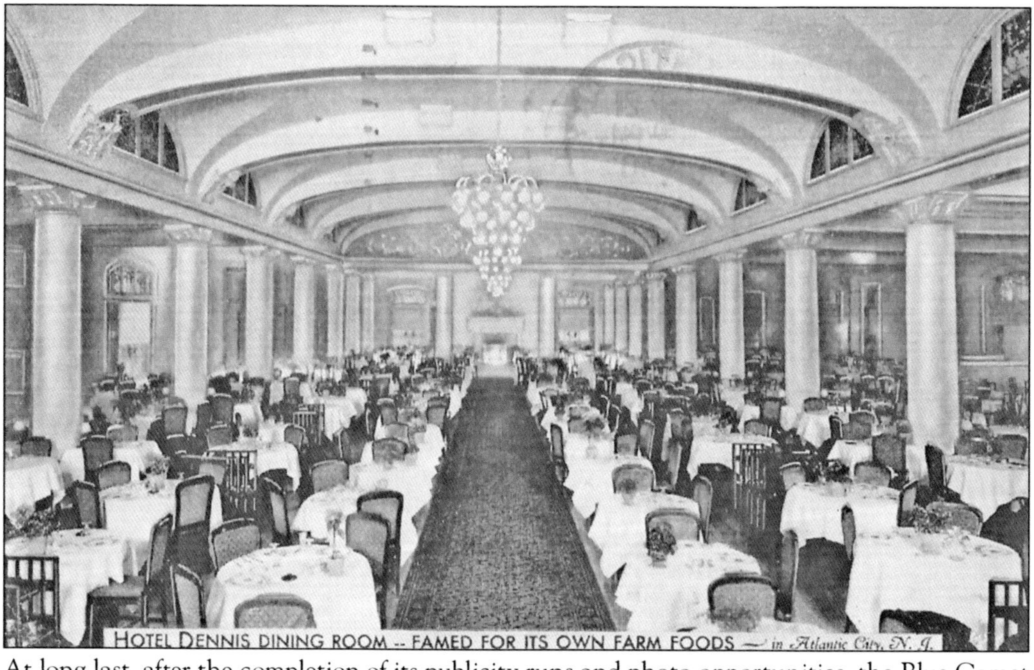

At long last, after the completion of its publicity runs and photo opportunities, the Blue Comet was finally inaugurated on February 21, 1929. The first revenue passengers to board the NJC's new flagship at the Jersey City terminal were Miss Beatrice Winter and Miss Helen Lewis of New York. Following its first arrival in Atlantic City, a formal dinner was held for railroad officials at the magnificent Hotel Dennis. (Author's collection.)

NEW YORK and ATLANTIC CITY
IN EFFECT MAY 26, 1929

NEW JERSEY SOUTHERN DIVISION

TRAIL OF THE

"BLUE COMET"

New Jersey Central

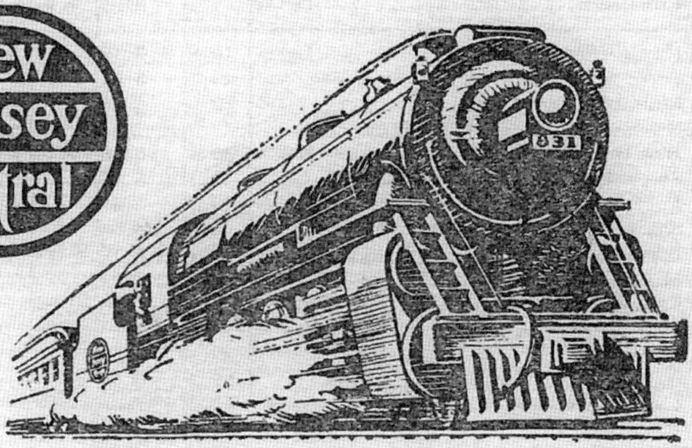

TIME TABLE

NEW YORK

LAKEWOOD LAKEHURST
TOMS RIVER BARNEGAT
VINELAND BRIDGETON

ATLANTIC CITY

IMPORTANT NOTICE
The time of trains shown in this time table is Eastern Standard Time; add one hour for Daylight Saving Time

W. V. SHIPLEY	B. D. BRANCH	H. E. SIMPSON
Passenger Traffic Manager	General Passenger Agent	Assistant General Passenger Agent

T. T. 103 (46-A) 5-20-29 (20M) Order No. 14934

The Blue Comet timetable No. 103 became effective on May 26, 1929. It was originally printed on blue paper, but this was only done for the first few years of the Blue Comet's run. Note the name of H.E. Simpson at the bottom. Simpson would later become president of the Baltimore & Ohio Railroad. (Courtesy Joel Rosenbaum and Tom Gallo.)

TABLE 1

NEW YORK—LAKEWOOD—LAKEHURST—ATLANTIC CITY

EASTERN STANDARD TIME — **WEEK-DAYS—SOUTHBOUND** — **SUNDAYS—SOUTHBOUND**

For Daylight Time Add One Hour

STATIONS	Miles	3303 4201	4205	4203	4209 (SATURDAYS ONLY)	4211	4215	4217	4229			4251	4257	4253	4261	4255	3381 4563
Leave		AM	AM	AM	AM	PM	PM	PM	PM			AM	AM	AM	PM	PM	PM
New York West 23d Street			8.47	9.47	11.45	12.07	2.17	2.25	3.45			6.47	8.47	9.47	1.15	2.17	7.47
New York Liberty Street		2.30	9.00	10.00	12.00	12.30	2.30	2.40	4.05			7.10	9.00	10.00	1.30	2.30	8.00
Jersey City	1.0	2.52	9.12	10.13	12.13	12.42	2.42	2.52	4.17			7.22	9.12	10.13	1.42	2.42	8.12
Jackson Avenue ... Leave			9.18	▴9.43	▴11.41	12.48	▴2.26	▴2.26	▴3.37			7.29	9.18	§9.27	▴1.10	▴2.10	8.18
Newark, Broad Street ... Leave			9.05	10.12	11.54	12.42	2.40	2.45	4.15			7.24	9.07	10.12	1.33	2.40	8.05
Newark Transfer ... Leave						12.54						7.36					
Elizabeth ... Leave		3.05	9.15	10.13	12.03	12.39	2.35	2.35	4.15			7.08	9.25	10.03	1.29	2.31	8.07
Elizabethport ... Leave	10.6	3.19	9.32	★10.28	a12.28	1.06	★2.57	a3.07	a4.32			7.48	9.34	★10.28	a1.57	★2.57	8.35
Perth Amboy	22.1	3.54	9.50			1.30						8.18					8.55
Matawan	29.5	4.30				1.51						8.33					9.07
Red Bank ... Leave	39.4	5.46	10.15	★11.04	1.10	2.16	★3.32	3.48	5.13			8.52	10.13	★11.04	2.39	★3.32	9.31
Shrewsbury	41.1	5.52		Dining Car		2.27								Dining Car			f9.37
Eatontown	42.7	5.57				2.30			5.20			8.59					9.41
Shark River	48.6	f6.08				f2.39			f5.34			f9.08					f9.49
Farmingdale	52.1	6.17	10.32		1.28	2.46			5.41			9.15	10.32		2.56		9.56
Maxim	54.8	6.23							f5.45			f9.19					10 f01
Lakewood ... Arrive	59.3	6.30	10.46		1.41	3.02		4.15	5.54			9.26	10.44		3.08		10.10
Lakewood ... Leave	59.3	6.48	10.46	★11.29	1.41	3.02	★3.57	4.15	5.54			9.26	10.44	★11.29	3.08	★3.57	10.10
South Lakewood	62.8	f6.55				3.09			f6.00			f9.32	f10.51				10 f17
Lakehurst ... Arrive	67.2	7.06	11.00		1.54	3.16		4.29	6.05			9.47	10.58		3.19		10.23
Lakehurst ... Leave	67.2	7.06	Parlor Car	★11.41 (The Blue Comet)	Parlor Car, Dining-Club Car	3.21	★4.08 (The Blue Comet)	Parlor Car					Parlor Car	★11.41 (The Blue Comet)	Parlor Car	★4.08 (The Blue Comet)	
Whitings	73.0	7.22				3.31											
Pasadena	77.7	f7.27				f3.36											
Woodmansie	80.5	f7.33				f3.41											
Chatsworth	85.6	7.40				3.48											
Pine Crest (Harris)	88.4	f7.44				f3.52											
Sandy Ridge	91.0	f7.48				f3 56											
Atsion	96.8	7.55				4.03											
Parkdale	99.2	f7.57				f4.05											
Elm	103.8	f8.06				f4.20											
Winslow Junction ... Arrive	105.3	8.10				4 23											
Winslow Junction ... Leave	105.3	⊕8.39				⊕5.16											
Hammonton	108.3	⊕8.45		12.29		⊕5.22	4.59							12.29		4.59	
Egg Harbor	119.4	⊕9.05				⊕5.40	♁5.28									♁5.22	
Atlantic City (Atlantic and Arkansas Aves.)	136.3	⊕9.30		1.00		⊕6.06	5.30							1.00		5.30	
Arrive		AM	AM	PM	PM	PM	PM	PM	PM			AM	AM	PM	PM	PM	PM

3381/4563: No Baggage Carried. Passengers for stations Shrewsbury to Lakehurst incl., change at Red Bank.

EXPLANATION OF REFERENCE MARKS

a—Stops on notice to Agents to take passengers.
b—Stops on notice to Conductor to leave passengers.
f—Stops on notice to Agent to take passengers and on notice to Conductor to leave passengers.
★—Stops only on notice to Agent to take passengers for Hammonton and points beyond.

The timetable for the southbound segment (New York to Atlantic City) of the New Jersey Central for May 26, 1929, is shown here. The timetable shows both the regular local rail service as well as the Blue Comet train. The timetable cleverly denotes Blue Comet trains with the streaking Blue Comet logo. The two daily Blue Comet southbound trains to Atlantic City were Nos. 4203 and 4213. On Sundays, they were Nos. 4253 and 4255. A dining car was provided only on Nos. 4203 and 4253. (Courtesy Joel Rosenbaum and Tom Gallo.)

ATLANTIC CITY—LAKEHURST—LAKEWOOD—NEW YORK

E 2

ERN STANDARD TIME	WEEK-DAYS—NORTHBOUND							SUNDAYS—NORTHBOUND				
Daylight Time Add One Hour STATIONS	4200	4206	4208	4212 3318	4214	4218	4224	4250	4252	4550 3380	4264	4268
	AM	AM	AM	AM	PM	PM	PM	AM	AM	PM	PM	PM
ic City { Atlantic and Arkansas Aves. } ..Leave	....	8.15	....	....	....	3.35	①3.00	8.15	....	....	4.30	....
arbor	....	δ8.22	....	....	....	δ3.19	①3.19	δ7.50	....	Passengers from stations Lakehurst to Shrewsbury, incl., change at Red Bank.	....	....
onton	....	8.43	....	....	....	4.03	①3.21	8.43	....		4.58	....
w Junction ... Arrive	....	....	....	....	....	....	①3.36	....	....		....	....
w Junction ... Leave	....	THE BLUE COMET	Parlor Car	8.50	Parlor Car	THE BLUE COMET	4.55	THE BLUE COMET	Parlor Car		THE BLUE COMET	....
	....			8.55			f4.59					....
le	....			f9.00			f5.06					....
	....			9.05			5.11					....
Ridge	..			f9.13			f5.19					....
est (Harris)	....			f9.17			f5.23					....
orth	....			9.23			5.29					....
nansie	....			f9.31			f5.37					....
na	....			f9.37			f5.43					....
gs	....			9.44			5.50					....
urst ... Arrive	..	C9.32		9.58		C4.55	5.59	C9.32			C5.47	....
urst ... Leave	5.57	....	9.35	9.58	2.35	....	6.05	....	10.00	2.28	....	6.45
Lakewood	f6.05	....	....	10.06	....	....	6.13	....	....	f2.32	....	f6.52
ood ... Arrive	6.15	C9.44	9.48	10.16	2.47	C5.06	6.24	C9.44	10.14	2.40	....	7.06
ood ... Leave	6.15	....	9.48	10.16	2.47	Dining Car	6.24	....	10.14	2.40	Dining Car	7.00
	f6.23	....	....	f10.25	....		f6.30	....	....	f2.46		....
gdale	6.28	....	....	10.33	2.58		6.34	....	10.33	2.56		7.10
River	f6.35	....	....	f10.41	....		f6.40	....	....	f3.08		f7.18
own	6.45	....	....	10.53	....		6.51	....	....	3.20		f7.27
bury	6.50	....	....	f10.57	....		f6.55	....	....	f3.24		....
ank ... Arrive	6.55	C10.08	10.12	11.02	3.15	C5.30	7.00	C10.08	10.51	3.29	C6.23	7.34
an	7.12	....	....	11.44	....	....	7.40	....	....	4.07	....	....
Amboy	7.27	....	....	12.02	3.40	....	7.59	....	....	....	....	....
ethport ... Arrive	7.48	C10.47	b10.52	12.26	b3.58	C6.08	8.20	C10.47	b11.32	4.35	C7.02	8.18
eth ... Arrive	8.34	11.05	11.05	12.47	4.12	6.21	9.06	11.45	11.45	5.25	7.16	8.33
k Transfer ... Arrive	....	....	....	....	....	....	....	....	....	4.45	....	8.28
k, Broad Street ... Arrive	8.25	11.02	11.16	1.01	4.16	6.23	8.40	11.02	11.59	4.55	7.17	8.37
n Avenue ... Arrive	*8.38	§11.29	*11.29	*1.36	*4.32	*6.42	*9.07	*11.22	*12.20	4.51	*7.30	8.34
City	8.05	11.03	11.08	12.46	4.13	6.23	8.38	11.03	11.48	4.58	7.18	8.41
Liberty Street	8.20	11.15	11.20	1.00	4.25	6.35	8.50	11.15	12.00	5.10	7.30	8.54
West 23d Street	8.42	11.27	11.33	1.12	4.37	6.49	....	11.27	12.12	5.25	7.42	9.12
Arrive	AM	AM	AM	PM	PM	PM	PM	AM	PM	PM	PM	PM

EXPLANATION OF REFERENCE MARKS—Continued

C—Stops only on notice to conductor to leave passengers from Hammonton and points beyond.

⊕—Change at Winslow Junction.
δ—Change at Hammonton.
*—Change at East Ferry Street.
*—Change at Jersey City.
§—Change at Newark.
①—Change at Winslow Junction, first trip June 1.

TIME: 12.01 Midnight to 12.00 noon is indicated by light-faced type.
12.01 noon to 12.00 midnight is indicated by heavy-faced type.

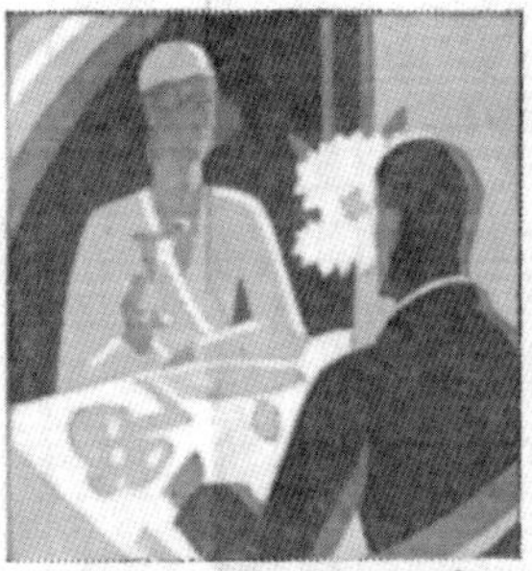

BLUE!

—even to napery and china—featuring an appetizing blue platter luncheon at 75 cents also special $1.25 Steak Dinner.

The Blue Comet
to ATLANTIC CITY

DeLuxe Coach Train with,
Individual seats
Observation car
Unique smoking car
Special ladies' lounge
Special train porter
Three hours flat

ALL these features at the standard coach fare. No Extra Charge.

The northbound segment (Atlantic City to New York) of the May 26, 1929, timetable is shown here. The northbound Blue Comet trains to New York, during the week, were Nos. 4206 and 4218. On Sundays, they were Nos. 4250 and 4264. A dining car was provided only on Nos. 4218 and 4264. Note the Art Deco advertisement for the Blue Comet's deluxe features, dining car décor, and appetizing blue platter lunch and special steak dinner prices. (Courtesy Joel Rosenbaum and Tom Gallo.)

EFFECTIVE APRIL 30, 1933

THE BLUE COMET
NEW YORK AND ATLANTIC CITY

Through Express Train Schedule

New York and Atlantic City

Observation Car—Individual Seat Coaches

THIS TIME TABLE is printed in DAYLIGHT SAVING TIME for the convenience of our patrons. EASTERN STANDARD TIME is one hour earlier.

DAYLIGHT SAVING TIME

TO ATLANTIC CITY

STATIONS	WEEKDAYS 4203		WEEKDAYS 4209		WEEKDAYS 4215	SUNDAYS 4253
	AM	Saturdays Only	PM	Fridays Only	PM	AM
New York, West 23d St. ......Lv.	9.47		1.07		3.17	9.47
New York, Liberty St. .... "	10.00		1.20		3.30	10.00
Jersey City .... "	10.13		1.32		3.42	10.13
Jackson Ave., J. City.... "	‡9.38		‡12.41		‡3.21	§9.20
Newark, Broad St........ "	10.10		1.32		3.40	10.10
Elizabeth .... "	10.18		1.36		3.46	10.19
Elizabethport .... "	a10.28		a1.48		a3.57	a10.28
Atlantic City (Atlantic and Arkansas Avs.) Ar.	1.00 PM		4.20 PM		6.30 PM	1.00 PM

FROM ATLANTIC CITY

STATIONS	WEEKDAYS	WEEKDAYS 4218	WEEKDAYS	SUNDAYS 4262
		PM		PM
Atlantic City (Atlantic and Arkansas Ave.) Lv.	....	3.30	....	3.30
Elizabethport ....Ar.	....	b6.02	....	b6.02
Elizabeth .... "	....	6.17	....	6.13
Newark, Broad St....... "	....	6.20	....	6.20
Jackson Ave., J. City.... "	....	‡6.59	....	‡7.20
Jersey City .... "	....	6.17	....	6.17
New York, Liberty St.......... "	....	6.30	....	6.30
New York, West 23d St...... "	....	6.42 PM	....	6.42 PM

a—Stops only on notice to receive passengers.
b—Stops only on notice to discharge passengers.
§—Change at Newark. ‡Change at Jersey City.
A.M. time in light type. P.M. time in heavy type.

Passenger Traffic Manager
Central Railroad of New Jersey

Passenger Traffic Manager
Reading Company

Declining ridership on the Blue Comet resulted in a reduction in service to only one daily round-trip service, as shown in this train schedule dated April 30, 1933. By 1932, the total number of passengers carried by the Blue Comet had dramatically fallen as the economic effects of the worsening Depression began to have an effect on ridership. In 1929, ridership stood at 62,105, but by 1932, it had fallen to 29,774. (Courtesy Mitch Dakelman.)

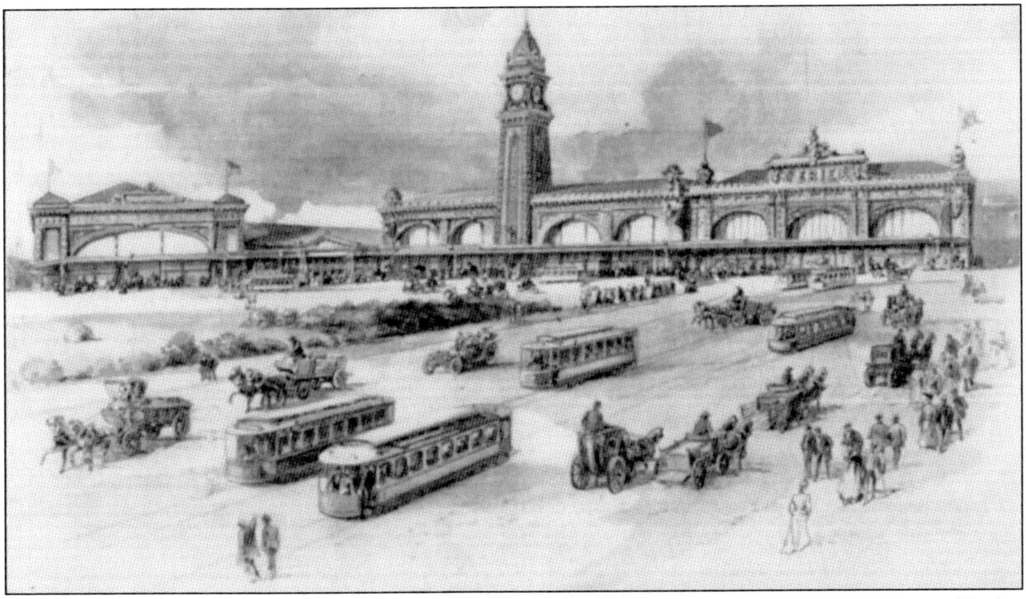

As in the case of all the NJC pre–Blue Comet trains, as well as the Blue Comet itself, the legendary journey to and from Atlantic City began at one of the two ferry locations in downtown Manhattan. Depicted here are ferry stations occupied by the Erie, Lackawanna, and NJC at the foot of West Twenty-Third Street in New York City. This was one of two ferry terminals used by the NJC to transport passengers from Lower Manhattan to its railroad terminal in Jersey City. Before proceeding to the NJC's main ferry terminal on Liberty Street, passengers would be loaded onto ferries at this location. The Twenty-Third Street Terminal was closed on November 14, 1941, due in part to the waning popularity of the Blue Comet service to Atlantic City. This 1905 illustration shows passengers arriving and leaving at the terminal by different modes of travel. (Courtesy New York Public Library.)

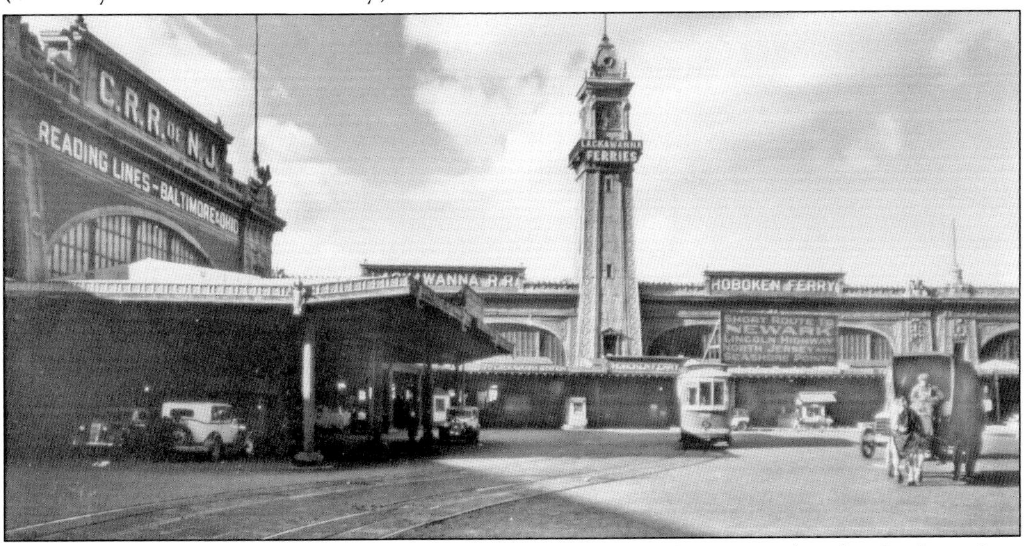

This 1935 photograph is from a special collection of historical images taken by the legendary New York City photographer Berenice Abbott (1898–1991) and reproduced from the archives of the New York Public Library. It shows ferry services at the West Twenty-Third Street Terminal, which also served the NJC and Lackawanna Railroad. (Courtesy New York Public Library.)

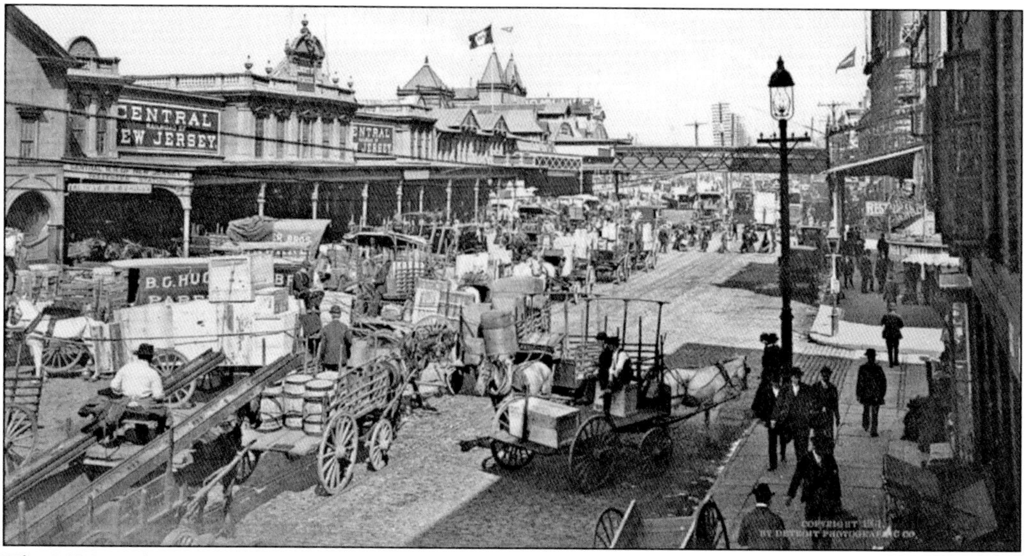

The NJC's Liberty Street Ferry Terminal was at the foot of Liberty and West Streets and served as the main NJC ferry terminal, transporting passengers to its train terminal in Jersey City until 1967. During the years of the Blue Comet, it provided this service for the NJC. The hustle and bustle of Lower Manhattan can be seen here as passengers and merchandise vendors crowd the busy street. (Courtesy Library of Congress.)

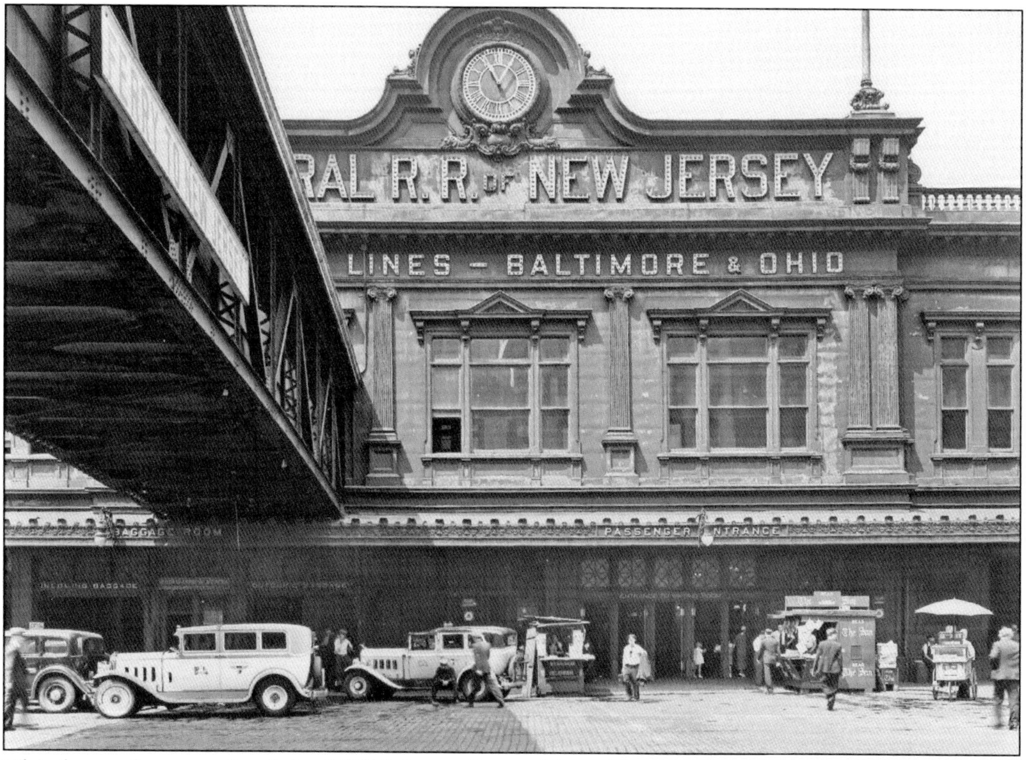

This later photograph of the NJC Liberty Street Ferry Terminal was taken in 1936. Sharing the NJC Terminal is the Reading Lines and the Baltimore & Ohio Railroad. Note the elevated covered walkway to the ferries. (Courtesy New York Public Library.)

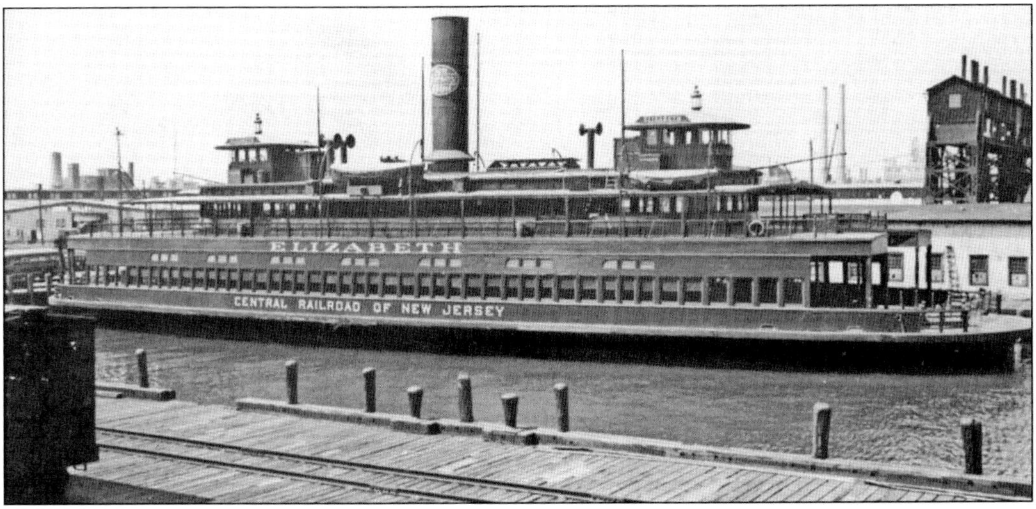

The ferry *Elizabeth* was one of the NJC's ferries that transported both passengers and vehicles from Lower Manhattan across the Hudson River to the railroad's massive terminal in Jersey City. These ferries serviced both the NJC's Liberty Street and Twenty-Third Street Terminals. These ferry operations were a vital and indispensable part of NJC's operations since it did not have a direct rail link to Lower Manhattan, as did the Pennsylvania Railroad, which operated under the Hudson River through the PRR's own tunnel to its Pennsylvania Station in New York City. (Above, author's collection; below, courtesy Information Works Inc.)

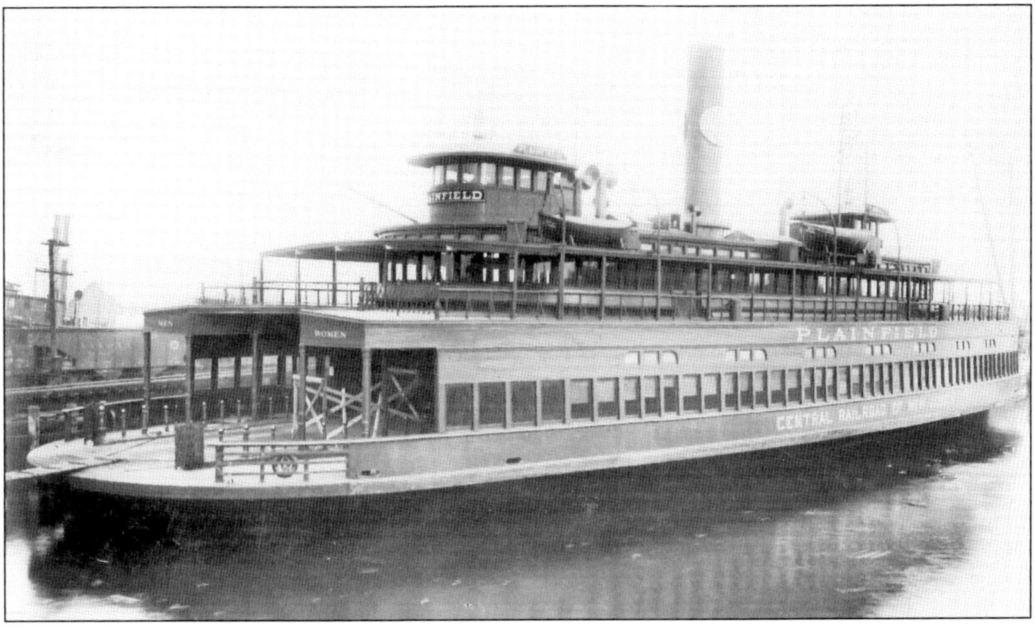

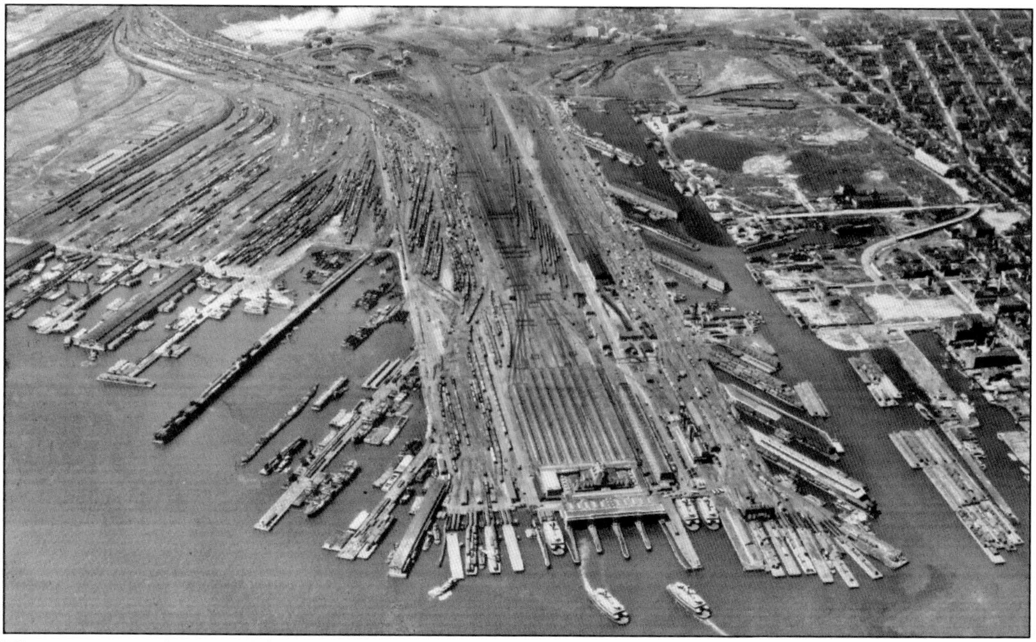

This is an aerial view of the approach to the NJC Jersey City Passenger Terminal. The terminal is at bottom, behind the ferry wharves. The NJC tracks and yards are behind the terminal. Additional docks flank the terminal itself on either side. The terminal, along with its docks and yards, was one of several terminal complexes that dominated the western waterfront of New York Harbor from the mid-19th to the mid-20th century. (Courtesy Robert A. Emmons.)

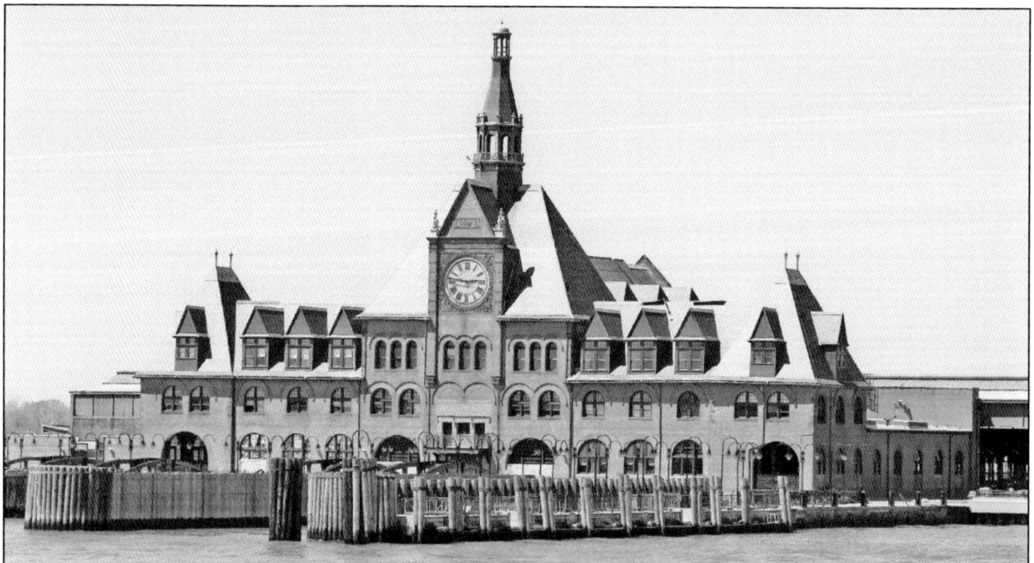

The NJC terminal in Jersey City also served the Reading Railroad, Baltimore & Ohio Railroad, and Lehigh Valley Railroad during various periods in its 78 years of operation from 1889 to 1967. At the turn of the 20th century, the NJC terminal accommodated from 30,000 to 50,000 people per day on 128 ferry runs and 275 trains. By 1914, the train and ferry sheds were enlarged to accommodate the growing numbers of commuters. The terminal claimed a record use of 21 million passengers in 1929. (Author's collection.)

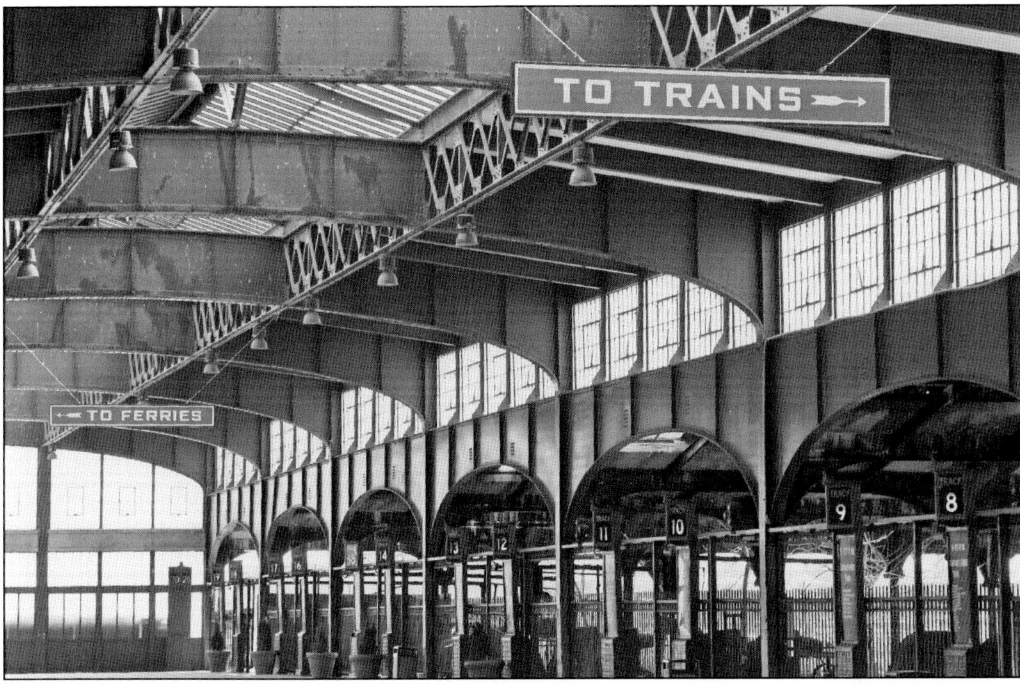

The three-story Victorian main terminal opened in 1889 and was built by the firm of Peabody & Steans of Boston. The red brick structure displays Richardson-Romanesque architectural elements characterized by the steep pitched roof with dormers on the third floor, prominent arched windows, cupola, and tower with a clock facing the waterfront. The interior included a concourse, ticket office, and waiting room of English buff-colored glazed brick walls on the first floor. The ceiling of the waiting room was supported by red iron trusses in a starburst design. (Courtesy Library of Congress.)

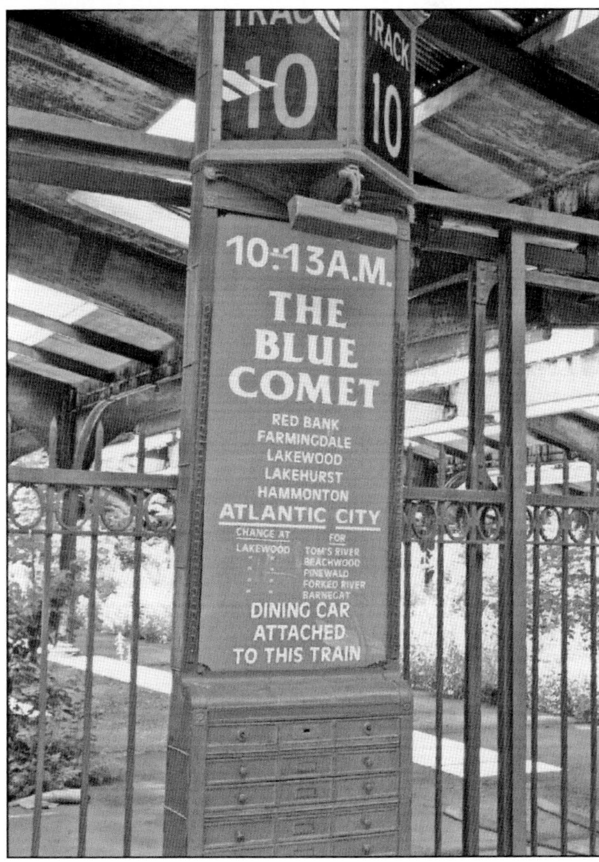

This is a reproduction of the Blue Comet train sign that was used at the Jersey City terminal. Passengers were directed to Track No. 10 for the 10:13 a.m. departure to Atlantic City with a dining car assigned to the train. This was the Blue Comet train No. 4203, which would have arrived in Atlantic City at 1:00 p.m. (Author's collection.)

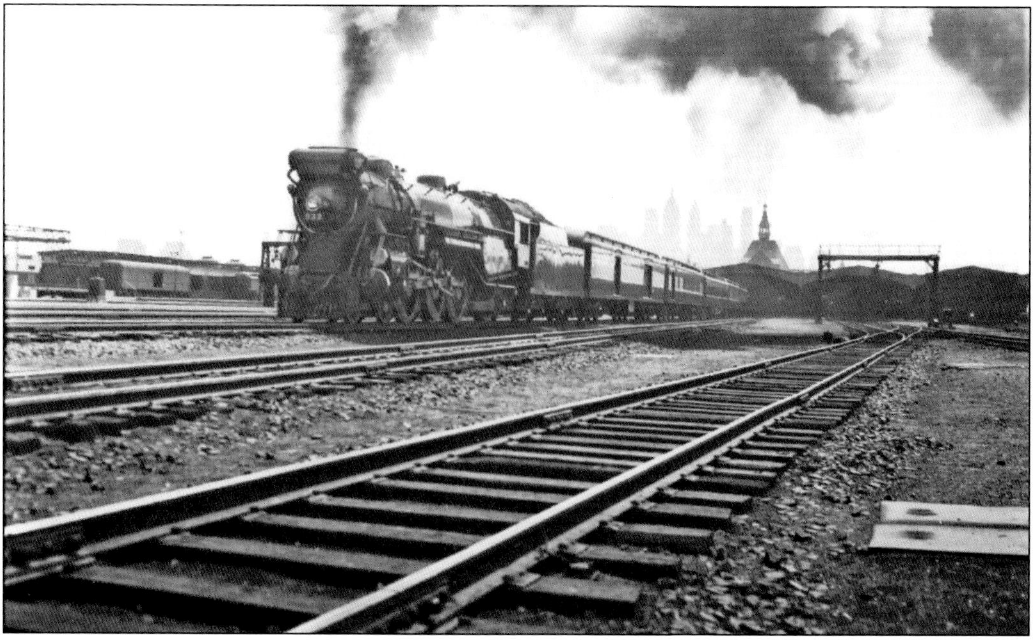

In 1935, the Blue Comet is building up steam as it departs the Jersey City terminal with the skyline of New York City, cloaked in an early morning haze, standing majestically in the background. This locomotive is Pacific No. 833. (Author's collection.)

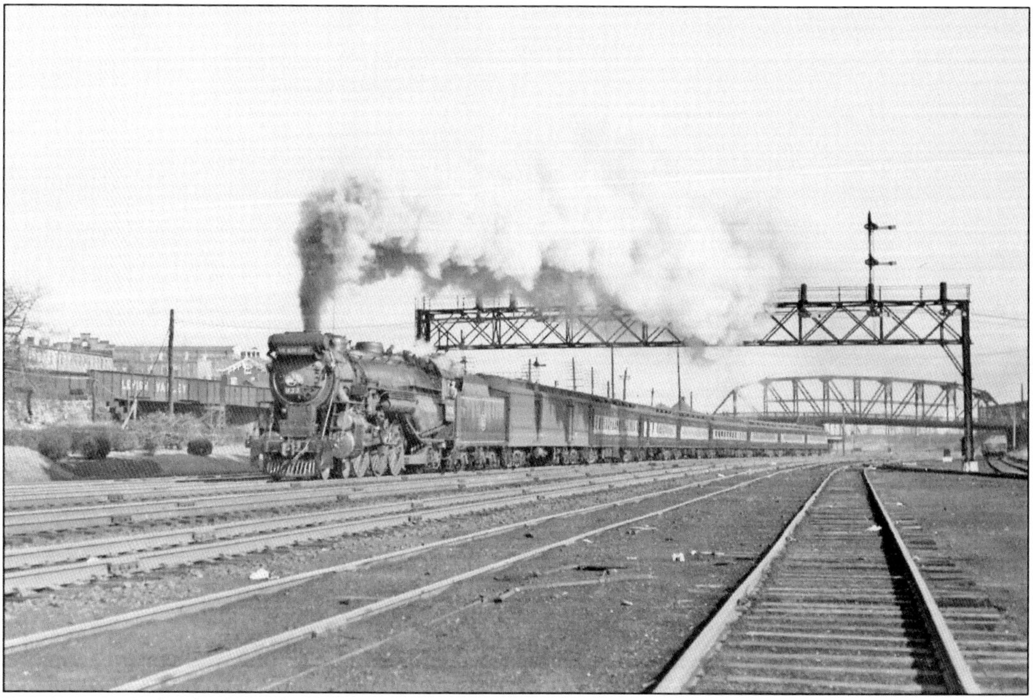

Pacific No. 833 leads the eight-car southbound Blue Comet train No. 4253 through the Communipaw section of Jersey City on November 14, 1937. Train No. 4253 left the Jersey City terminal on 10:13 a.m. on Sunday, which accounts for the long train. (Photograph by George Votava, courtesy Joel Rosenbaum and Tom Gallo.)

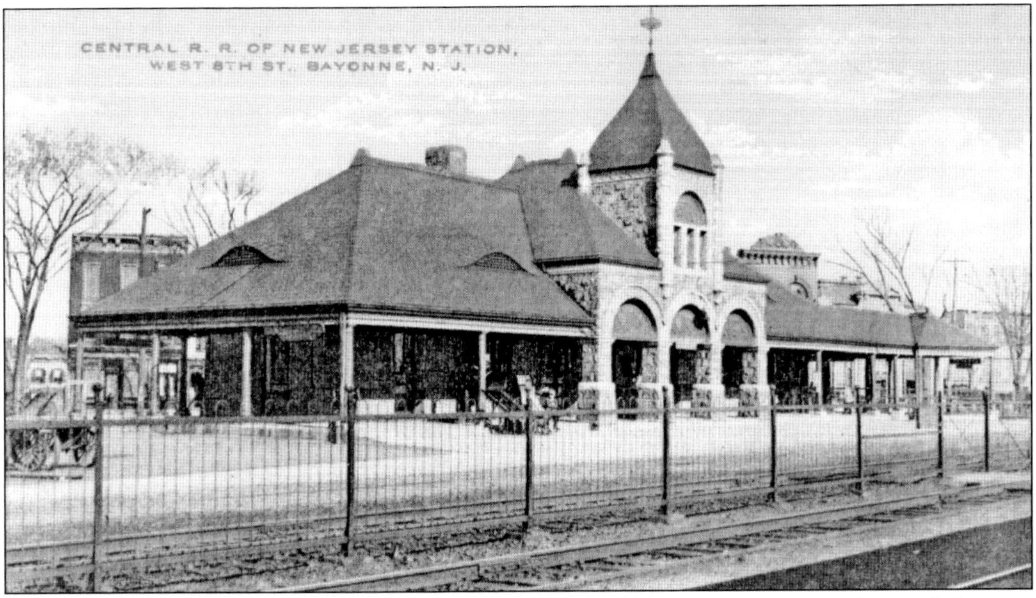

The NJC station at West Eighth Street in Bayonne, New Jersey, was not a regular weekday stop for the Blue Comet, although the train regularly passed the station on its way to Atlantic City. However, sometime after 1932, it was used on Sundays for southbound Blue Comet service. This service continued until the end of the Blue Comet in 1941. In the NJC timetable, effective April 27, 1941, on Sundays, the Blue Comet train No. 4253 would stop at Bayonne "only on notice to [the] Agent to take passengers for Hammonton and points beyond." (Author's collection.)

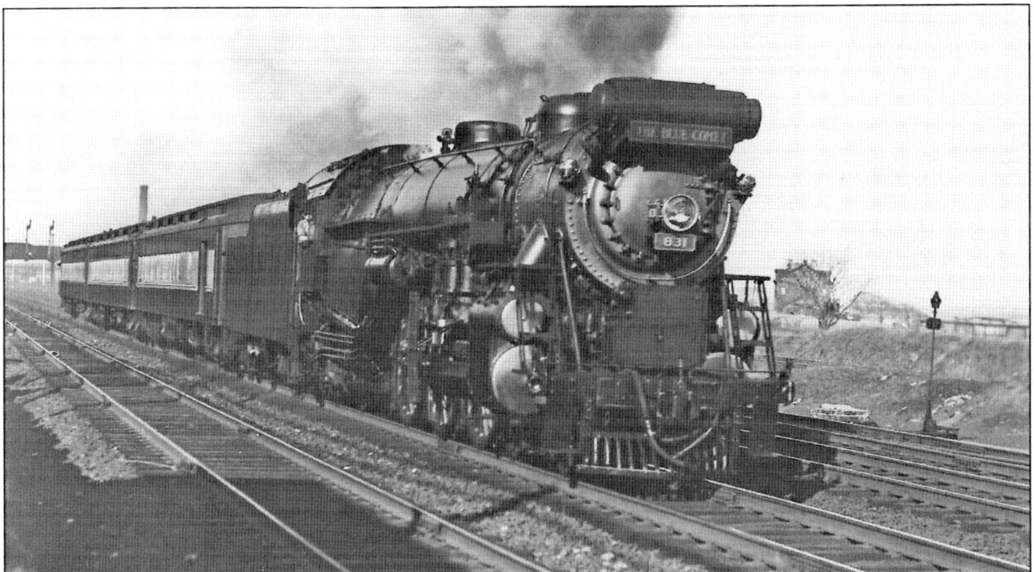

The date is Thursday, March 30, 1933. The G-3 Pacific No. 831 leads three cars of the Blue Comet southbound at Thirty-Seventh Street in Bayonne. The abbreviated consist of combine, coach, and observation car would be the second Blue Comet round trip conducted on that particular day and did not include a diner car. This service was discontinued on April 30, 1933, leaving only one daily round trip to Atlantic City. (Photograph by Tony Formaneck, courtesy Joel Rosenbaum and Tom Gallo.)

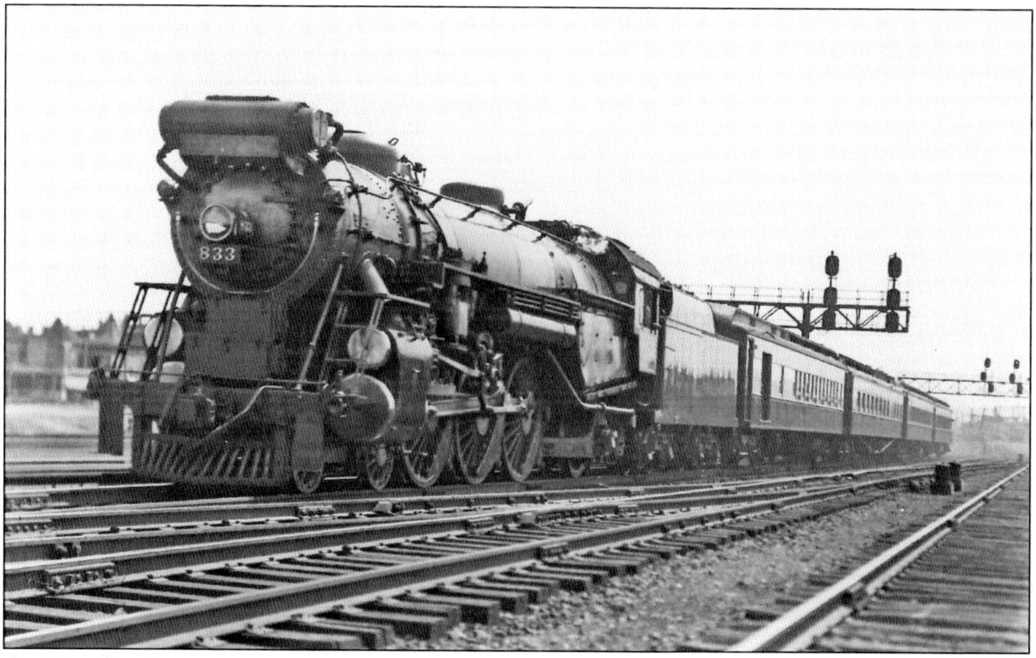

On Tuesday, June 25, 1935, the G-3 No. 833 leads four cars of the Blue Comet, including the diner *Giacobini*, the second car in the consist. By that date, the Blue Comet was running only one daily round trip to Atlantic City. (Photograph by Tony Formaneck, courtesy Joel Rosenbaum and Tom Gallo.)

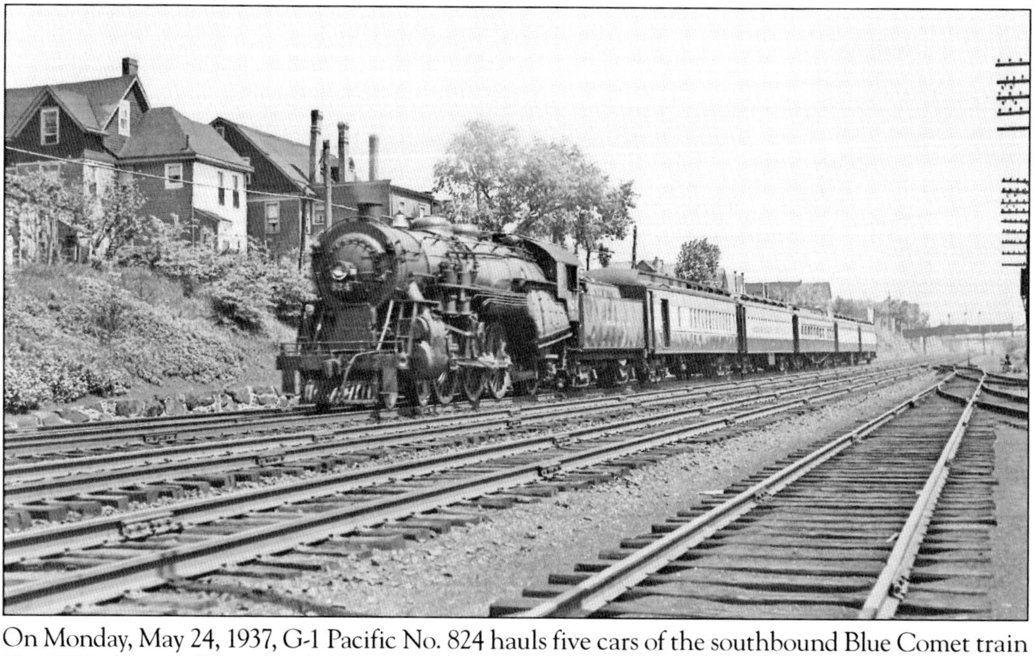

On Monday, May 24, 1937, G-1 Pacific No. 824 hauls five cars of the southbound Blue Comet train No. 4203 through Bayonne. As passenger counts decreased on the Blue Comet train, sometimes the more powerful G3s locomotives were sent to haul long passenger trains on the New York & Long Branch and other routes. (Photograph by George Votava, courtesy Joel Rosenbaum and Tom Gallo.)

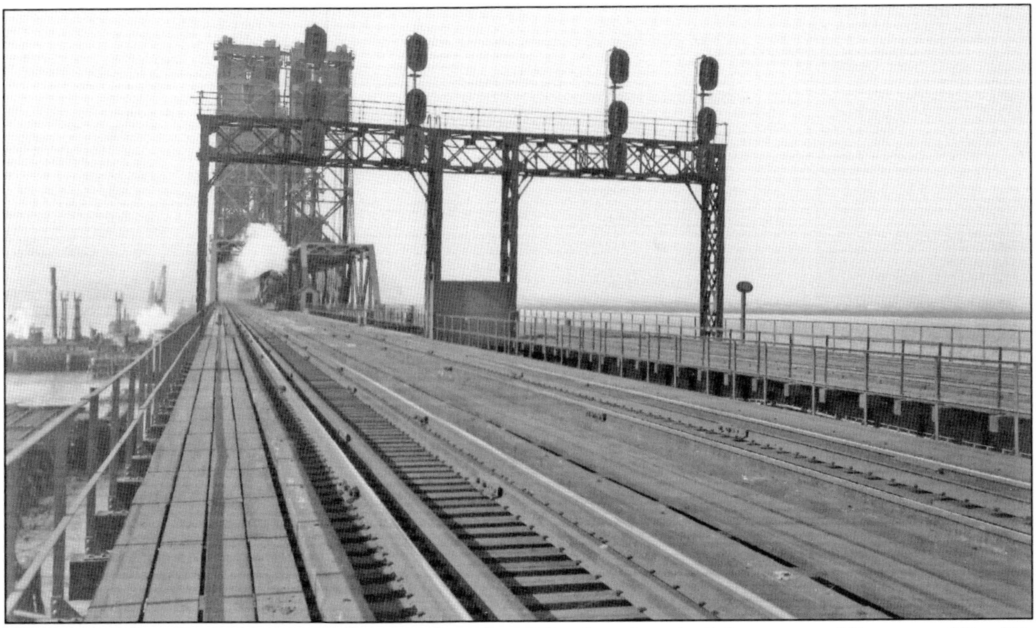

The Newark Bay Bridge was a four-track railroad bridge that had four main lift spans. The lift spans were a pair of two-track spans over two separate shipping channels. One span provided a clear opening of 200 feet, and the other had an opening of 125 feet. The bridge opened in 1926, and was hailed as the largest of its kind. It served the main line of the NJC, carrying daily interstate, intrastate, and commuter trains. The bridge connected Bayonne and Elizabethport at the southern end of Newark Bay. (Courtesy Mitch Dakelman.)

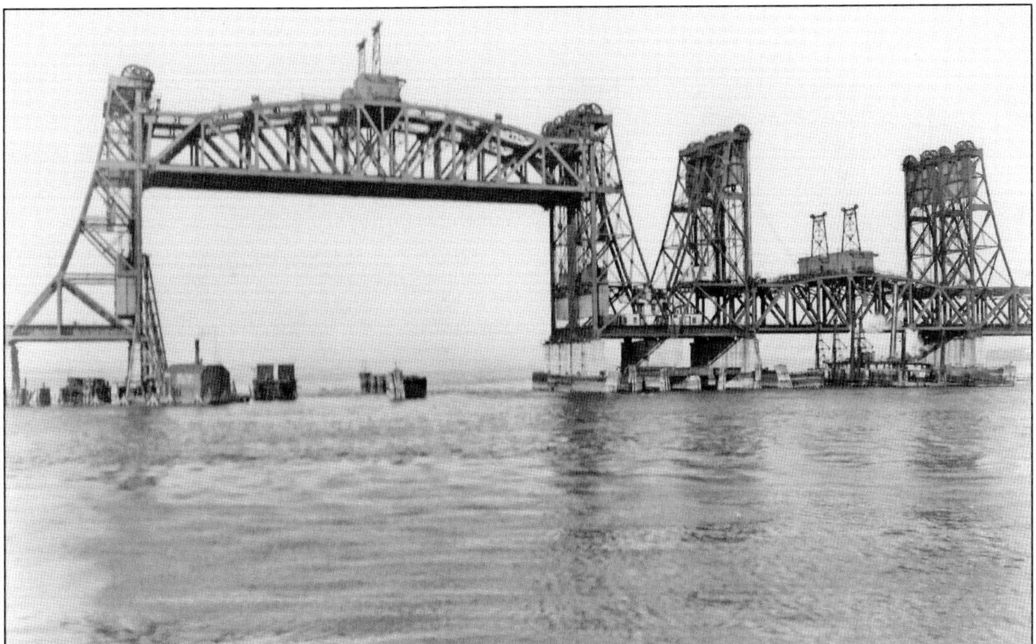

One of the four main lift spans of the Newark Bay Bridge is seen here in operation. (Courtesy Mitch Dakelman.)

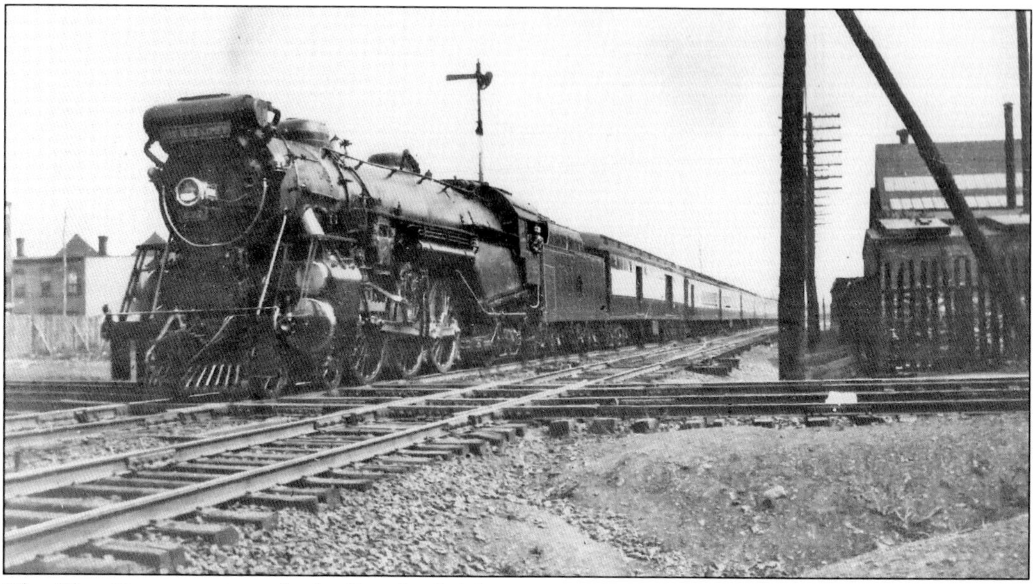

The Blue Comet train with the Pacific G-3 locomotive No. 832 at front is heading westbound, ready to enter the NJC's Elizabethport and Perth Amboy Branch at the Elizabethport station. (Courtesy Mitch Dakelman.)

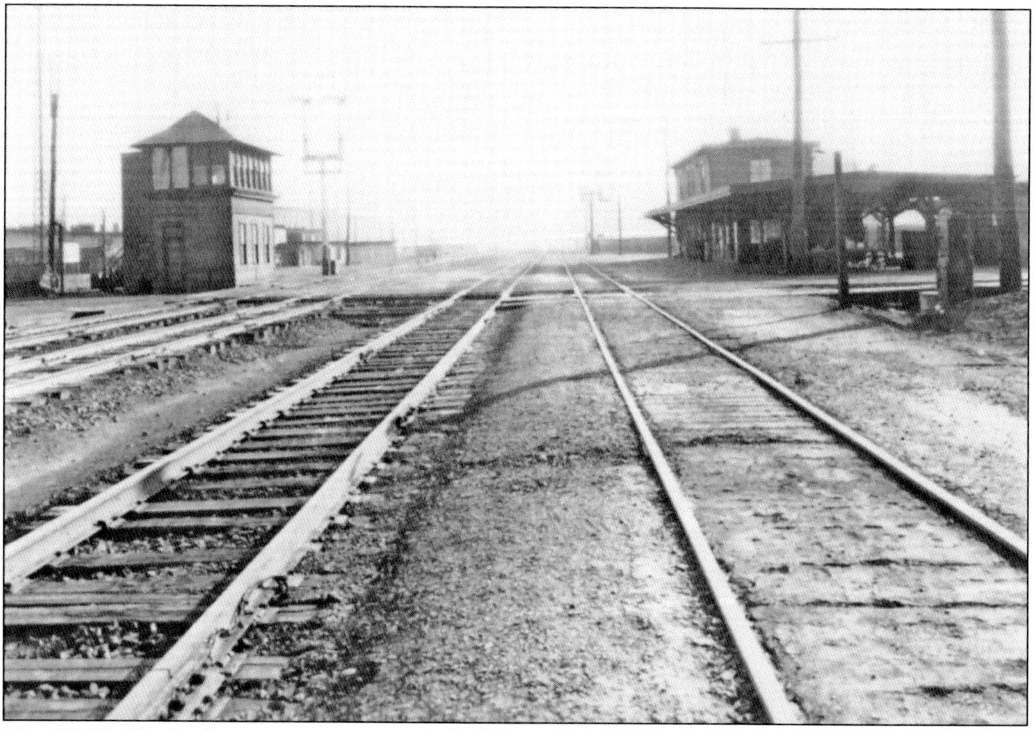

The NJC's Elizabethport station was in a highly industrial and residential section of Elizabeth, New Jersey, and was not considered an attractive station. It was a designated stop for the Blue Comet, and provided transfer service for NJC trains operating between the NJC Elizabeth Broad Street and the Newark Broad Street Stations. This photograph was taken sometime before a new Elizabethport station became operational on November 30, 1938. (Courtesy Elaine Anderson.)

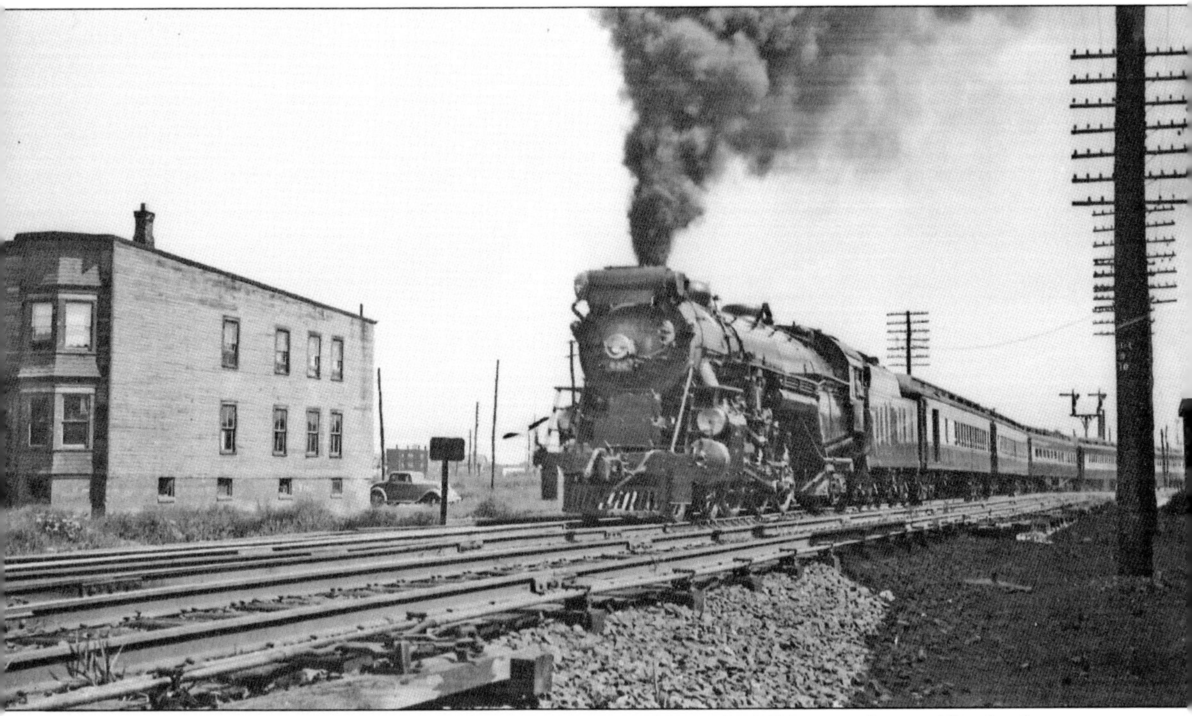

The Blue Comet train is led by the G-3 locomotive No. 832 on the NJC main line at Elizabethport. The 4-6-2 locomotive and the train's consist of six cars were photographed on August 27, 1934. (Author's collection.)

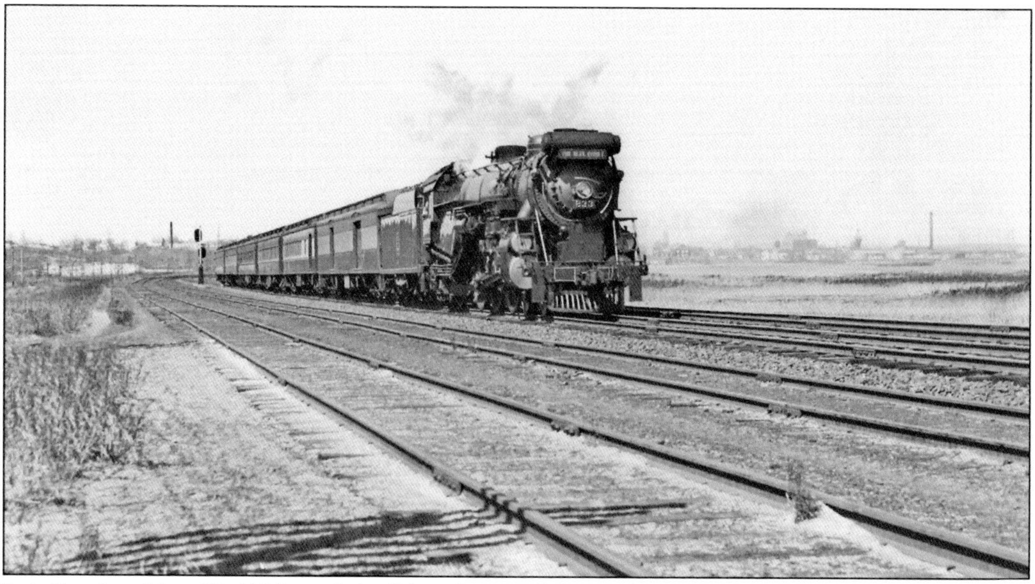

It is Sunday, May 27, 1938, and the Blue Comet G-3 Pacific No. 833 heads up the southbound six-car train No. 4253 at South Amboy, New Jersey. The Raritan River Railroad interchange tracks are visible. On April 17, 1938, the Raritan River Railroad discontinued its last regularly scheduled passenger train between New Brunswick, New Jersey, and South Amboy. (Photograph by George Votava, courtesy Joel Rosenbaum and Tom Gallo.)

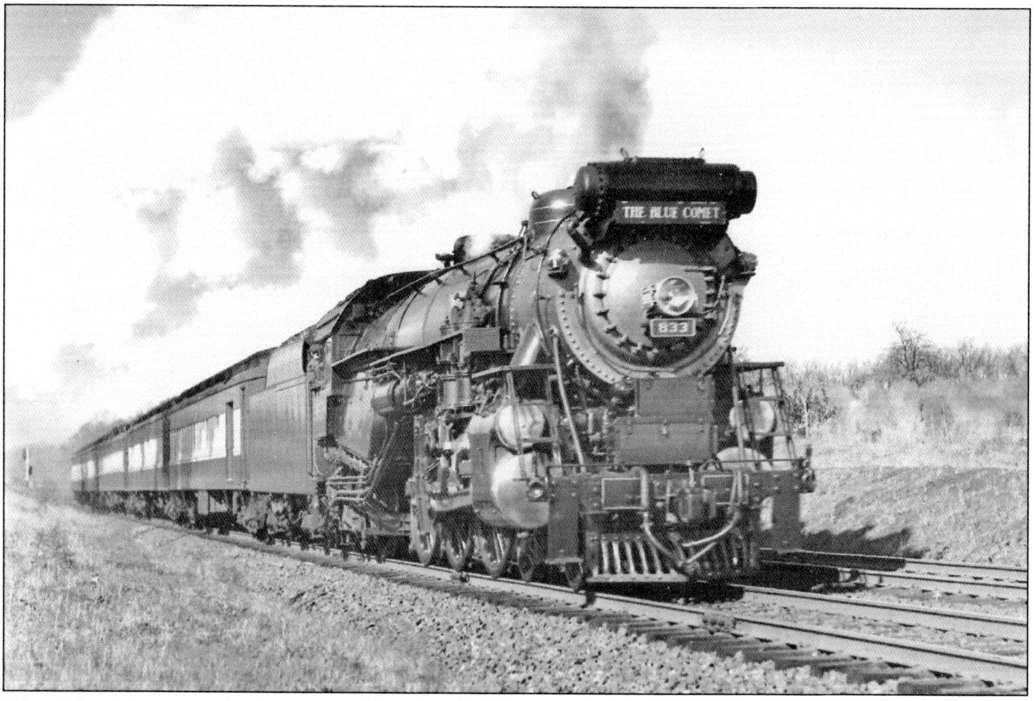

This Blue Comet train is powered by the G-3 Pacific 4-6-2 No. 833 and is roaring through the Oak Hill section of Middletown, New Jersey. This Central Railroad of New Jersey photograph was taken in the early 1930s. (Photograph by Robert P. Morris, courtesy Joel Rosenbaum and Tom Gallo.)

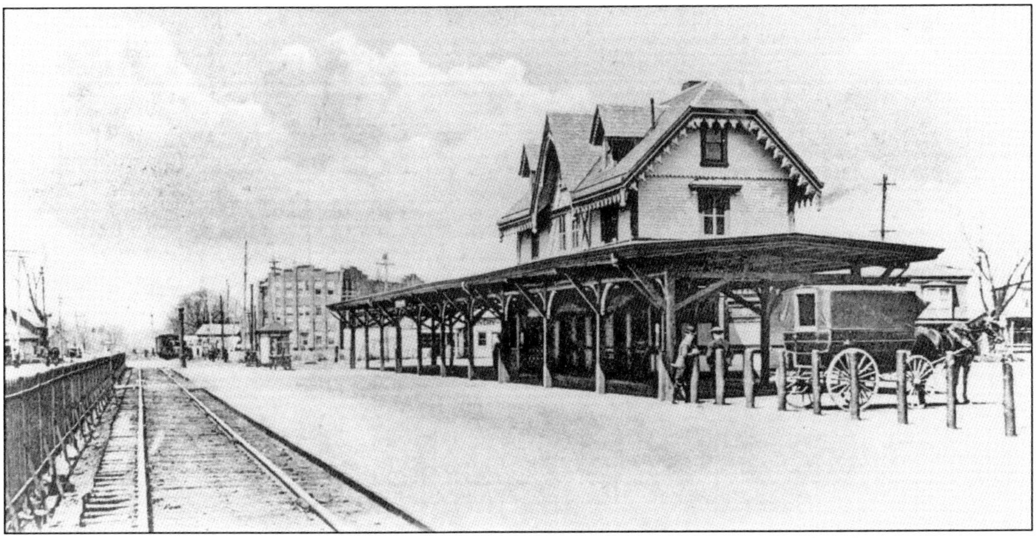

The Red Bank station is on Monmouth Street and Bridge Avenue. Red Bank's distinctive station house is one of the last remaining examples of the Stick-style station houses built by the New York & Long Branch Railroad in the 1870s. It served the Blue Comet throughout its service life. (Courtesy Robert A. Emmons.)

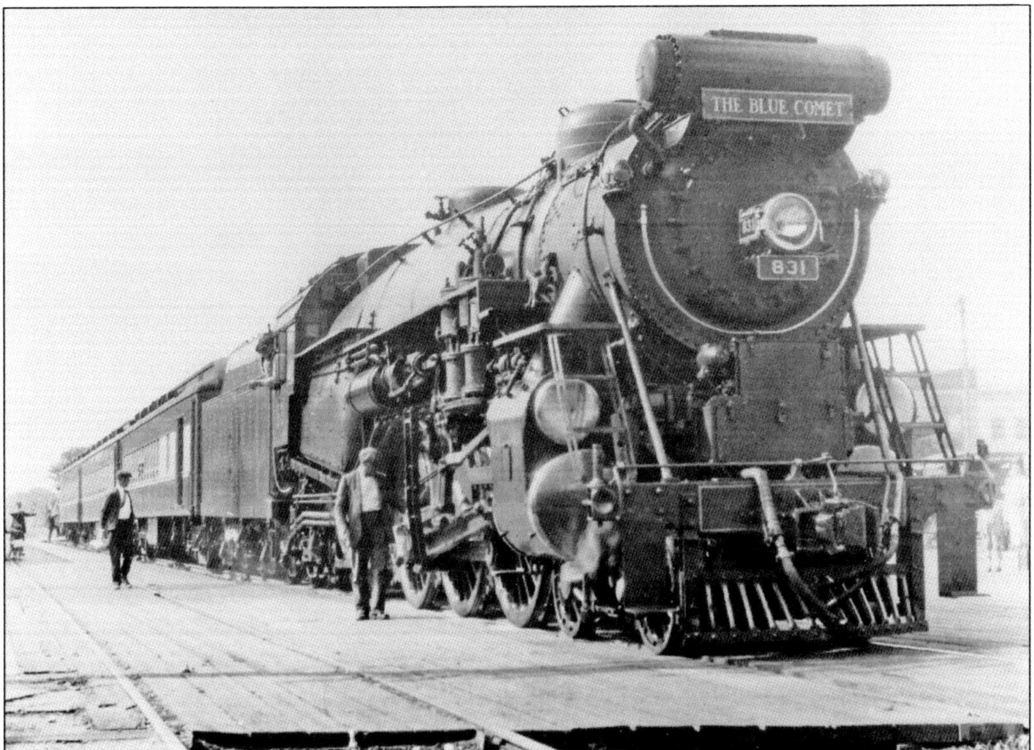

This is the Blue Comet train No. 4215, which left Jersey City daily at 2:42 p.m. It was the second round trip of the day and did not carry a dining car. The photograph was taken in the spring of 1929 at Red Bank. This train was scheduled to leave Red Bank on its southbound trip to Atlantic City at 3:32 p.m. (Photograph by Charles Foxwell, courtesy Joel Rosenbaum and Tom Gallo.)

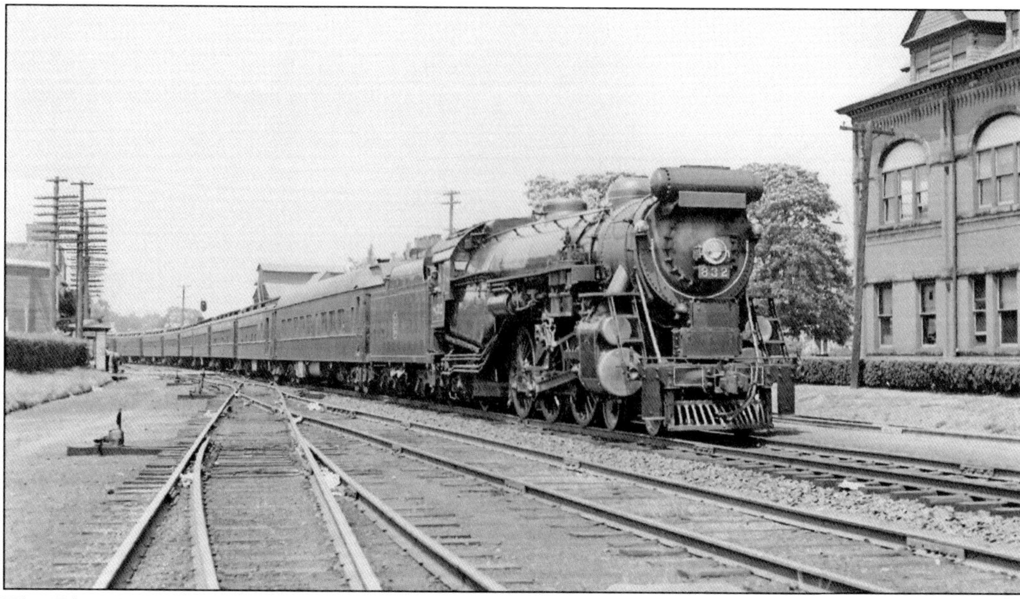

The Blue Comet G-3 Pacific No. 832 heads up a nine-car southbound Saturday-only train No. 3313 on July 24, 1937, from Jersey City to Bay Head Junction, New Jersey. The train's consist includes a parlor car next to the engine and a dining-club car at the end of the train. The train is arriving at Long Branch with the New York & Long Branch Railroad office building at right. Note that the Blue Comet sign has been covered over. Waning passenger demand for Blue Comet service allowed the NJC to use the powerful Baldwin Pacific locomotives for other passenger runs. (Photograph by George Votava, courtesy Joel Rosenbaum and Tom Gallo.)

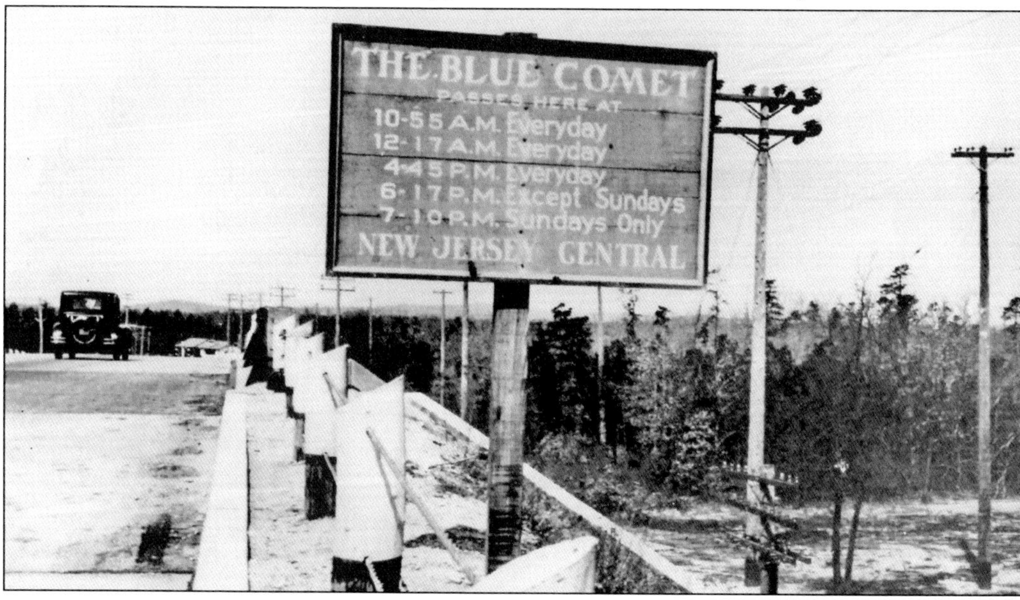

This innovative advertising method drew attention to the Blue Comet on the highway overpass that the train passed under. Curious onlookers and spectators would gather on the overpass in order to get a view of the Blue Comet as it passed. The sign painter made an error with the 12:17 a.m. passage; it should read p.m. This particular sign was located at the Route 33/34 overpass at Collingwood Park, New Jersey. (Courtesy Joel Rosenbaum and Tom Gallo.)

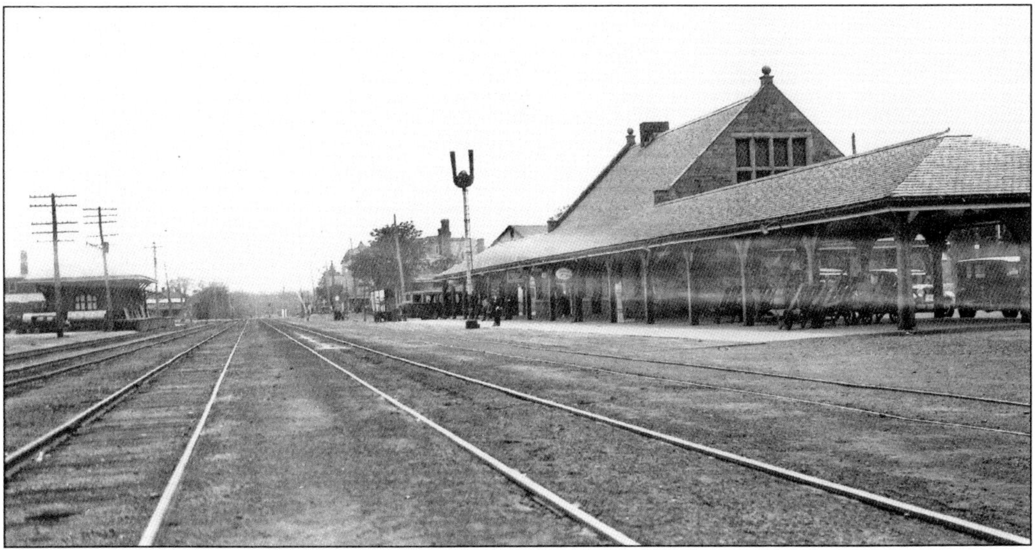

The Lakewood station was located at mile marker No. 58.0 along the NJC main line from Jersey City. It was named Bricksburg in 1865 but was renamed Lakewood in 1880. It was built in 1891 and located at Monmouth and Second Avenues, replacing an earlier station on the south side of Main Street. The station served the Blue Comet. In response to the spirit of goodwill shown by the Blue Comet crew to residents all along the entire route of the train, folks would bring baskets of berries to the train crew while the train was taking on passengers at Lakewood and Lakehurst, New Jersey. (Photograph by Francis Palmer, courtesy Robert A. Emmons.)

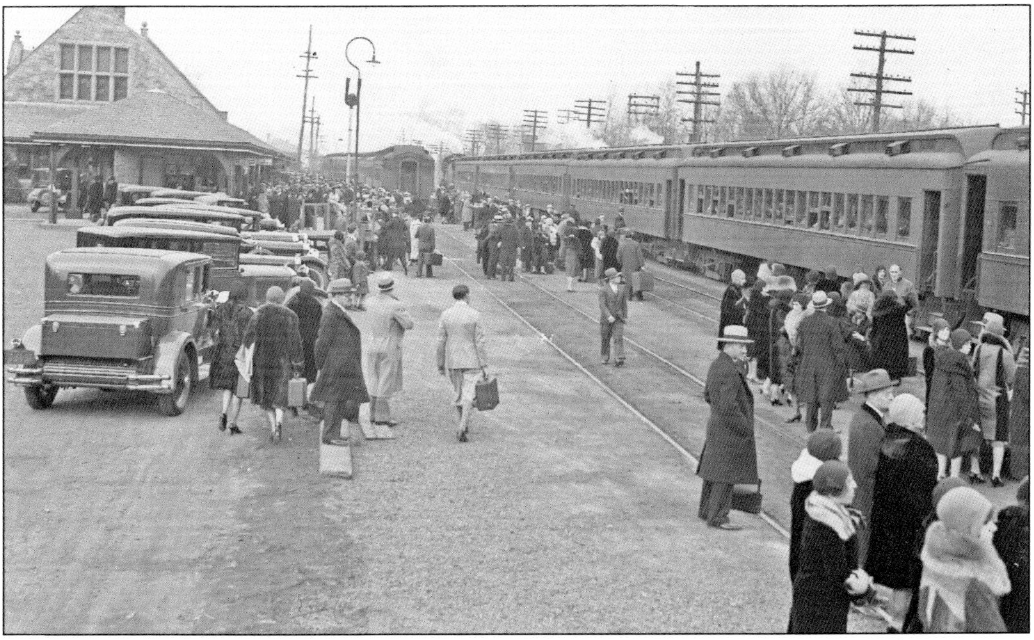

It has been four months since the Wall Street crash of 1929, which began on October 24, 1929, Despite this catastrophic economic event, crowds still flock to Lakewood for the traditional Washington's Birthday holiday. However, within another four months, this festive scene would become a thing of the past as the economy spiraled into a complete tailspin. (Courtesy Ocean County Historical Society.)

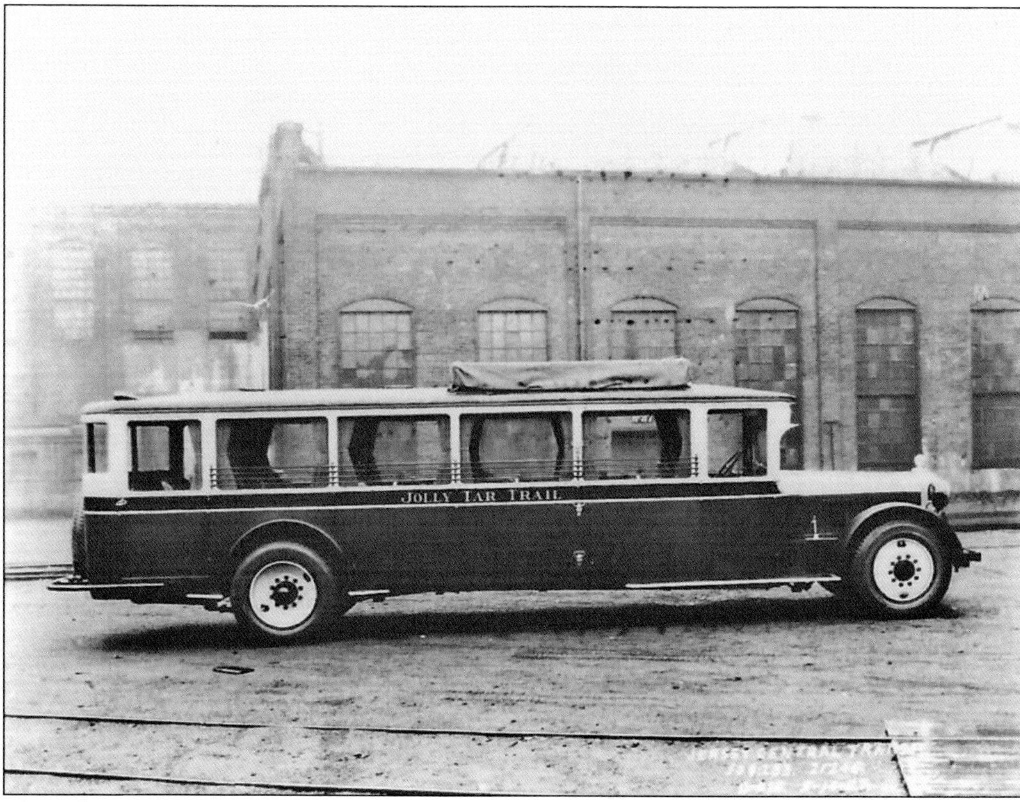

The Jolly Tar Trail bus of the Jersey Central Transportation Company is seen at the ACF Motor Company's Detroit factory on May 14, 1927. The NJC began operating buses on its Barnegat Branch between Lakewood and Barnegat to replace some trains as an economy measure. The buses were painted dark green and cream with a black belt rail and gold lettering. (Courtesy Joel Rosenbaum and Tom Gallo.)

SERVICE NEW YORK AND INTERMEDIATE STATIONS AND POINTS ON THE BARNEGAT BRANCH

TABLE 4

JERSEY CENTRAL TRANSPORTATION COMPANY

"Jolly Tar Trail"—MOTOR COACH SERVICE LAKEWOOD AND BARNEGAT *Included*

Eastern Standard Time—*add one hour for Daylight Saving Time*

ALL MOTOR COACH STOPS will be made on signal to operators

SOUTHBOUND

	STATIONS		Miles	Week Days 4263	Week Days 4209 (SATURDAYS ONLY)	Week Days 4229 (THROUGH TRAIN FROM JERSEY CITY)	Sunday 4251 (THROUGH TRAIN FROM JERSEY CITY)
				AM	PM	PM	AM
Lv.	New York (West 23d St)	Train Service	....	9.45	12.15	3.45	6.58
″	New York (Liberty St.)	″	....	10.00	12.30	4.05	7.10
″	Jersey City Terminal	″	1.0	10.13	12.44	4.17	7.22
″	Jackson Avenue (Jersey City)	″	....	*9.47	§12h21	*3.37	7.20
″	Newark, Broad Street	″	....	10.10	12.43	4.13	7.23
″	Newark Transfer	″	....	....	....	....	7.36
″	Elizabeth	″	....	10.08	....	4.22	7.17
″	Elizabethport	″	10.6	10a28	a1.00	a4.32	7.46
″	Perth Amboy	″	22.1	....	....	....	8.04
″	Matawan	″	29.5	....	....	....	....
″	Red Bank	″	39.4	11.04	1.36	5.12	8.28
″	Farmingdale	″	53.1	11.20	1.58	5.40	8.50
Ar.	Lakewood	″	59.3	11.29	2.06	5.52	9.03
Lv.	Lakewood	″	59.3	....	....	5.52	9.08
″	Lakewood (C. R. R. Station)	Motor Coach	59.3	11.35	2.10	....	....
Ar.	Paul Kimball Hospital	″	60.9	11.41	2.15	....	....
Lv.	Lakehurst	Train Service	67.2	....	....	6.10	9.21
Ar.	Seven Stars	Motor Coach	62.2	11.44	2.17	....	....
″	White Oak Tea Room	″	64.7	11.50	2.22	....	....
″	Pleasant Plains	″	65.7	11.52	2.24	....	....
″	Trenery's	″	67.2	11.55	2.27	....	....
″	Toms River (Baptist Church)	″	69.1	11.59	2.31	....	....
″	Toms River (Ocean Co. Title Bldg.)	″	69.4	12.02	2.34	....	....
″	Toms River (C. R. R. Station)	″	69.8	12.07	2.38	....	....
″	Toms River	Train Service	74.0	....	....	6.27	9.40
″	Beachwood	″	75.5	....	....	6.30	9.43
″	Beachwood	Motor Coach	70.7	12.10	2.41	....	....
″	Pine Beach (P. B. Service Sta.)	″	71.6	12.14	2.45	....	....
″	Mott's Corners (Kormann's Rest't)	″	73.2	12.18	2.49	....	....
″	Bayville (Post Office)	″	74.1	12.20	2.51	....	....
″	Bayville (Rosedge Farm)	″	74.6	12.22	2.53	....	....
″	Pinewald	Train Service	78.7	....	....	6.36	9.50
″	Pinewald (Pinewald Inn)	Motor Coach	75.4	12.23	2.54	....	....
″	Lanoka Harbor	Train Service	80.7	....	....	f6.42	9.56
″	Lanoka Harbor (Post Office)	Motor Coach	76.9	12.28	2.58	....	....
″	Murray Grove (Piedmont Inn)	Motor Coach	77.7	12.30	3.00	....	....
″	State Game Farm	″	78.9	12.32	3.02	....	....
″	Forked River	Train Service	83.0	....	....	6.47	10.02
″	Forked River (Post Office)	Motor Coach	79.3	12.33	3.03	....	....
″	Ostrom (Dewey's Garage)	Motor Coach	80.0	12.35	3.05	....	....
″	Waretown	Train Service	86.2	....	....	6.55	10.10
″	Waretown (C. R. R. Station)	Motor Coach	82.7	12.39	3.08	....	....
″	Barnegat	Train Service	89.3	....	....	7.02	10.18
″	Barnegat (C. R. R. Station)	Motor Coach	85.8	12.45	3.13	....	....
Ar.				PM	PM	PM	AM

NORTHBOUND

	STATIONS		Week Days 4260 (THROUGH TRAIN TO JERSEY CITY)	Week Days 4218	Sundays 4268 (THROUGH TRAIN TO JERSEY CITY)
			AM	PM	PM
Lv.	Barnegat (C. R. R. Station)	Motor Coach	....	3.49	....
″	Barnegat	Train Service	5.01	....	5.50
″	Waretown (C. R. R. Station)	Motor Coach	....	3.55	....
″	Waretown	Train Service	5.09	....	5.57
″	Ostrom (Dewey's Garage)	Motor Coach	....	3.59	....
″	Forked River (Post Office)	Motor Coach	....	4.01	....
″	Forked River	Train Service	5.18	....	6.05
″	State Game Farm	Motor Coach	....	4.02	....
″	Murray Grove (Piedmont Inn)	″	....	4.04	....
″	Lanoka Harbor (Post Office)	″	....	4.06	....
″	Lanoka Harbor	Train Service	5.24	....	6.11
″	Pinewald (Pinewald Inn)	Motor Coach	....	4.11	....
″	Pinewald	Train Service	5.26	....	6.14
″	Bayville (Rosedge Farm)	Motor Coach	....	4.12	....
″	Bayville (Post Office)	″	....	4.14	....
″	Mott's Corners (Kormann's Rest't)	″	....	4.16	....
″	Pine Beach (P. B. Service Sta.)	″	....	4.20	....
″	Beachwood	″	....	4.24	....
″	Beachwood	Train Service	5.36	....	6.23
″	Toms River	″	5.39	....	6.26
″	Toms River (C. R. R. Station)	Motor Coach	....	4.27	....
″	Toms River (Ocean Co. Title Bldg.)	″	....	4.32	....
″	Toms River (Baptist Church)	″	....	4.35	....
″	Trenery's	″	....	4.38	....
″	Pleasant Plains	″	....	4.41	....
″	White Oak Tea Room	″	....	4.43	....
″	Seven Stars	″	....	4.48	....
Ar.	Lakehurst	Train Service	5.53	....	6.40
Lv.	Paul Kimball Hospital	Motor Coach	....	4.51	....
Ar.	Lakewood (C. R. R. Station)	″	....	4.57	....
″	Lakewood	Train Service	6.15	....	7.06
Lv.	Lakewood	″	6.15	5.04	7.09
Ar.	Farmingdale	″	6.29	5.13	7.16
″	Red Bank	″	6.54	5.30	7.34
″	Matawan	″	7.10	....	....
″	Perth Amboy	″	7.23	....	....
″	Elizabethport	″	7.42	b6.05	8.14
″	Elizabeth	″	....	6.13	8.30
″	Newark Transfer	″	....	....	8.23
″	Newark, Broad St.	″	8.07	6.24	8.33
″	Jackson Avenue (Jersey City)	″	*8h38	*6.41	8.29
″	Jersey City Terminal	″	7.58	6.21	8.36
″	New York (Liberty Street)	″	8.10	6.33	8.50
″	New York (West 23d St.)	″	8.33	6.47	9.03
Ar.			AM	PM	PM

*—Change at Jersey City.
†—Change at East Perry St.
§—Change at Newark.

a—Stop on notice to Agent to take passengers.
b—Stop on notice to Conductor to leave passengers.
f—Stops on notice to Agent or Conductor.
h—Will not stop July 4 and Sept. 7.

The Blue Comet timetable No. TT103, effective June 21, 1936, shows train and connecting bus service from Lakewood on the Barnegat Branch courtesy of the Jolly Tar Trail. The weekday bus connection at Lakewood to Barnegat met the Blue Comet train No. 4203 at the Lakewood station. The Barnegat Branch came off at Lakehurst, but the bus connection at Lakewood was a more convenient location. (Courtesy Joel Rosenbaum and Tom Gallo.)

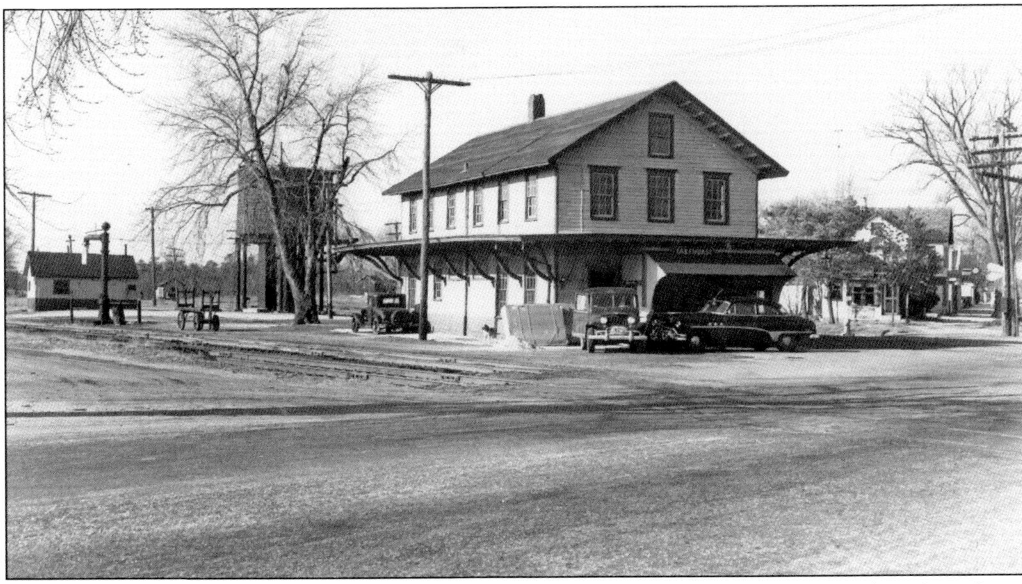

The Lakehurst station was located at mile marker No. 65.9 along the NJC main line from Jersey City. It was established in 1862 and named Manchester, but later renamed Lakehurst in 1897. It was built in 1863. The station served the Blue Comet and was razed in May 1962. It provided rail service to the naval station located nearby. In addition to the station, Lakehurst provided the NJC with a freight house, roundhouse, and the Lakehurst Shops, which included a car shop, an engine house with a 50-foot turntable, and a host of additional service facilities. (Photograph by Francis Palmer, courtesy Robert A. Emmons.)

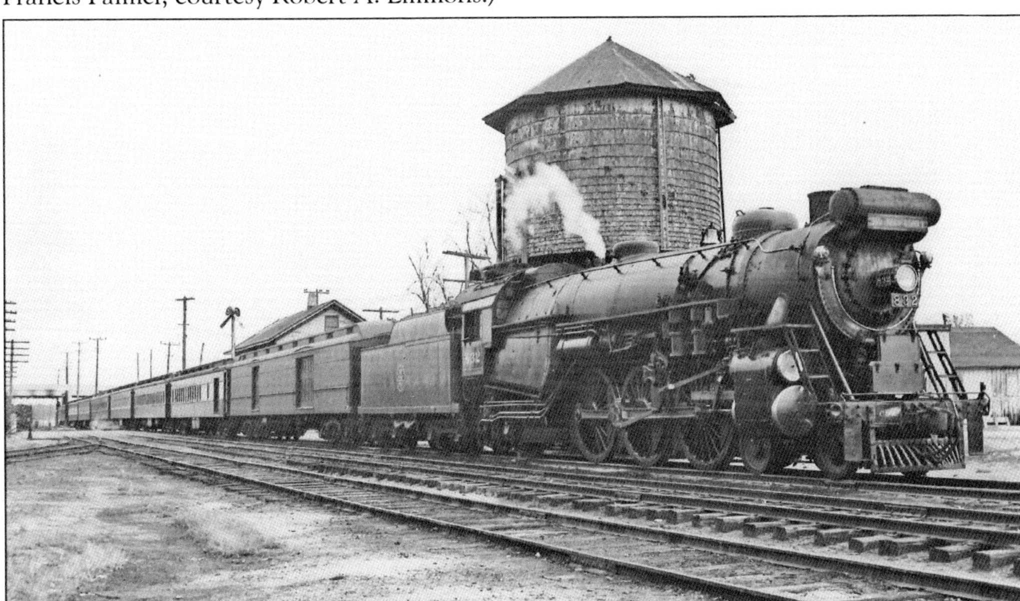

On Sunday, November 13, 1938, the southbound Blue Comet to Atlantic City is making a station stop at Lakehurst. Its consist includes eight cars headed by Pacific No. 832. By this time in its service run, the Blue Comet consist was not always solid Blue Comet livery. Note the use of a standard NJC baggage car following the locomotive and tender. (Photograph by George Votava, courtesy Joel Rosenbaum and Tom Gallo.)

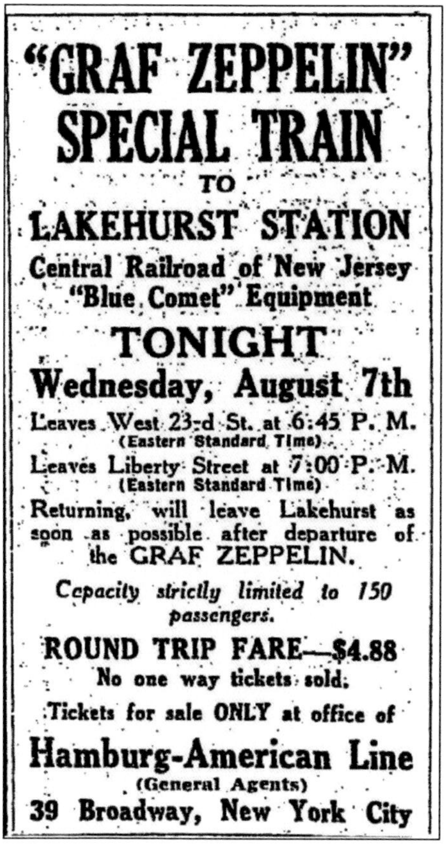

"GRAF ZEPPELIN"
SPECIAL TRAIN
TO
LAKEHURST STATION
Central Railroad of New Jersey
"Blue Comet" Equipment
TONIGHT
Wednesday, August 7th
Leaves West 23-d St. at 6:45 P. M.
(Eastern Standard Time)
Leaves Liberty Street at 7:00 P. M.
(Eastern Standard Time)
Returning, will leave Lakehurst as soon as possible after departure of the GRAF ZEPPELIN.
Capacity strictly limited to 150 passengers.
ROUND TRIP FARE—$4.88
No one way tickets sold.
Tickets for sale ONLY at office of
Hamburg-American Line
(General Agents)
39 Broadway, New York City

An NJC Blue Comet special train was operated on Wednesday, August 7, 1929, to Lakehurst in commemoration of the arrival of the *Graf Zeppelin* from Germany. A *New York Times* advertisement announced this obviously staged publicity stunt. The *Graf Zeppelin* had left Friedrichshafen, Germany, on July 27, 1929, and arrived in Lakehurst on August 7. (Courtesy *The New York Times*.)

The *Graf Zeppelin* was a passenger-carrying, hydrogen-filled rigid airship. When it entered service in 1928, it became the first commercial passenger transatlantic flight service in the world. It was named after the German pioneer of airships, Ferdinand Von Zeppelin, who was a count (graf) in the German nobility. During its operating life, the airship made 590 flights covering more than a million miles. The airship was retired in 1937 and was scrapped for fighter plane parts in 1940. (Courtesy barnstmr.blogspot.com.)

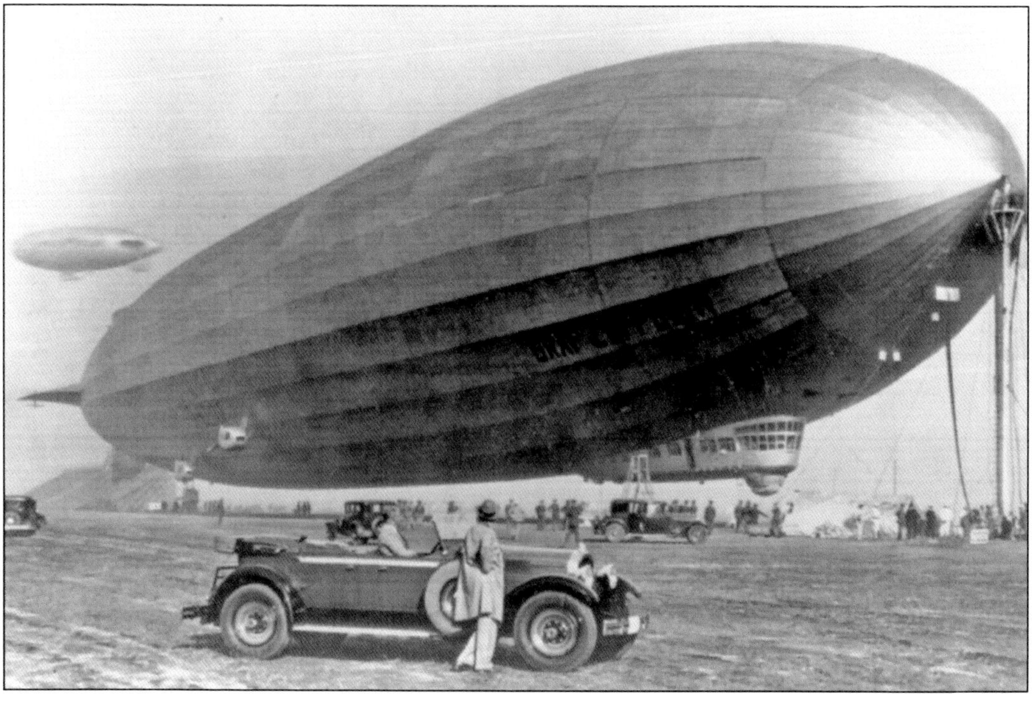

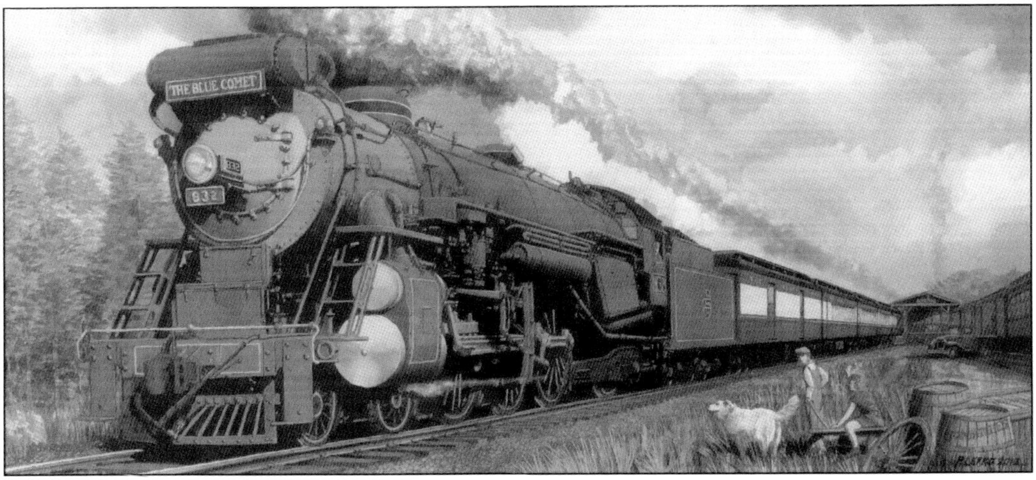

Artist Peter Lerro painted the Blue Comet as she races through the New Jersey Pine Barrens. In the spirit of spreading goodwill, the Blue Comet train crew would throw off newspapers from the moving train to residents in the more isolated sections of the Pine Barrens who were without radios or electricity. The Barrens are still a largely rural and undisturbed area of New Jersey. (Author's collection.)

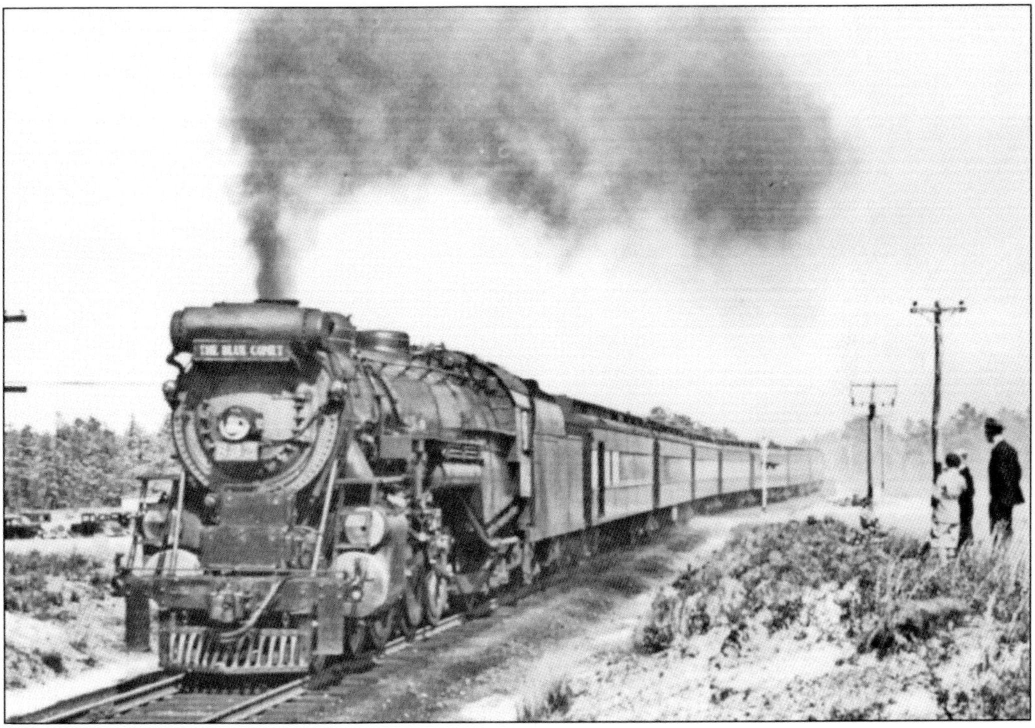

The Blue Comet G-3 Pacific No. 832 speeds through the Pine Barrens of Southern New Jersey with a full consist. The locomotive and consist painted in its blue livery with the cream stripe, when in motion, represented a comet streaking through space. The Pine Barrens were the home of the legendary Jersey Devil, a dragon-like creature first reported in Lenni-Lenape Indian folklore. (Courtesy Joel Rosenbaum and Tom Gallo.)

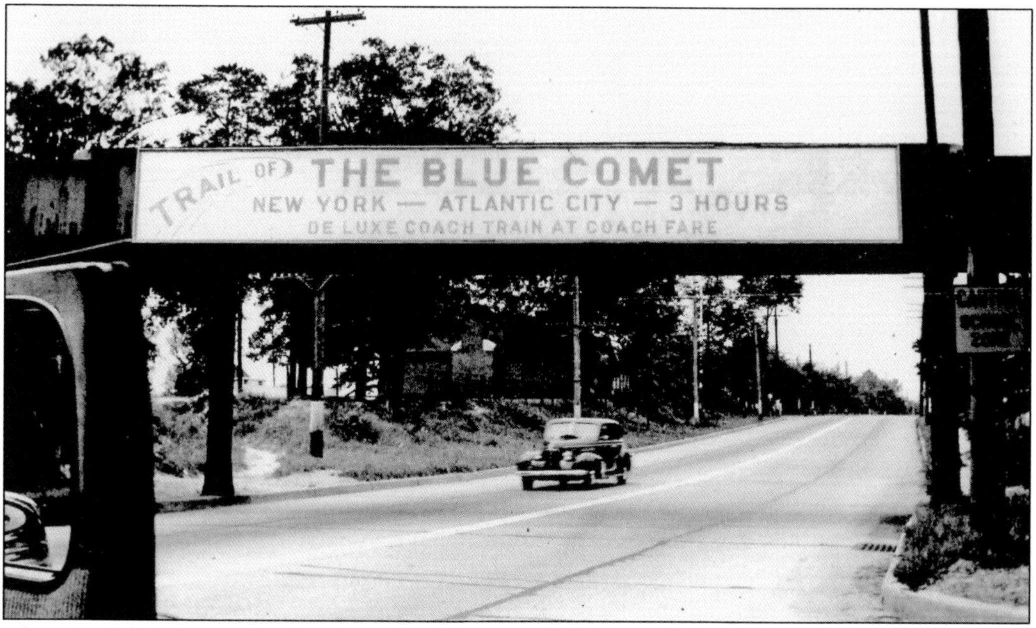

This 1940 photograph shows the NJC overpass over White Horse Pike at Elm, New Jersey, on the route of the Blue Comet. This method of advertising was innovative for passenger train promotion. As the Blue Comet aged, New Jersey built a highway system that at the time was second only to California. The improving highway system reduced the passenger counts on the train. (Photograph by Don Wentzel, courtesy Joel Rosenbaum and Tom Gallo.)

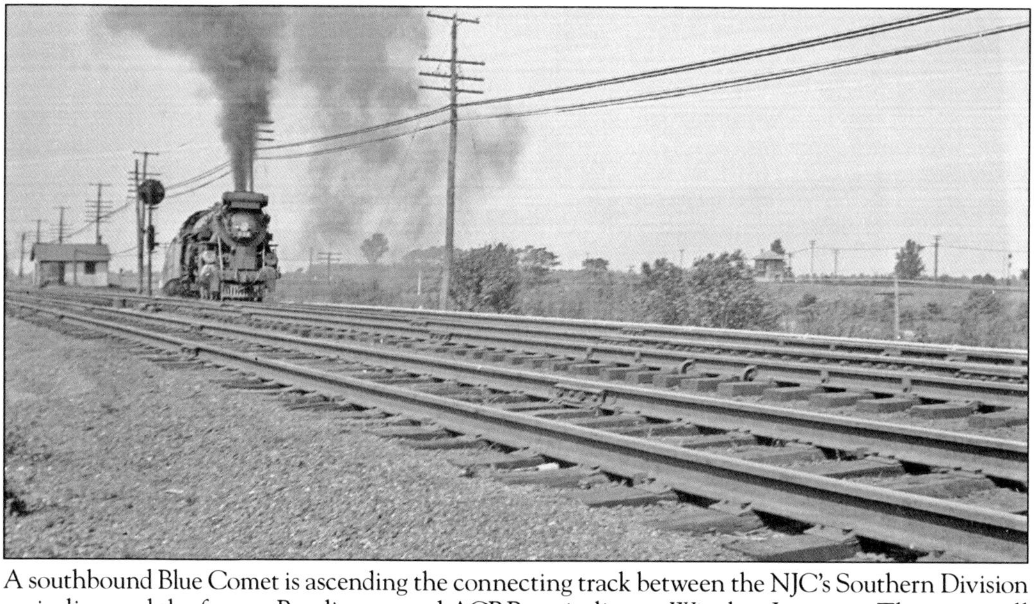

A southbound Blue Comet is ascending the connecting track between the NJC's Southern Division main line and the former Reading-owned ACRR main line at Winslow Junction. The train will then proceed on a connecting track between the former ACRR main line and the former West Jersey & Seashore Atlantic City main line, which was built after the PRSL consolidation in 1933 for the last leg of its journey to Atlantic City. The locomotive heading this train is the NJC class G-3 Pacific (4-6-2) No. 832. (Courtesy Edward Trebino Collection, West Jersey Chapter of the National Railway Historical Society.)

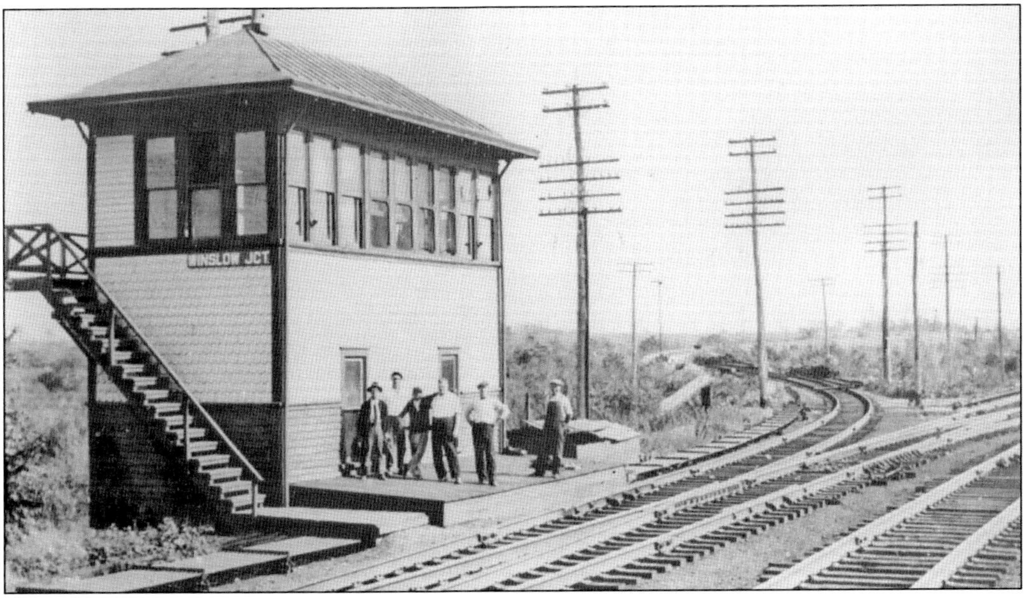

The Reading Winslow Junction tower was built in 1906. On the right is the crossover between the two main tracks that were used daily by southward joint NJC-Reading passenger trains to Atlantic City. The Winslow Junction tower was continuously staffed by three operators and a relief man. This photograph was taken shortly before it was abandoned on June 3, 1934, when the new brick PRSL Winslow tower alongside the former Pennsylvania Railroad was placed into service. (Courtesy Robert A. Emmons.)

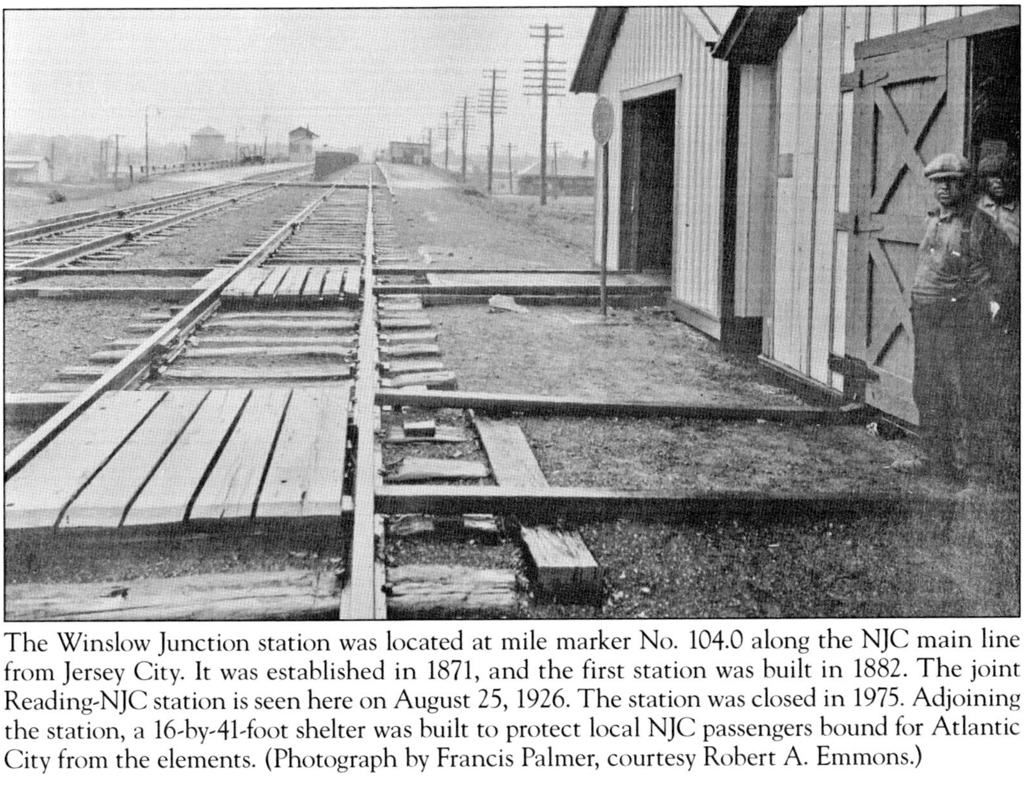

The Winslow Junction station was located at mile marker No. 104.0 along the NJC main line from Jersey City. It was established in 1871, and the first station was built in 1882. The joint Reading-NJC station is seen here on August 25, 1926. The station was closed in 1975. Adjoining the station, a 16-by-41-foot shelter was built to protect local NJC passengers bound for Atlantic City from the elements. (Photograph by Francis Palmer, courtesy Robert A. Emmons.)

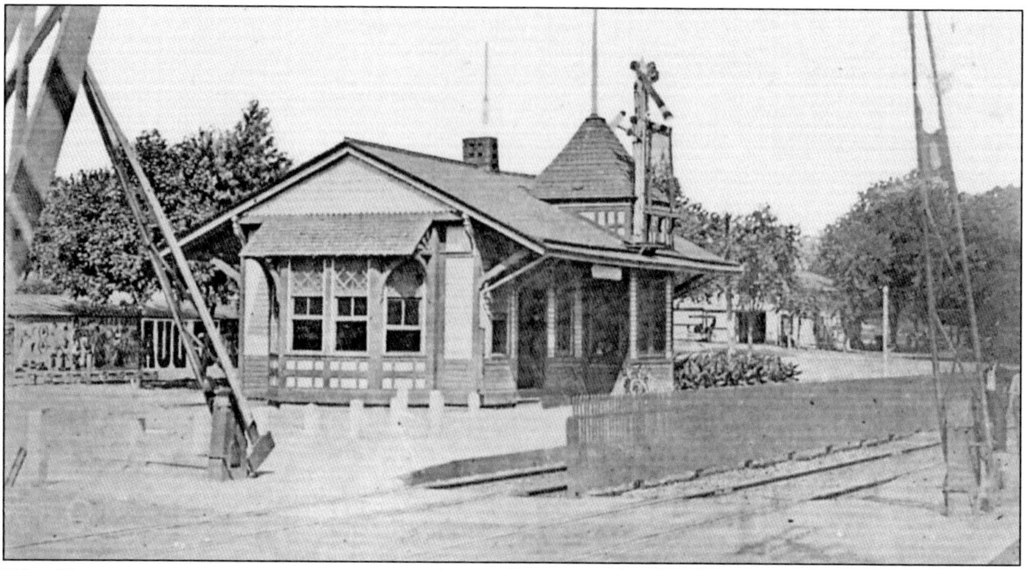

The Hammonton passenger station was located just north of Bellevue Avenue adjacent to the southbound track. A shelter served northbound passengers. The 20-by-42-foot one-story frame station was built in the late 1870s by the Philadelphia & Atlantic City Railway and was improved in 1912. The station was later jointly used by the Reading Railroad and the NJC. This photograph was taken in 1915 shortly after improvements were made to the station. NJC used the station as the terminus for a special bus service, which connected the Blue Comet train with outlying areas of southern New Jersey, beginning in 1929. (Courtesy R.L. Long.)

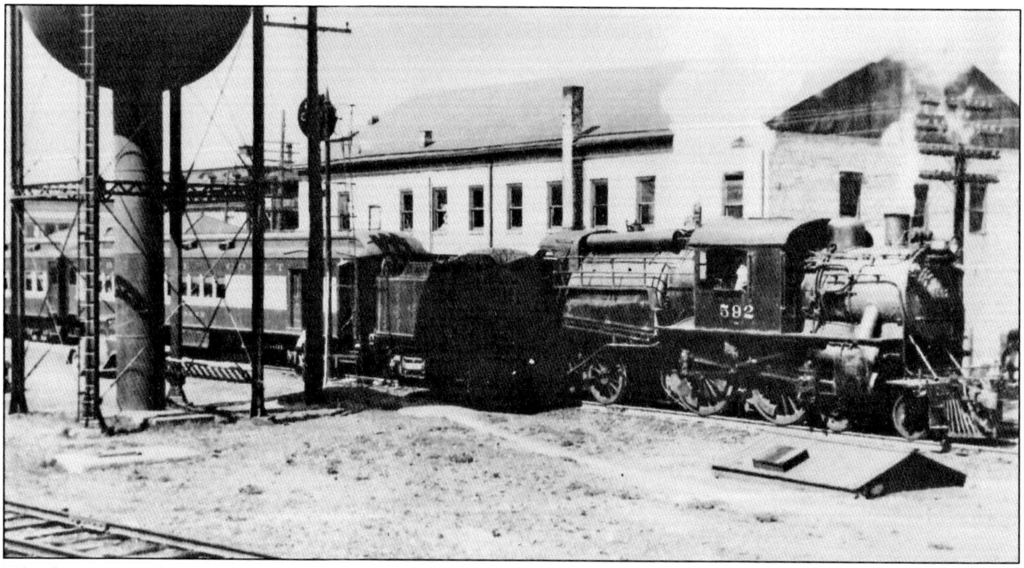

The historic NJC No. 592, a 4-4-2 class P-6s Camelback locomotive, was built by the Brooks Works of the American Locomotive Company (ALCO) in September 1901. In this photograph, it is pulling the Blue Comet though Hammonton, New Jersey. This locomotive was utilized when low passenger counts diverted the G3s Pacifics to routes carrying heavier passenger loads. It was known as the "Speed Queen," as it sometimes reached speeds of 100 miles per hour when assigned to the Jersey City–Philadelphia runs. Locomotive No. 592 is now on display at the Baltimore & Ohio Railroad Museum in Baltimore. (Photograph by Granville Thomas, courtesy E. Lewis Pardee collection.)

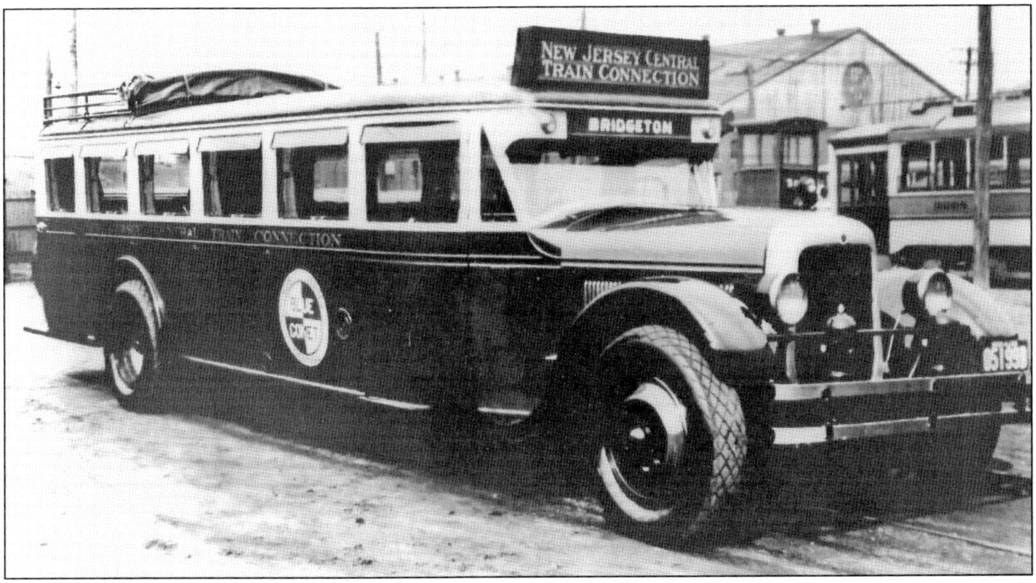

A special bus service provided Hammonton-Vineland-Bridgeton passengers a connection with the Blue Comet. The bus was operated by the Public Service Company under contract with the NJC and replaced a costly steam train connection at Winslow Junction, which was eliminated with the inauguration of the Blue Comet service. The bus was painted blue and cream to match the Blue Comet. It had a large sign above the destination sign, which read, "New Jersey Central Train Connection." The attractive color scheme of the bus and the good connections to the Blue Comet resulted in support from communities having their train service replaced by a bus. (Photograph by The Motor Bus Society, Inc., courtesy Joel Rosenbaum and Tom Gallo.)

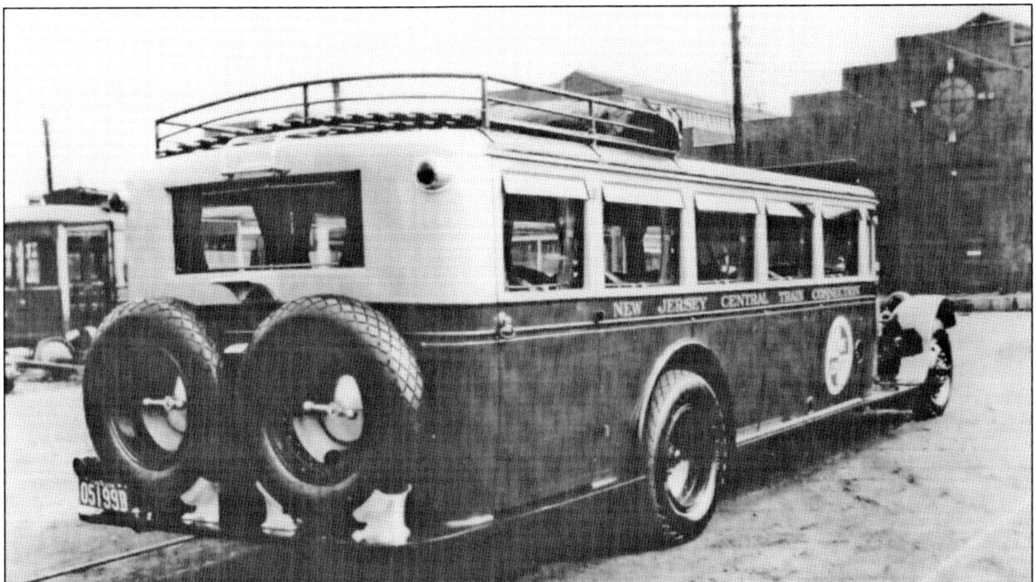

Pictured is a Blue Comet bus connection between Hammonton and Bridgeton, operated by the Public Service Company. The side of the bus carried the same Blue Comet logo as the drumhead on the Blue Comet observation car. The bus connection was eliminated on April 26, 1936. (Photograph by the Motor Bus Society Inc., courtesy Joel Rosenbaum and Tom Gallo.)

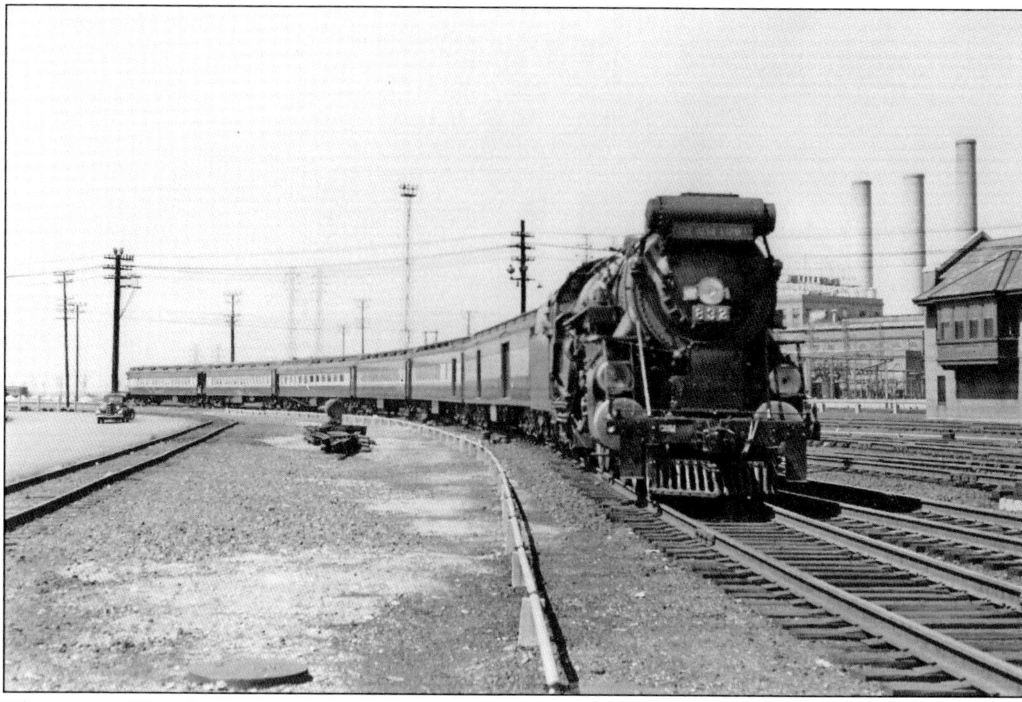

The six-car Blue Comet train No. 4253 arrives in Atlantic City on Sunday, August 30, 1936. The train is headed by the G-3 Pacific No. 832 and is composed of the classic Blue Comet consist of a baggage car, combine, two coaches, diner car *Giacobini*, and an observation car. (Photograph by George Votava, courtesy Joel Rosenbaum and Tom Gallo.)

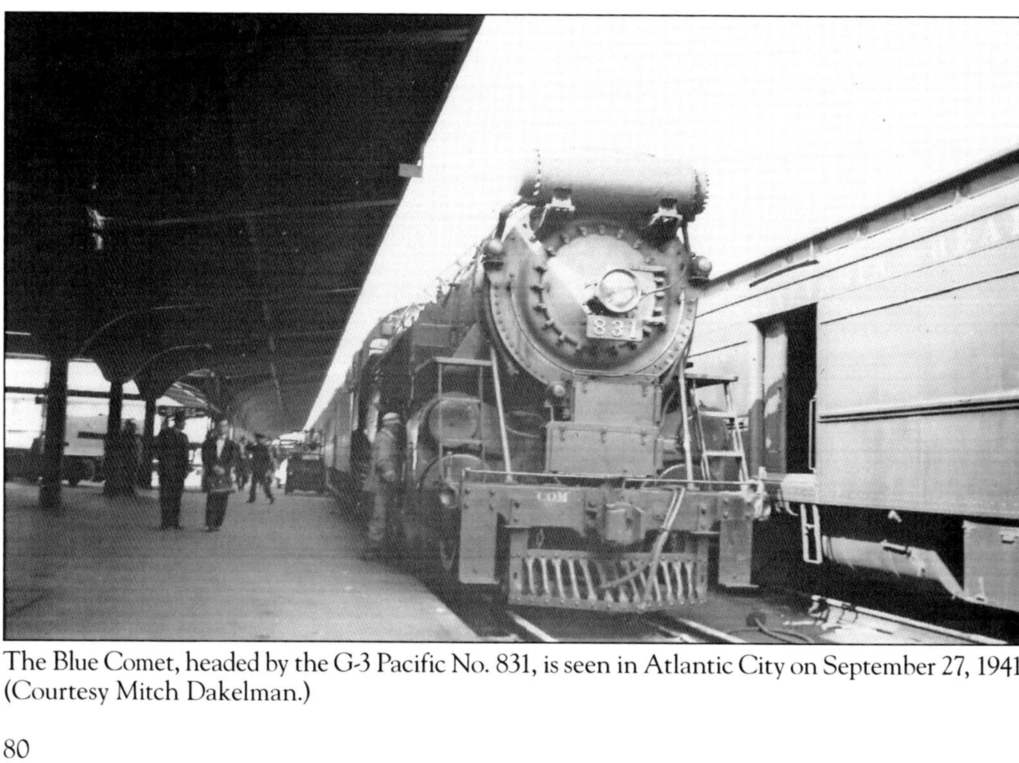

The Blue Comet, headed by the G-3 Pacific No. 831, is seen in Atlantic City on September 27, 1941. (Courtesy Mitch Dakelman.)

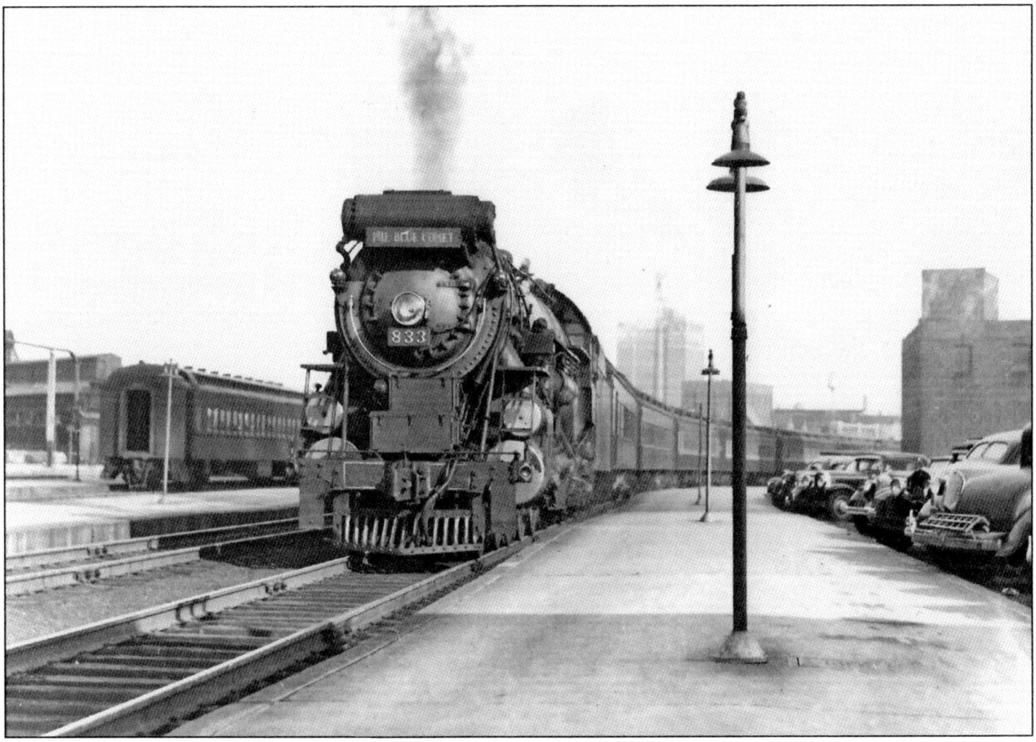

The Blue Comet G-3 Pacific No. 833 is preparing to depart the Pennsylvania-Reading Seashore Lines Atlantic City Terminal on Saturday, April 23, 1938. Behind the tender is the Claridge Hotel, the last of Atlantic City's great hotels from that era. It was built in 1930 and became a hotel-casino; however, it is currently just a hotel. (Photograph by Bruce G. Saylor, courtesy Joel Rosenbaum and Tom Gallo.)

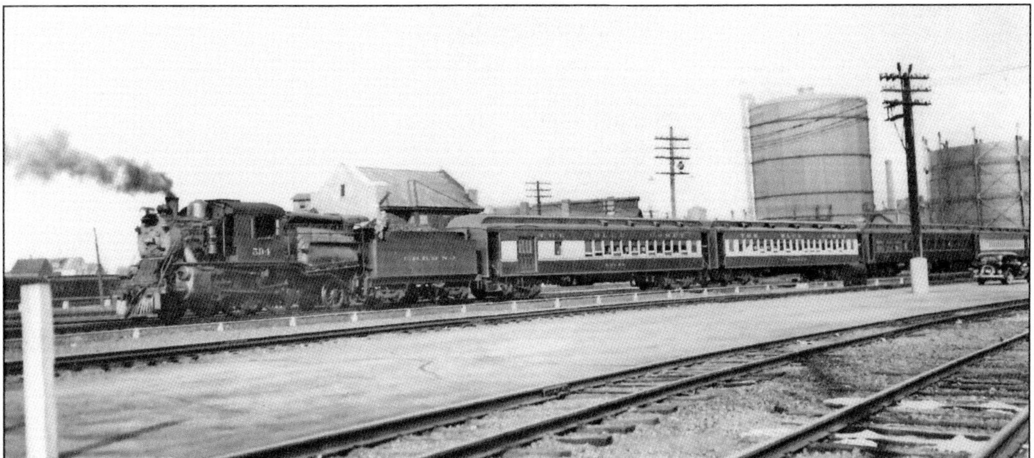

The P-6s Atlantic 4-4-2 Camelback No. 594 is seen backing the Blue Comet into the Pennsylvania-Reading Seashore Lines Atlantic City terminal on Sunday, July 17, 1938. This might be one of the additional trips of the Blue Comet added on some Fridays southbound and Sundays northbound with food service provided on some of the trips. Note that the steel Reading Company café car, the third car from the engine, provided dining service and was obtained from a pool of Reading/NJC café cars. (Courtesy Joel Rosenbaum and Tom Gallo.)

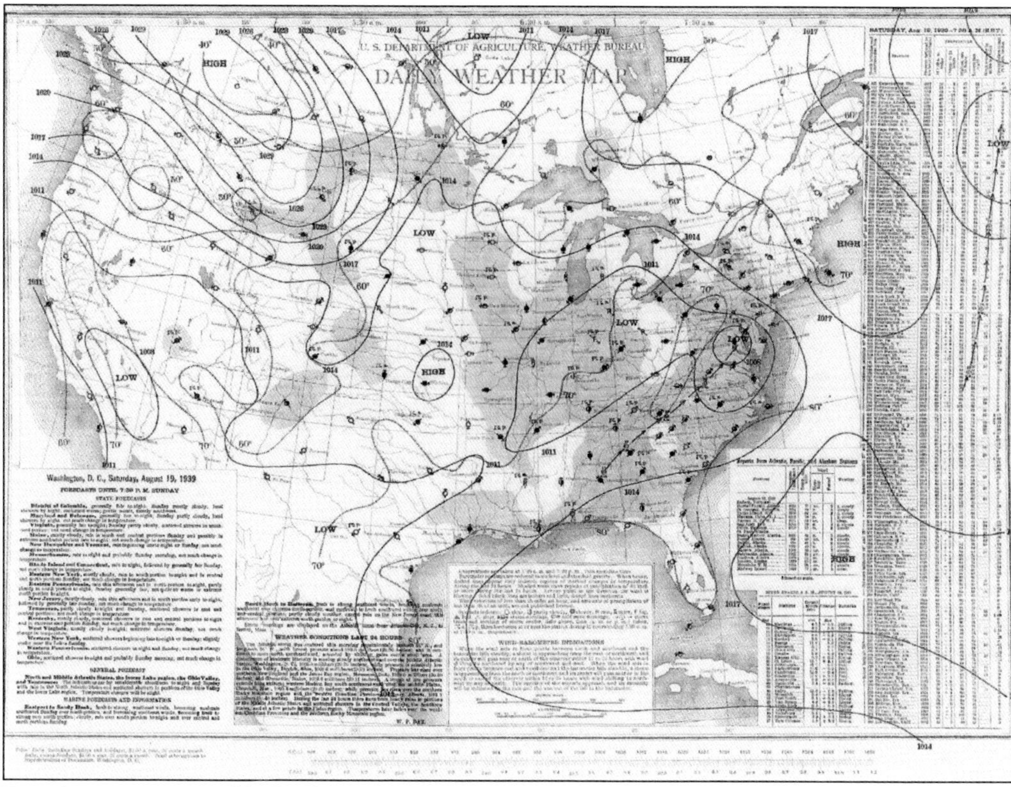

Weather was responsible for the most serious accident to befall the Blue Comet. Very heavy rain had been falling on August 19, 1939, due to an intense and stationary low-pressure system that had settled over the area. Water-gauge readings recorded by the Chatsworth Cranberry Association indicated that 13.5 inches of rain fell that day, with 10.25 inches having fallen between 2:00 p.m. and 6:00 p.m. In just four hours, Chatsworth received almost a quarter of its average yearly precipitation of 45 inches. (Courtesy Robert A. Emmons.)

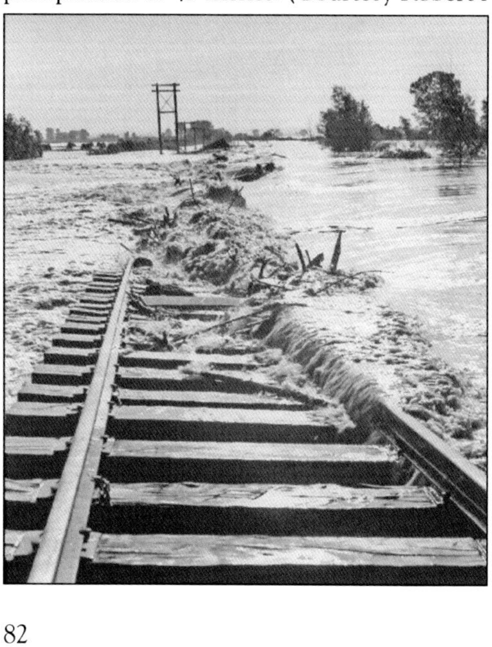

Just south of Chatsworth, the intense rain caused the sandy roadbed to wash across the track to a depth of several feet. At Winslow Junction, 19.7 miles west of Chatsworth, the crew of the northbound train No. 4218 received an urgent message warning them of hard rains and advising them to keep a sharp lookout for sand washed down on crossings. The Blue Comet reduced its speed to about 35 miles per hour instead of its usual 70. However, by the time engineer Thomas saw the impending disaster just south of Chatsworth and pulled the brake, the momentum of the locomotive carried it into the deluge. The locomotive derailed, separating from the rest of the train and ripping up 600 feet of track as it did. Its five cars also derailed, with some toppling over. (Courtesy Robert A. Emmons.)

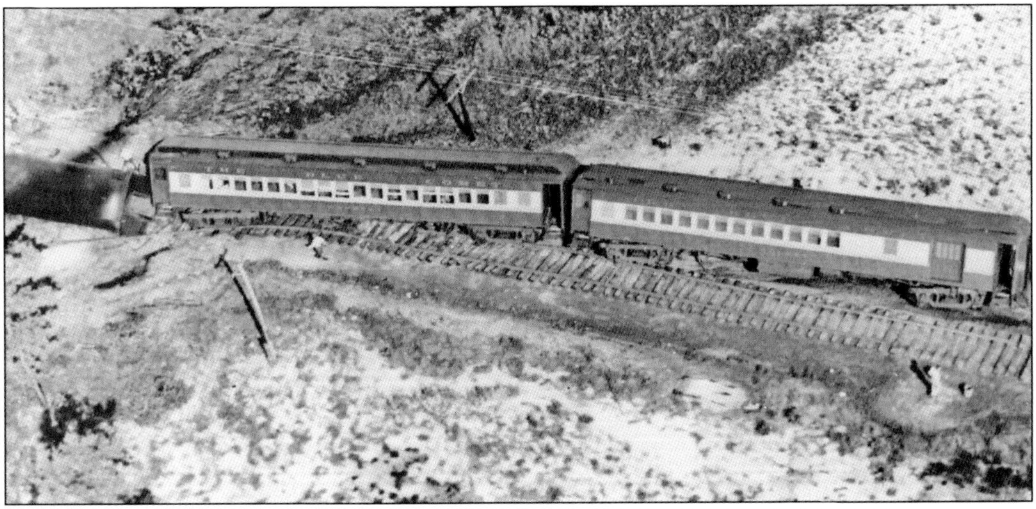

The consist of the Blue Comet when it derailed included the G-3 Pacific No. 820, two coaches (*D'Arrest* and *Winnecke*), one combine-smoker (*Halley*), a diner (*Giacobini*), and an observation car (*Biela*). The decline in the Blue Comet's popularity was evident by the passenger count that day: only 49. Luckily, just 32 passengers were injured, along with a dining car employee, one porter, and one train service employee. All the equipment involved in the wreck was repaired and returned to service except for the dining car *Giacobini*. Being a steel-clad wooden car, it was unable to withstand the forces of the wreck and was too badly damaged to repair. An army of NJC railroad workers replaced the 600 feet of damaged track in approximately 48 hours. (Photograph by Ed Brown, courtesy Joel Rosenbaum and Tom Gallo.)

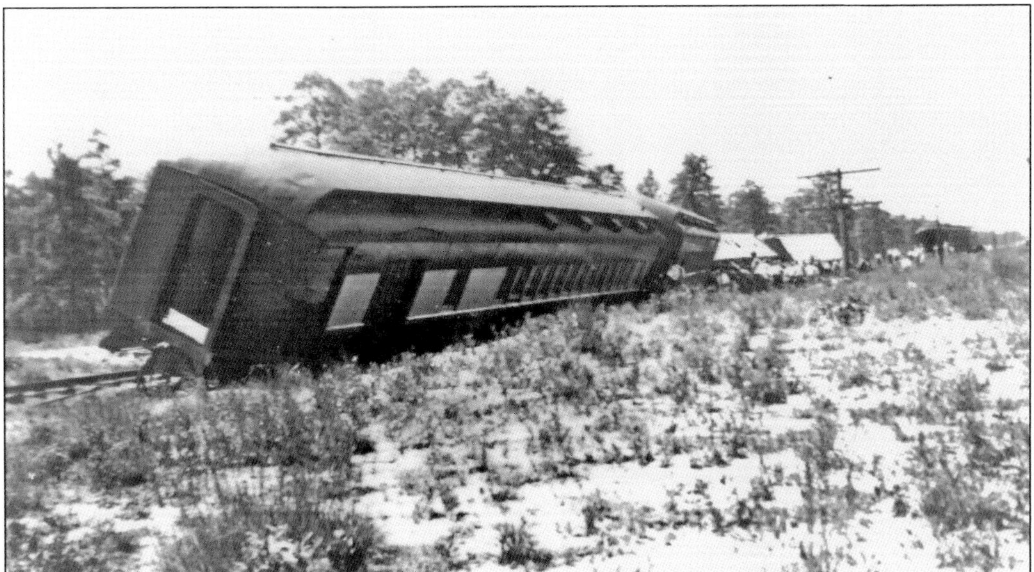

The day after the Blue Comet wreck, the combine-smoker *Halley* is seen leaning on its side. At the time of the wreck, there was smoke in the diner *Giacobini* where a small oil stove caused a fire. I.L. Gordon, of the railroad's public relations department, noted that if the wreck had been the next day, which would have been a Sunday, there might have been several hundred passengers on board instead of 49. (Photograph by John Brinckmann, courtesy Joel Rosenbaum and Tom Gallo.)

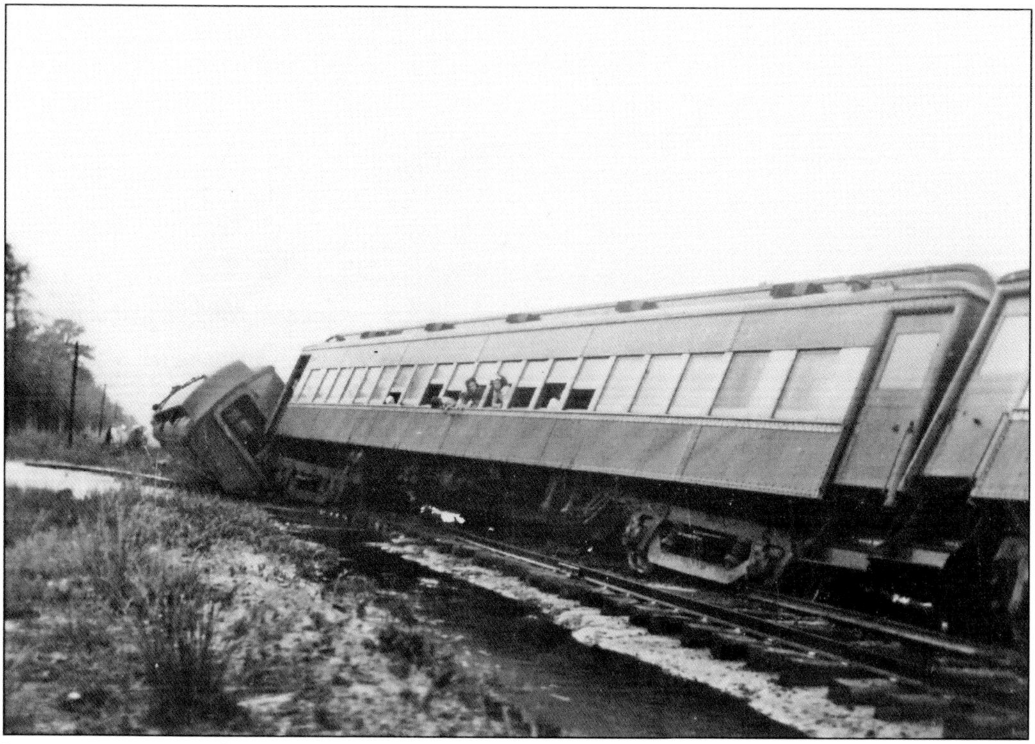

It appears passengers leaning out of the windows of the coach *D'Arrest* are anxiously waiting rescue after the Blue Comet derailed on August 19, 1939. (Courtesy Joel Rosenbaum and Tom Gallo.)

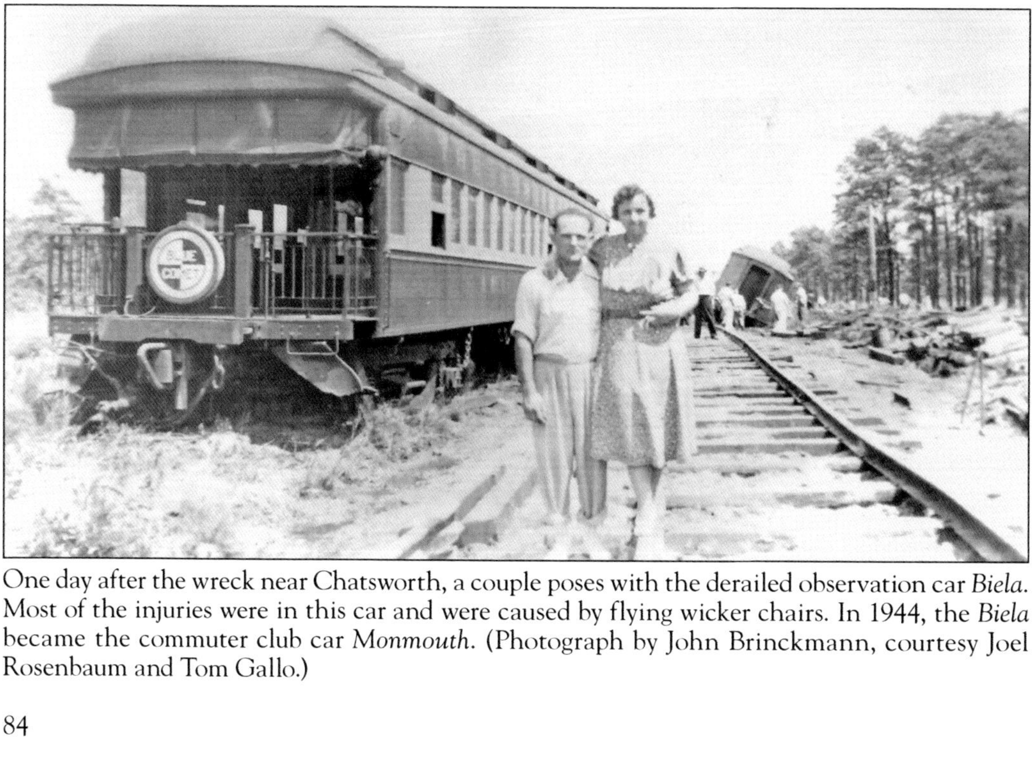

One day after the wreck near Chatsworth, a couple poses with the derailed observation car *Biela*. Most of the injuries were in this car and were caused by flying wicker chairs. In 1944, the *Biela* became the commuter club car *Monmouth*. (Photograph by John Brinckmann, courtesy Joel Rosenbaum and Tom Gallo.)

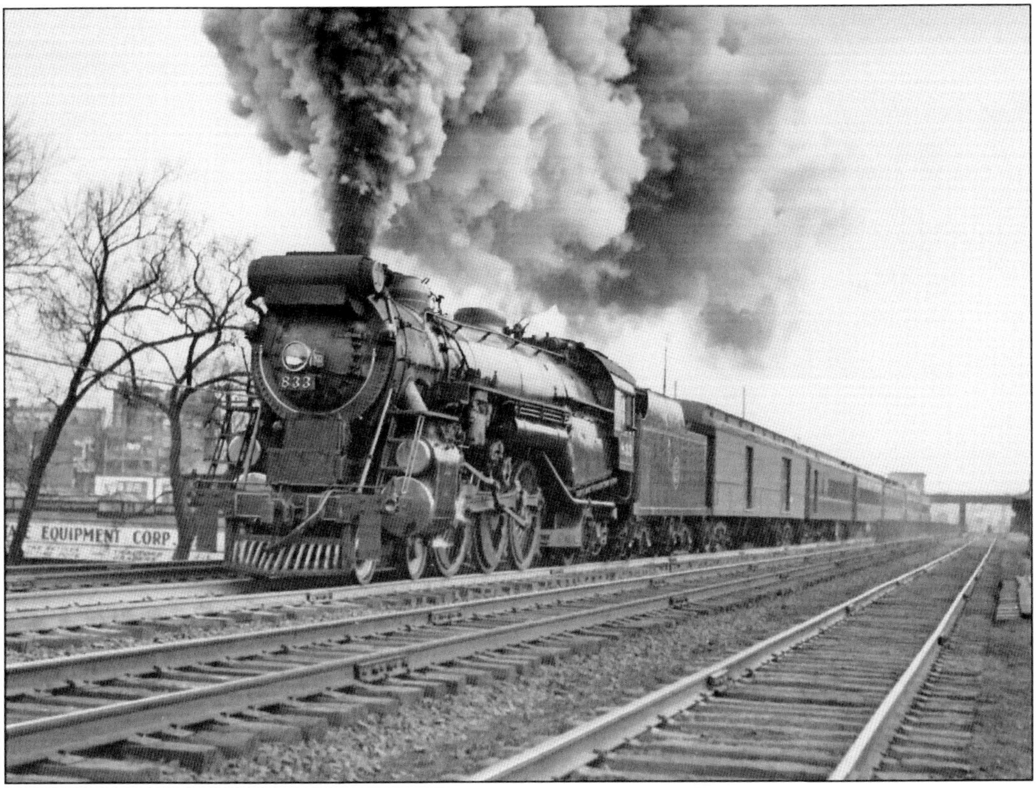

Passenger numbers on the Blue Comet continued to plummet after 1932 due to the Depression. As a result, the powerful G-3 Pacifics were pressed into long-haul passenger service on other trains operated by the NJC. In this photograph, NJC engine No. 833 is shown with its Blue Comet sign covered. The photograph was taken just west of the NJC Broad Street Elizabeth Station in 1933 or later. The train itself is probably the Harrisburg Special or the Queen of the Valley. (Author's collection.)

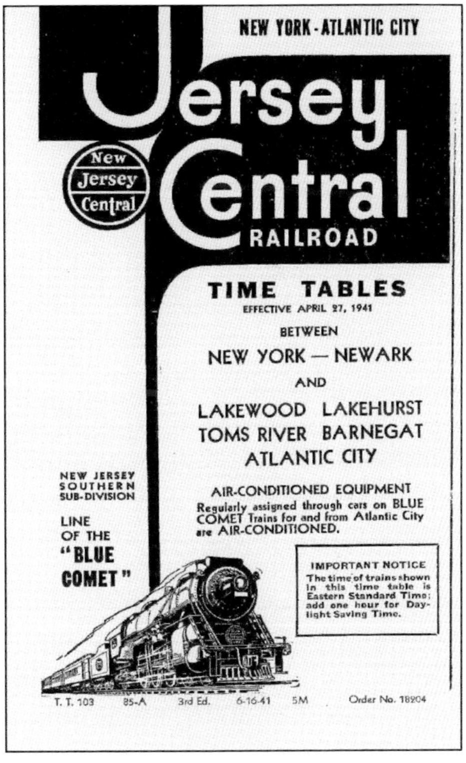

This Blue Comet timetable was put in place on April 27, 1941. This was one of the last timetables issued for the Blue Comet, perhaps the very last, as the train made its last run on September 27, 1941. Note that the Blue Comet name is no longer prominent on the front of the timetable. Dining service is still provided, on the one daily Blue Comet round trip to Atlantic City, even though the *Giacobini* was taken out of service after the August 19, 1939, wreck. (Courtesy Joel Rosenbaum and Tom Gallo.)

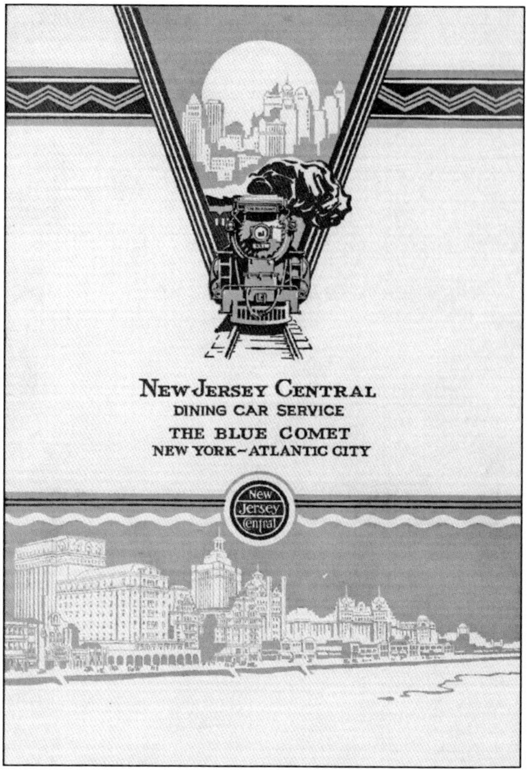

The Blue Comet made its last run on September 27, 1941. Passengers included 157 members of Railroad Enthusiasts Inc., from the New York Division. The NJC made every possible effort to make the last run memorable, which included a special dinner with a commemorative menu for the occasion. The front cover of the souvenir menu is richly decorated with the same Art Deco designs used by the NJC in its earlier advertisements for the Blue Comet service. (Courtesy Joel Rosenbaum and Tom Gallo.)

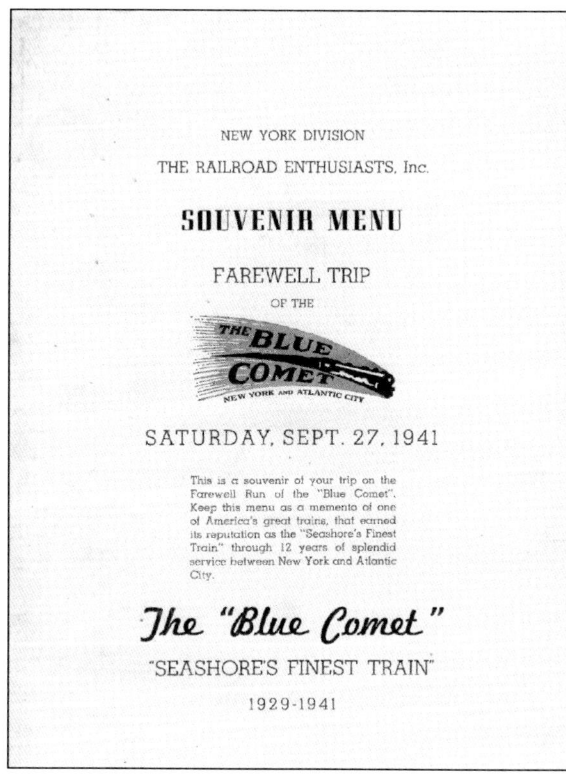

NEW YORK DIVISION

THE RAILROAD ENTHUSIASTS, Inc.

SOUVENIR MENU

FAREWELL TRIP

OF THE

THE BLUE COMET
NEW YORK AND ATLANTIC CITY

SATURDAY, SEPT. 27, 1941

This is a souvenir of your trip on the Farewell Run of the "Blue Comet". Keep this menu as a memento of one of America's great trains, that earned its reputation as the "Seashore's Finest Train" through 12 years of splendid service between New York and Atlantic City.

The "Blue Comet"

"SEASHORE'S FINEST TRAIN"

1929-1941

The left inside panel of the souvenir menu urges members of the Railroad Enthusiasts to "keep this menu as a memento of one of America's great trains, that earned its reputation as the 'Seashore's Finest Train' through 12 years of splendid service between New York and Atlantic City." (Courtesy Joel Rosenbaum and Tom Gallo.)

The right inside panel of the souvenir menu is seen here. To start, passengers were served an appetizer of olives and gherkins; either vegetable soup, tomato juice, or a fruit cup; rolls; and a salad with dressing. Riders could pick from three entrees, which were served with side dishes of potatoes (fried or mashed) and either corn or peas. For dessert, they could have either ice cream and cake or apple pie and cheese. All was served for the low price of $1. (Courtesy Joel Rosenbaum and Tom Gallo.)

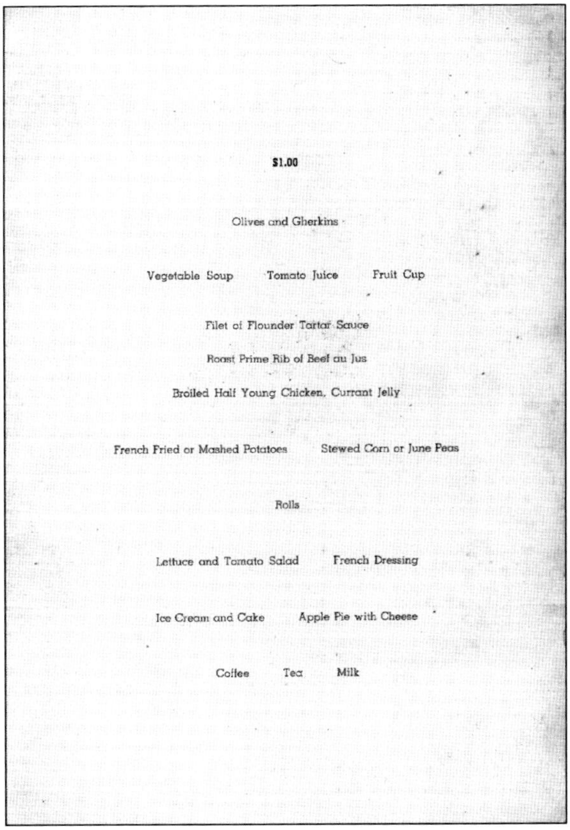

$1.00

Olives and Gherkins

Vegetable Soup Tomato Juice Fruit Cup

Filet of Flounder Tartar Sauce

Roast Prime Rib of Beef au Jus

Broiled Half Young Chicken, Currant Jelly

French Fried or Mashed Potatoes Stewed Corn or June Peas

Rolls

Lettuce and Tomato Salad French Dressing

Ice Cream and Cake Apple Pie with Cheese

Coffee Tea Milk

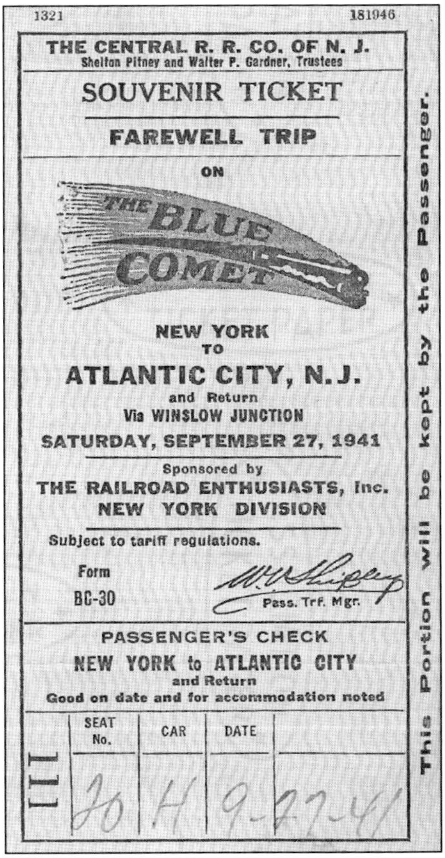

1321 181946

THE CENTRAL R. R. CO. OF N. J.
Shelton Pitney and Walter P. Gardner, Trustees

SOUVENIR TICKET

FAREWELL TRIP

ON

THE BLUE COMET

NEW YORK
TO
ATLANTIC CITY, N. J.
and Return
Via WINSLOW JUNCTION
SATURDAY, SEPTEMBER 27, 1941

Sponsored by
THE RAILROAD ENTHUSIASTS, Inc.
NEW YORK DIVISION

Subject to tariff regulations.

Form
BC-30

Pass. Trf. Mgr.

PASSENGER'S CHECK
NEW YORK to ATLANTIC CITY
and Return
Good on date and for accommodation noted

SEAT No.	CAR	DATE
20	H	9-27-41

This Portion will be kept by the Passenger.

For the final run of the Blue Comet, a special souvenir ticket was printed on red stock. The passenger count on the last day was 173 southbound and 171 northbound. The passengers were permitted to keep their tickets as a memento of the farewell trip of the Blue Comet. (Courtesy Ben Kranefeld.)

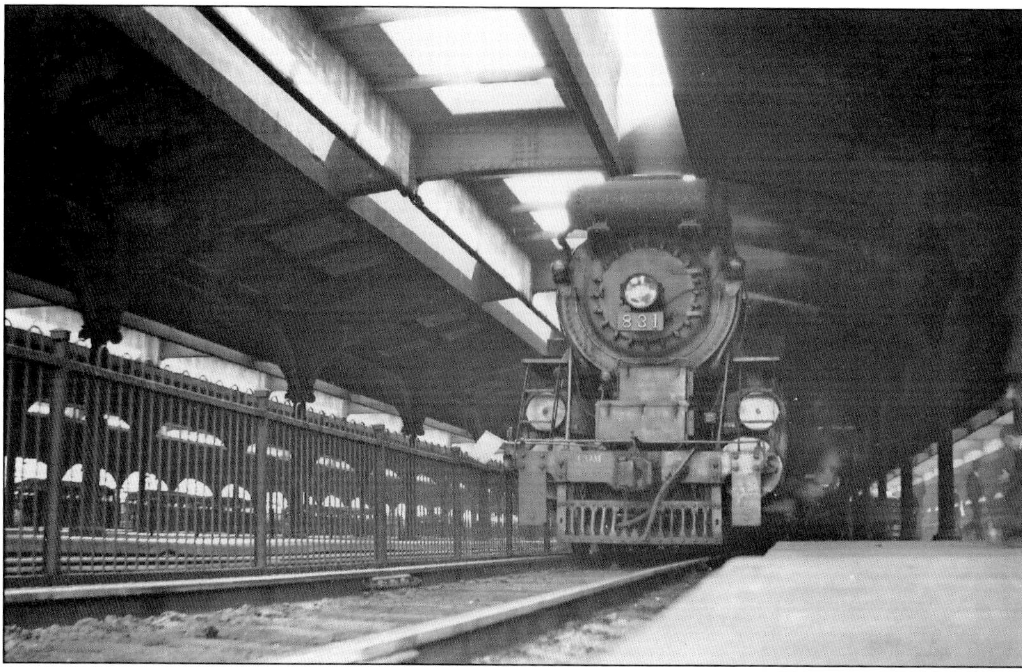

The final run of the Blue Comet was hauled by the G-3 Pacific No. 831. The Blue Comet sign was removed from the front of the locomotive below the Elesco feedwater heater. The train is seen here ready for departure in the Communipaw Jersey City Terminal on the morning of September 27, 1941. (Courtesy Mitch Dakelman.)

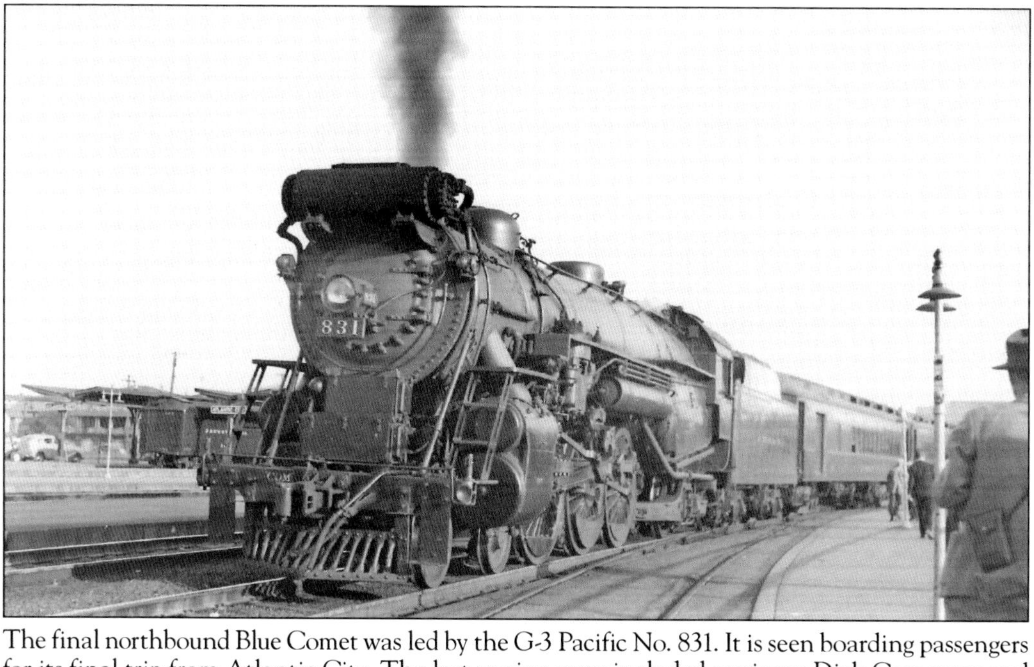

The final northbound Blue Comet was led by the G-3 Pacific No. 831. It is seen boarding passengers for its final trip from Atlantic City. The last engine crew included engineer Dick Carpenter and fireman Howard Schuyler. The train crew included conductor Joseph F. Walsh and trainman Paul Kennedy. (Photograph by John Brinckmann, courtesy Joel Rosenbaum and Tom Gallo.)

The consolidation of the Reading Company's Atlantic City Railroad and the Pennsylvania Railroad's West Jersey & Seashore Lines (PRSL) in 1933 had an adverse effect on the Blue Comet. Prior to this, the Blue Comet traveled over the tracks of the friendly Reading Company's Atlantic City Railroad. With the formation of the PRSL, the PRR owned a controlling two-thirds of the consolidated line. The Blue Comet was now forced to play second fiddle to the PRR New York to Atlantic City trains, as the PRR trains were given the choice departure times. (Courtesy South Jersey Rails.)

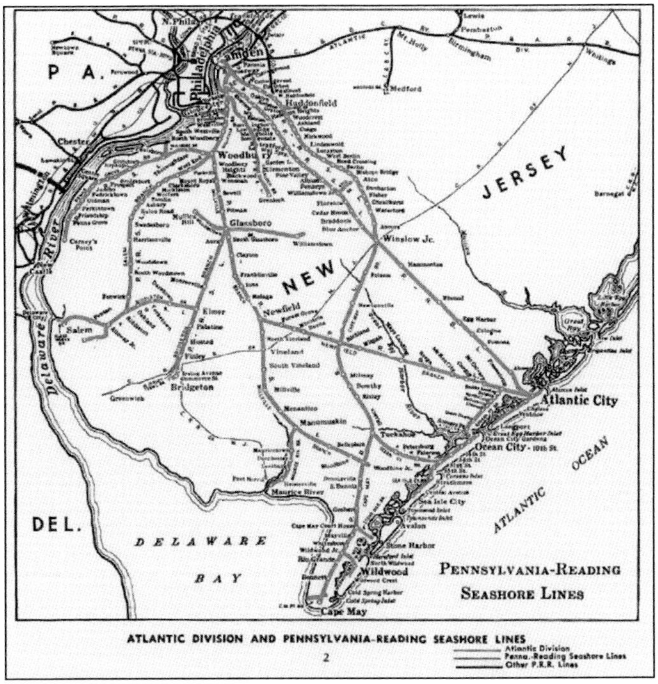

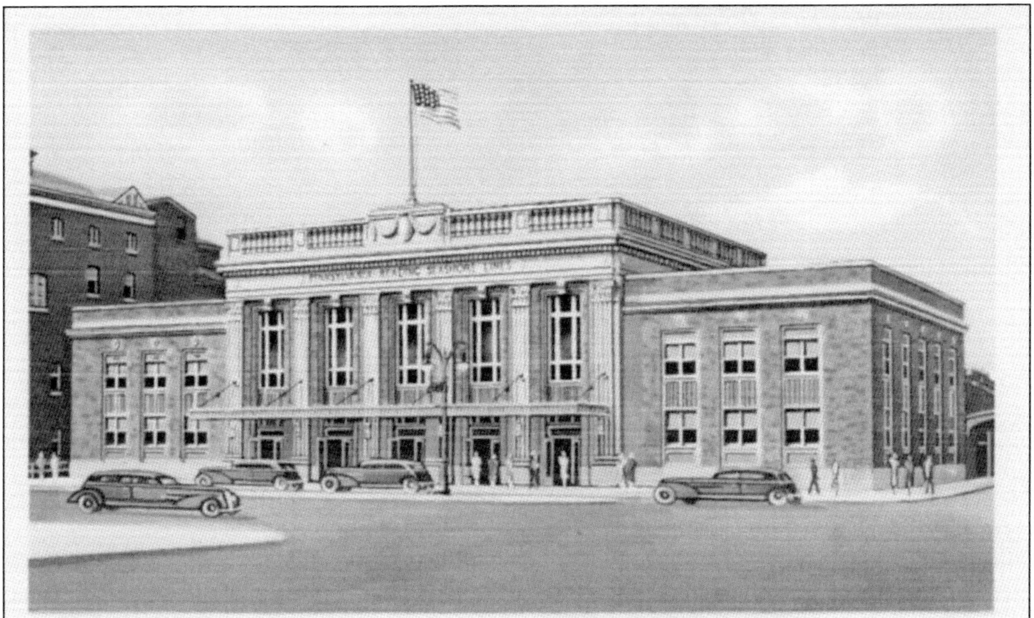

The PRSL's Union Terminal in Atlantic City was opened on October 30, 1934. The headhouse bore the new railroad's name on its limestone cornice and fronted five platforms serving eight 15-car stub-end tracks. With the new Union Terminal, the Blue Comet began using the formerly owned PRR trackage from Winslow Junction to the Atlantic City Union Terminal, which allowed the PRR the opportunity to manipulate track usage and affect Blue Comet scheduling. Also, the train information clerk at Union Terminal would give out information about the Blue Comet service to New York only when such information was specifically asked for. (Courtesy South Jersey Rails.)

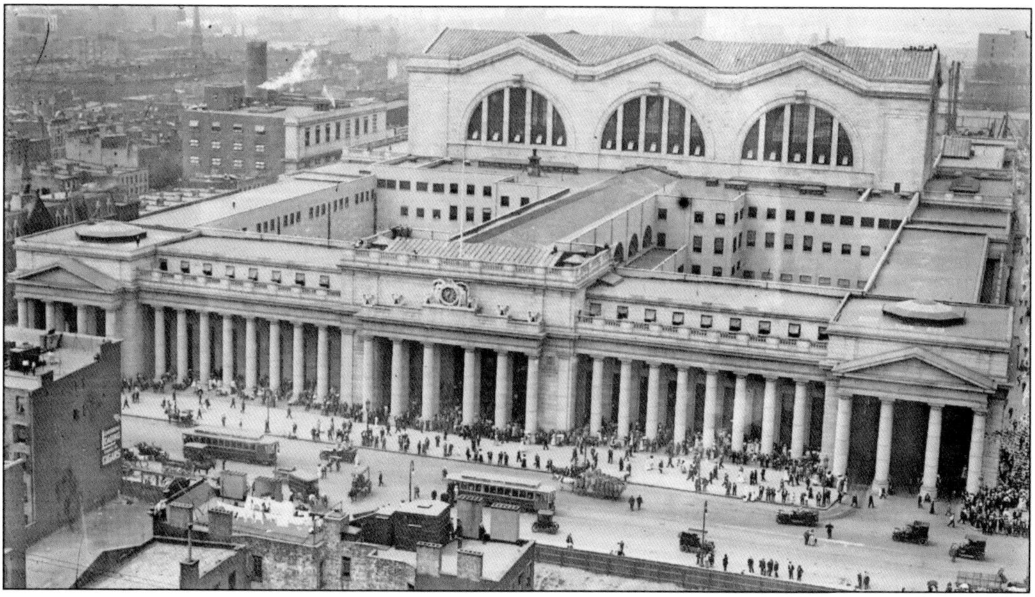

The Pennsylvania Railroad already had a number of distinct advantages over the NJC Atlantic City rail passenger service at the time, even before the creation of the PRSL and the inauguration of the Blue Comet service. The Pennsylvania provided direct rail service to mid-town Manhattan, via the Hudson River Tunnels, at Pennsylvania Station. Here, passengers bound for Atlantic City had a choice of taking a through train from New York or making connections at North Philadelphia. Pennsylvania Station opened in 1910 and served the PRR until it was demolished in 1963. (Courtesy South Jersey Rails.)

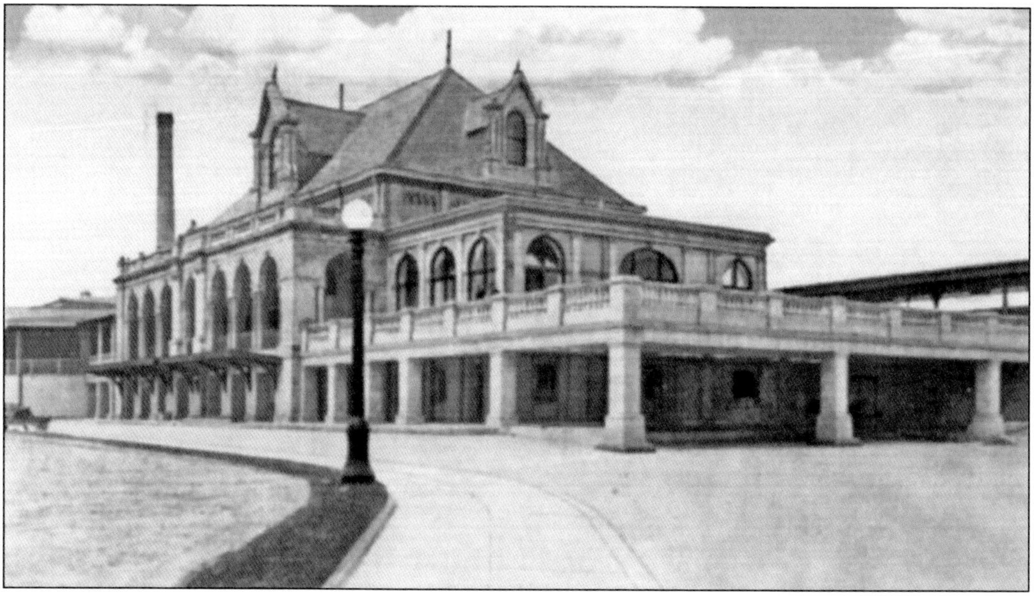

The PRR provided frequent Atlantic City connecting service from New York at its North Philadelphia station, and fast connecting service to Atlantic City for passengers coming up from the south and west. The main structure of the station was built from 1896 to 1901 for the Pennsylvania Railroad. It served as Philadelphia's sole stop for virtually the entire PRR east/west main line traffic. (Author's collection.)

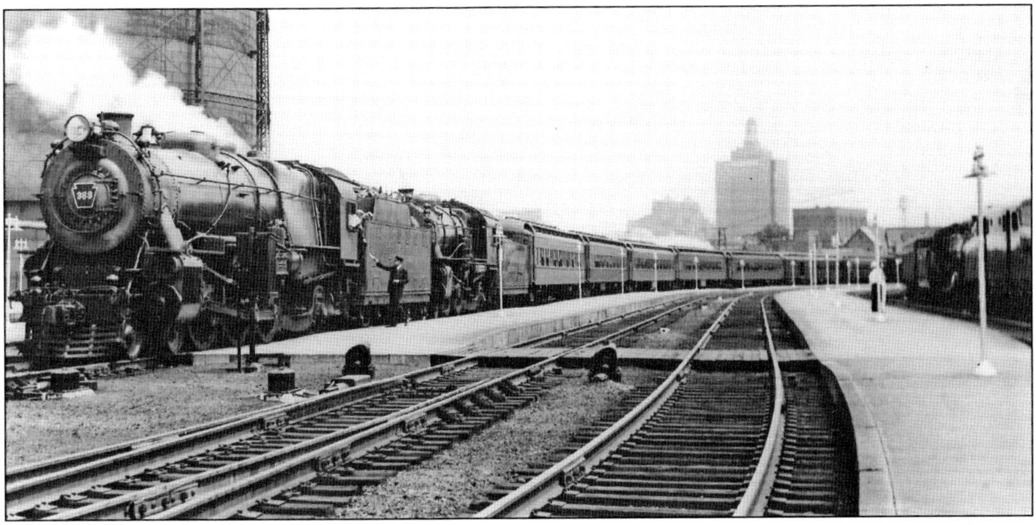

A double-headed PRSL train is seen here at the Atlantic City terminal. The PRR K4 Pacific No. 389 leads the duo. The Pennsylvania Railroad operated frequent service from New York to North Philadelphia, connecting there with PRSL for Atlantic City. The Claridge Hotel can be seen in the background. (Courtesy Joel Rosenbaum and Tom Gallo.)

Through and Connecting Trains—New York and Atlantic City

	179-1003	179-1005	201-1005	111-1007	25-1009	t ★1073	115-1011	115-1019	121-1013	121-1013
	Sat., Sun. and Sept. 2	Daily	Week-days	Daily	Sun. and Sept. 2	Daily	See Note	Sat. only	Sat., Sun. and Sept. 2	Except Sat., and Sun.
	Last trip September 15. Connects at Broad Street Station, Philadelphia.	Connects at Broad Street Station, Philadelphia.	Connects at North Philadelphia.	Connects at North Philadelphia.	Last Trip September 15. Connects at North Philadelphia.	Through Train Pennsylvania Station to Atlantic City.	Runs daily until September 8, inc., also Sunday, September 15 and 22. Connects at North Philadelphia.	First trip September 14. Connects at North Philadelphia.	Last Trip September 8. Connects at North Philadelphia.	First trip September 9. Connects at North Philadelphia.
Lv New York (Penna. Station)	AM 4.30	AM 4.30	AM 6.00	AM 7.05	AM 8.00	AM 9.20	AM 9.30	AM 9.30	AM 10.30	AM 10.30
Lv New York (Hudson Terminal)	*4.15	*4.15	5.50	7.00	7.50	9.10	9.20	9.20	10.20	10.20
" Jersey City (Exchange Place)	*4.18	*4.18	u5.53	u7.03	u7.53	u9.13	u9.23	u9.23	u10.23	u10.23
Ar Manhattan Transfer (v)	4.32	4.32	6.07	7.16	8.07	9.26	9.37	9.37	10.37	10.37
Lv Manhattan Transfer (v)	4.43	4.43	6.13	7.18	8.13	9.33	9.43	9.43	10.43	10.43
" Newark (Penna. Station)	4.47	4.47	6.17	7.22	8.17	9.37	9.47	9.47	10.47	10.47
" Elizabeth	§4.55	§4.55	....	7.30	....	9.45	....	....	....	....
" New Brunswick	5.19	5.19	....	7.48	....	....	....	....	....	....
" Princeton Junction	....	....	....	....	....	....	....	....	....	....
" Trenton	5.57	5.57	7.03	8.14	9.03	10.32	10.33	10.33	11.33	11.33
Ar North Philadelphia	....	....	7.32	8.43	9.31	....	11.01	11.01	12.06	12.06
" Philadelphia, Broad Street Station	6.45	6.45	....	....	....	....	....	....	....	....
Lv Philadelphia, Broad Street Station	7.05	7.50	....	....	....	....	....	....	....	....
" North Philadelphia	....	....	8.05	9.08	10.09	....	11.09	11.29	12.09	12.09
Ar Absecon—Pleasantville	....	....	....	b10.08	....	e12.00	....	....	....	....
" Atlantic City	8.30 AM	9.15 AM	9.15 AM	10.20 AM	11.15 AM	12.10 PM	12.20 PM	12.35 PM	1.20 PM	1.20 PM

	75-1015	t ★1075	125-1017	217-1021	t ★1077	219-1025	t ★1085	223-1029	227-1031	449-1033
	See Note	Sat. only	Sat., Sun. and Sept. 2	Daily	Week-days	Week-days Except Sept. 2	Fri. only	Daily	Fri. and Sat. only	Daily
	Daily until September 8, inc., then Saturdays and Sundays only. Connects at North Philadelphia.	Through Train Pennsylvania Station to Atlantic City.	Last trip September 2. Connects at North Philadelphia.	Connects at North Philadelphia.	Through Train Pennsylvania Station to Atlantic City. Nellie Bly.	Connects at North Philadelphia.	Through Train Pennsylvania Station to Atlantic City.	Connects at North Philadelphia.	Last Trip August 31. Connects at North Philadelphia.	Connection will be held at North Philadelphia five minutes if necessary.
Lv New York (Penna. Station)	AM 11.00	PM 12.20	PM 12.30	PM 2.00	PM 2.10	PM 3.00	PM 4.50	PM 5.00	PM 7.00	PM 9.00
Lv New York (Hudson Terminal)	10.50	12.10	12.20	1.50	2.00	2.50	4.42	4.50	6.50	8.50
" Jersey City (Exchange Place)	u10.53	u12.13	u12.23	u1.53	u2.03	u2.53	u4.45	u4.53	u6.53	u8.53
Ar Manhattan Transfer (v)	11.07	12.26	12.37	2.07	2.16	3.07	4.59	5.07	7.07	9.07
Lv Manhattan Transfer (v)	11.13	12.33	12.43	2.13	2.23	3.13	5.03	5.13	7.13	9.13
" Newark (Penna. Station)	11.17	12.37	12.47	2.17	2.27	3.17	5.07	5.17	7.17	9.17
" Elizabeth	....	12.45	....	....	2.35	....	....	....	....	9.25
" New Brunswick	11.41	1.03	....	....	....	....	....	5.40	7.41	9.42
" Princeton Junction	....	1.19	....	....	3.08	3.55	....	5.54	7.57	....
" Trenton	12.05	1.34	1.35	3.03	3.24	4.05	6.03	6.05	8.11	10.10
Ar North Philadelphia	12.34	....	2.04	3.31	....	4.35	....	6.33	8.40	10.39
" Philadelphia, Broad Street Station	....	....	....	....	....	....	....	....	....	....
Lv Philadelphia, Broad Street Station	....	....	....	....	....	....	....	....	....	....
" North Philadelphia	1.09	....	2.09	3.39	....	4.40	....	6.59	9.09	10.59
Ar Absecon—Pleasantville	....	e3.00	....	b4.39	b4.50	....	....	....	....	....
" Atlantic City	2.15 PM	3.10 PM	3.15 PM	4.50 PM	5.00 PM	5.50 PM	7.40 PM	8.05 PM	10.15 PM	12.10 Night

	1002-202	1006-204	1008-206	t ★1070	1010-208	1012-212	t ★1072	1014-218	1016-218	1020-222
	Week-days Except Sept. 2	Daily Except Sun. Sept. 22	Week-days Except Sept. 2	Week-days	Daily	Week-days	Daily	Sun. only	Week-days	Daily
	Connects at North Philadelphia.	Connects at North Philadelphia.	Connects at North Philadelphia.	Through Train Atlantic City to Penna. Station. Nellie Bly.	Connects at North Philadelphia.	Connects at North Philadelphia.	Through Train Atlantic City to Pennsylvania Station.	Connects at North Philadelphia.	Connects at North Philadelphia.	Connects at North Philadelphia.
Lv Atlantic City	AM 5.55	AM 6.45	AM 7.30	AM 8.25	AM 8.40	AM 10.40	PM 1.30	PM 1.45	PM 1.50	PM 3.40
" Absecon—Pleasantville	....	....	....	a8.35	....	10.50	a1.40	....	....	a3.50
Ar North Philadelphia	7.01	7.51	8.41	....	9.46	12.04	....	3.00	3.00	4.50
" Philadelphia, Broad Street Station	....	....	....	....	....	....	....	....	....	....
Lv Philadelphia, Broad Street Station	....	....	....	....	....	....	....	....	....	....
" North Philadelphia	7.13	8.13	9.13	....	10.13	12.13	....	3.13	3.13	5.13
Ar Trenton	7.40	8.42	9.42	10.03	10.40	12.40	3.08	3.42	3.42	5.42
" Princeton Junction	7.51	8.53	....	10.19	§10.50	....	....	....	....	....
" New Brunswick	8.07	....	....	10.36	....	....	....	....	....	....
" Elizabeth	....	....	....	10.58	....	....	3.54	4.24	4.24	....
" Newark (Penna. Station)	8.31	9.31	10.29	11.08	11.27	1.28	4.02	4.32	4.32	6.29
Ar Manhattan Transfer (v)	d8.35	d9.35	d10.33	d11.12	d11.31	d1.32	d4.06	d4.36	d4.36	d6.33
Lv Manhattan Transfer (v)	8.35	9.35	10.34	11.14	11.34	1.34	4.08	4.44	4.38	6.34
Ar Jersey City (Exchange Place)	u8.48	u9.48	u10.48	u11.28	u11.48	u1.47	u4.22	u4.57	u4.52	u6.48
" New York (Hudson Terminal)	8.51	9.51	10.51	11.31	11.51	1.50	4.25	5.00	4.55	6.51
Ar New York (Penna. Station)	8.48 AM	9.48 AM	10.46 AM	11.25 AM	11.45 AM	1.45 PM	4.20 PM	4.49 PM	4.49 PM	6.46 PM

	t ★1080	1024-224	1026-226	t ★1078	1028-228	1032-74	1034-172	1036-178	1038-178
	Sun. and Sept. 2	Sun. and Sept. 2	Daily	Sun. and Sept. 2	See Note	Daily	Sun. and Sept. 2	See Note	Sun. and Sept. 2
	Through Train Atlantic City to Pennsylvania Station.	Connects at North Philadelphia.	Connects at North Philadelphia.	Through Train Atlantic City to Pennsylvania Station.	Runs Saturdays, Sundays and September 2; Except Saturdays Sept. 14, 21 and 28. Connects at North Philadelphia.	Connects at North Philadelphia.	Connects at North Philadelphia.	Runs daily until September 2, inc., then Sundays only. Connects at Broad Street Station, Philadelphia.	Last Trip September 8. Connects at North Philadelphia.
Lv Atlantic City	PM 4.40	PM 4.45	PM 5.45	PM 6.10	PM 6.45	PM 7.55	PM 8.55	PM 9.50	PM 10.45
" Absecon—Pleasantville	a4.50	....	....	a6.20	....	....	....	....	....
Ar North Philadelphia	....	5.54	6.55	....	7.55	9.09	10.02	10.59	11.52
" Philadelphia, Broad Street Station	....	....	....	....	....	....	....	11.13	....
Lv Philadelphia, Broad Street Station	....	....	....	....	....	....	....	11.50	....
" North Philadelphia	....	6.13	7.13	....	8.13	9.13	10.54	12.04	12.04
Ar Trenton	6.19	6.41	7.40	7.52	8.40	9.42	11.24	12.32	12.32
" Princeton Junction	....	6.52	7.51	....	....	....	....	....	....
" New Brunswick	....	....	....	....	9.06	10.06	....	....	....
" Elizabeth	7.05	....	....	8.38	9.27	10.26	....	....	....
" Newark (Penna. Station)	7.13	7.31	8.29	8.47	9.35	10.35	12.13	1.20	1.20
Ar Manhattan Transfer (v)	d7.17	d7.35	d8.33	d8.51	d9.39	d10.39	d12.17	d1.24	d1.24
Lv Manhattan Transfer (v)	7.24	7.35	8.34	8.54	9.44	10.49	12.34	1.34	1.34
Ar Jersey City (Exchange Place)	u7.38	u7.48	u8.48	u9.08	u9.58	u11.02	u12.47	u1.47	u1.47
" New York (Hudson Terminal)	7.41	7.51	8.51	9.11	10.01	11.05	12.50	1.50	1.50
Ar New York (Penna. Station)	7.30 PM	7.48 PM	8.46 PM	9.05 PM	9.54 PM	10.52 PM	12.30 Night	1.37 Night	1.37 Night

★Regularly assigned Parlor Cars Air-Conditioned.
§ Stops Sundays only.
* On Sundays leaves Hudson Terminal 1.30 A. M., Jersey City, 1.33 A. M.
a Stops only on signal or notice to Agent to receive passengers.
b stops only on notice to Conductor to discharge passengers.
d Stops only to discharge passengers.
e Stops only on notice to conductor to discharge passengers from New York and Newark.
t Through trains between New York and Atlantic City.
u Hudson and Manhattan R. R. Station.
v For transfer of passengers only.

This schedule shows both through and connecting trains between New York City and Atlantic City via the PRR and the PRSL. The schedule, dated June 23, 1935, illustrates the fact that the Pennsylvania Railroad provided more choices and trains from New York to Atlantic City than the NJC could offer. In addition, the PRR's electrification of its track from New York to Philadelphia further reduced travel time. This allowed the through PRR New York–Atlantic City Nellie Bly train to beat the Blue Comet by 15 minutes. (Courtesy Joel Rosenbaum and Tom Gallo.)

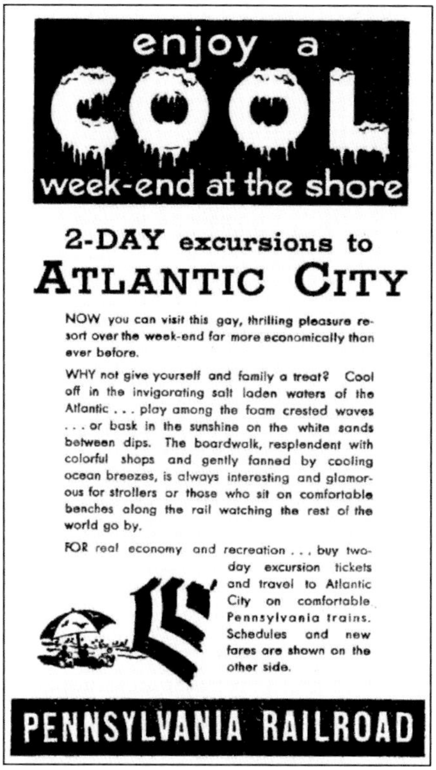

Despite all the advantages the PRR seemed to have over the NJC passenger service to Atlantic City, the inauguration of the Blue Comet service caused much consternation for the PRR. Employees of the PRR were sent to Jersey City and Elizabethport to physically count the number of passengers boarding and leaving the Blue Comet. The Pennsylvania Railroad engaged in a vigorous advertising campaign to counter the initial popularity of the Blue Comet. This advertisement promotes special-fare two-day excursions in the early 1930s from Washington, Baltimore, and Wilmington, Delaware, on summer Saturdays to Atlantic City. (Courtesy Joel Rosenbaum and Tom Gallo.)

With the creation of the Pennsylvania-Reading Seashore Lines in 1933 came a renewed round of advertising campaigns to counter the initial success of the NJC Blue Comet service to Atlantic City. Atlantic City's claim to fame as America's Favorite Playground was used in the PRSL advertisements beginning in 1933. (Courtesy West Jersey Chapter, National Railway Historical Society.)

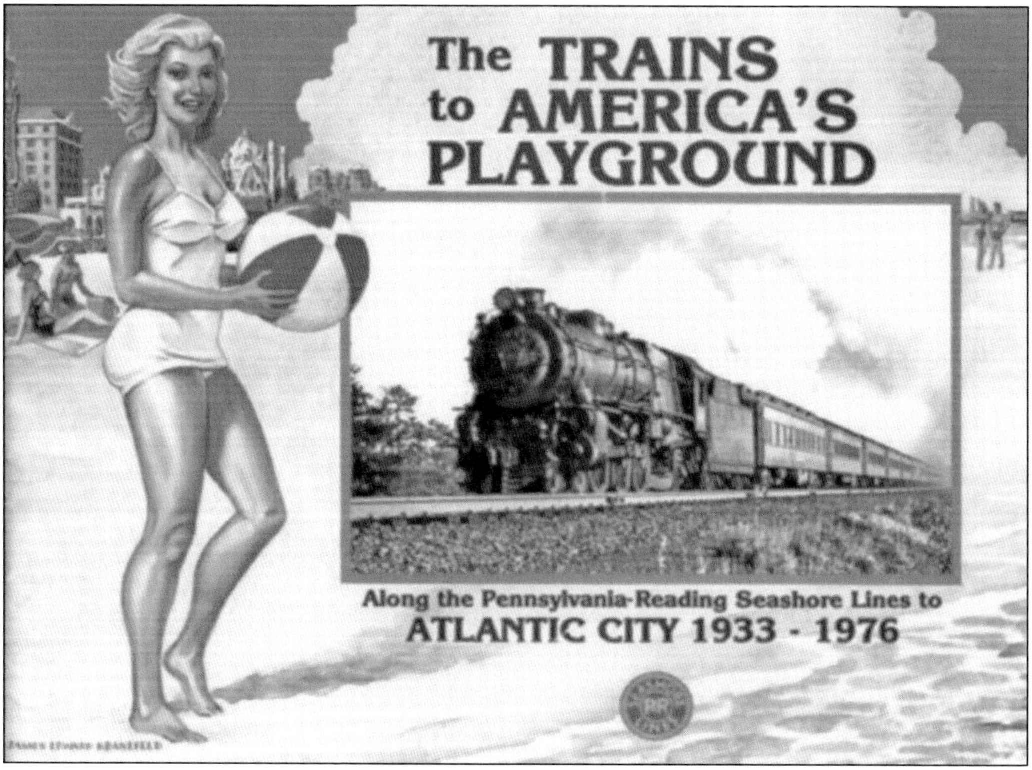

Three

Blue Comet Locomotives and Rolling Stock

The Baldwin Locomotive Works in Philadelphia, Pennsylvania, was commissioned to build a total of five class G-3 Pacific-type 4-6-2 locomotives for the NJC. These locomotives were Nos. 831–835. Locomotives 831, 832, and 833 were painted in a combination of Packard blue and royal blue and were used in Blue Comet service. No. 834 was painted olive green for service on the NJC Bullet, which provided first-class passenger service between Wilkes-Barre, Pennsylvania, and Jersey City. No. 835 was painted black and was usually assigned to the Queen of the Valley and Harrisburger trains. In later years, as ridership declined, the G-3 locomotives were sometimes used in other NJC rail services and other fast NJC Pacifics, such as No. 820, and the Camelback locomotives were assigned to Blue Comet train service. For those G-3 locomotives assigned to the Blue Comet, the round New Jersey Central emblem appeared on the tender on a dark-blue background against the rest of the tender, which was painted a lighter Packard blue. The tender truck frames were painted royal blue. The cab roof of the locomotive was painted royal blue. The train was known by its distinctive whistle. While the manufacturer or cadence of the whistle have never been verified, it is reported to have been a long bell, three-chime steamboat whistle. A plate carrying the Blue Comet name in gold letters against a blue background was attached to the front of the locomotive, below the Elesco feedwater heater. Eventually, 16 NJC cars were completely refurbished and assigned to the Blue Comet service. Each car was named for short-period comets. The outside surfaces of the passenger cars were finished in Packard blue and Jersey cream. The Jersey cream band extended from the belt rail up to the letter board. Initially, a gold stripe ran the length of the bottom edge of the car sides. The car roofs were finished in royal blue. The name of the train appeared in gold letters on the letter boards. The name of the comet each car was given also appeared in gold letters and was placed in the center of each car side, below the windows. Four-wheel die-cast bearing trucks were used in the combines, coaches, and observation cars, while the diner *Giacobini* and the full baggage cars had six-wheel die-cast trucks.

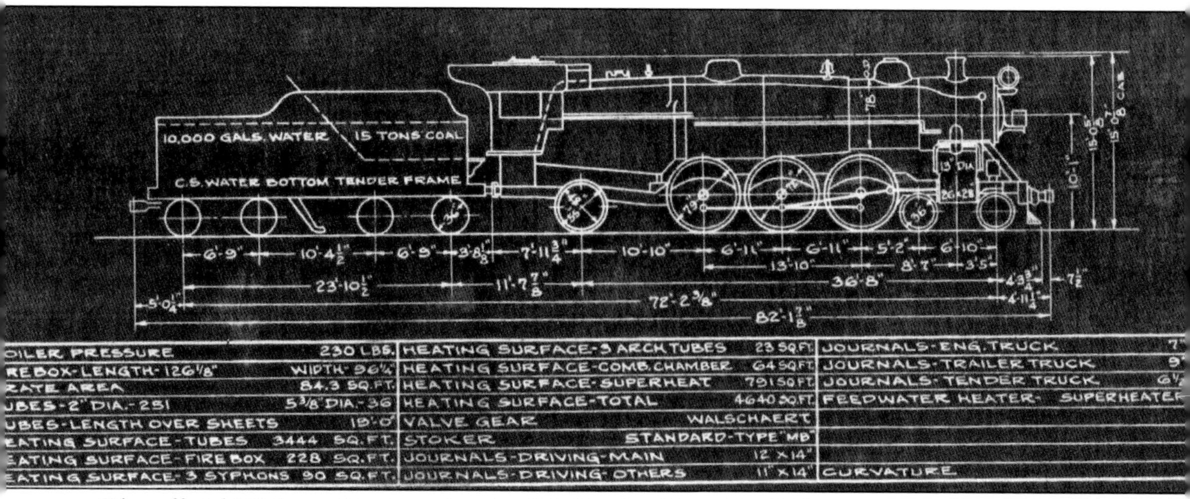

The official NJC specifications for the G-3 Pacifics Nos. 831–835, as submitted to the Baldwin Locomotive Works, can be seen in this blueprint. The five class G-3 Pacifics for the NJC were built in 1928. These locomotives, with high steaming capacity and lightweight reciprocating and revolving parts, were specially fitted for fast passenger service. The grate area of the locomotive for the NJC was designed for burning anthracite fuel or a mixture of anthracite and bituminous coal. (Courtesy Joel Rosenbaum and Tom Gallo.)

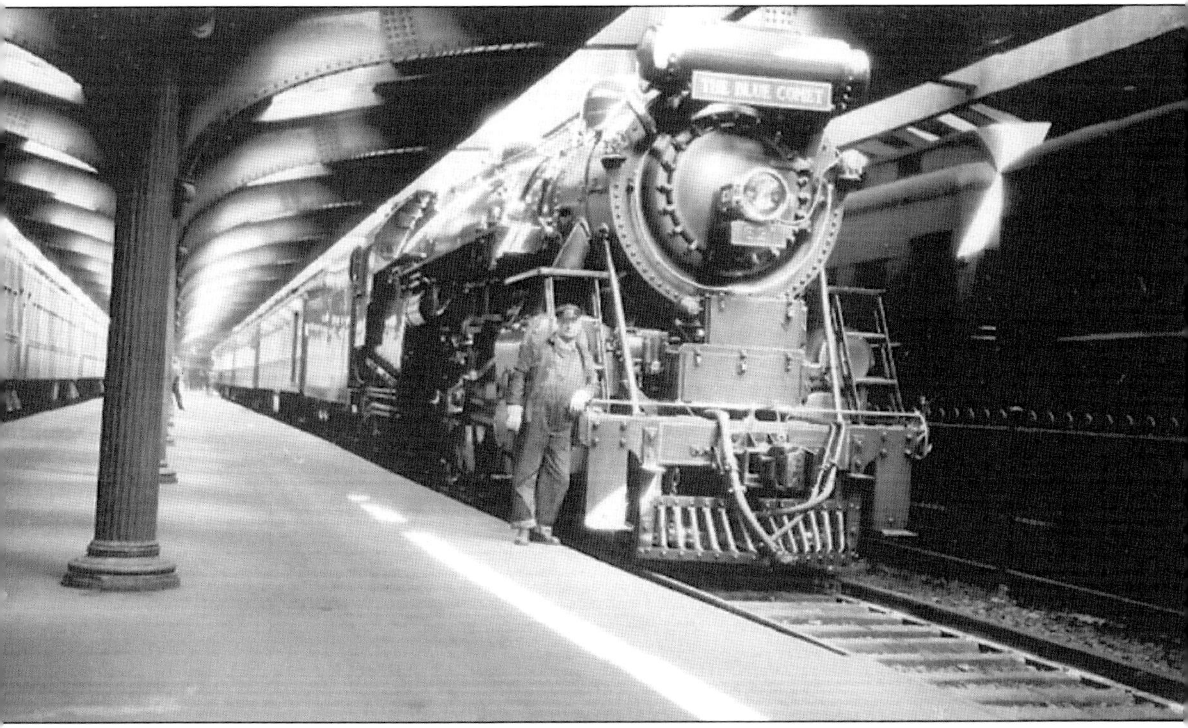

The engineer of a Blue Comet train poses proudly with locomotive No. 831 inside the NJC terminal in Jersey City, New Jersey, prior to its departure to Atlantic City. Don Wood's photographs focused on steam locomotives and early diesel locomotives. (Courtesy Don Wood collection.)

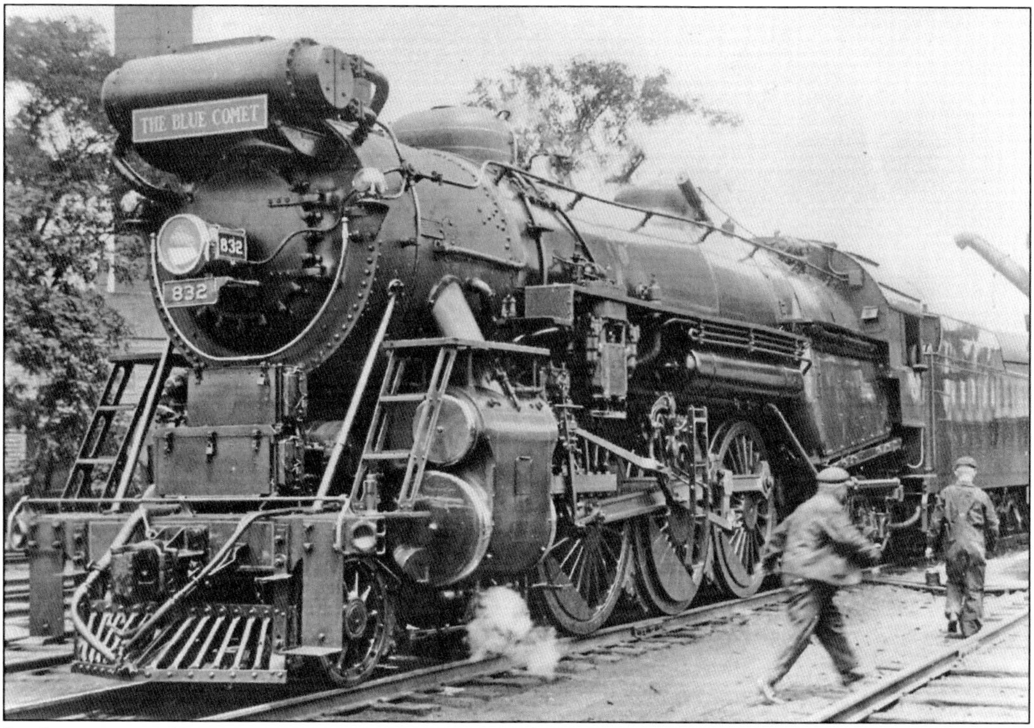

In this image of locomotive No. 832, it appears that the seasoned engineer Harvey Dunfee, in the foreground, is more anxious to get going than his foreman. Nonetheless, this was a ritual that would be repeated a thousand times, day after day, in the glory days of steam. (Photograph by Hank Webber, courtesy webbersphotography.)

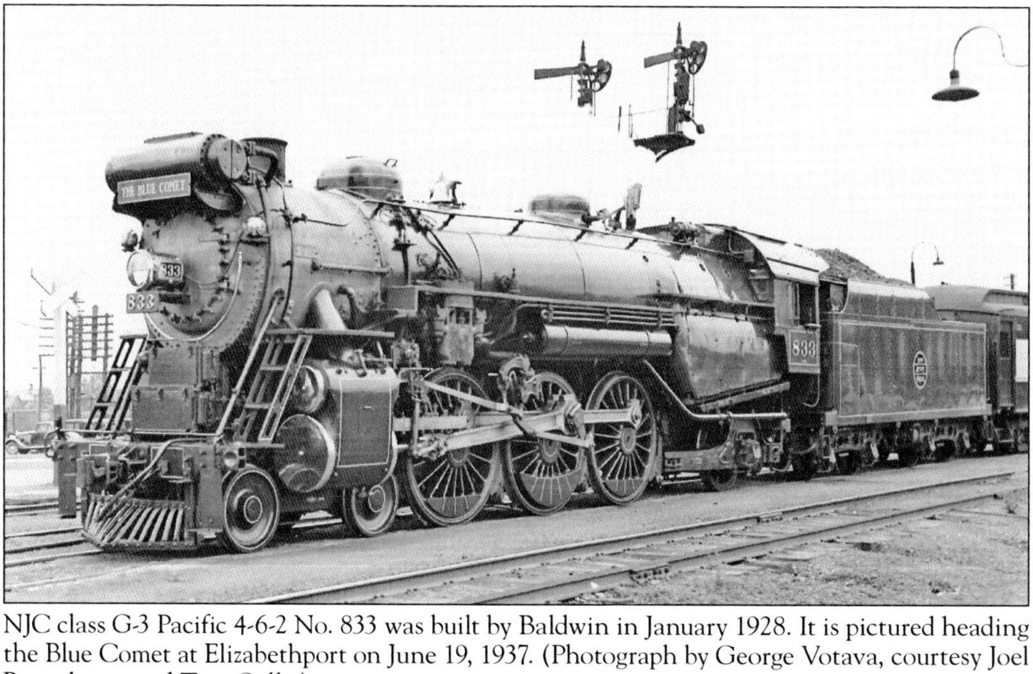

NJC class G-3 Pacific 4-6-2 No. 833 was built by Baldwin in January 1928. It is pictured heading the Blue Comet at Elizabethport on June 19, 1937. (Photograph by George Votava, courtesy Joel Rosenbaum and Tom Gallo.)

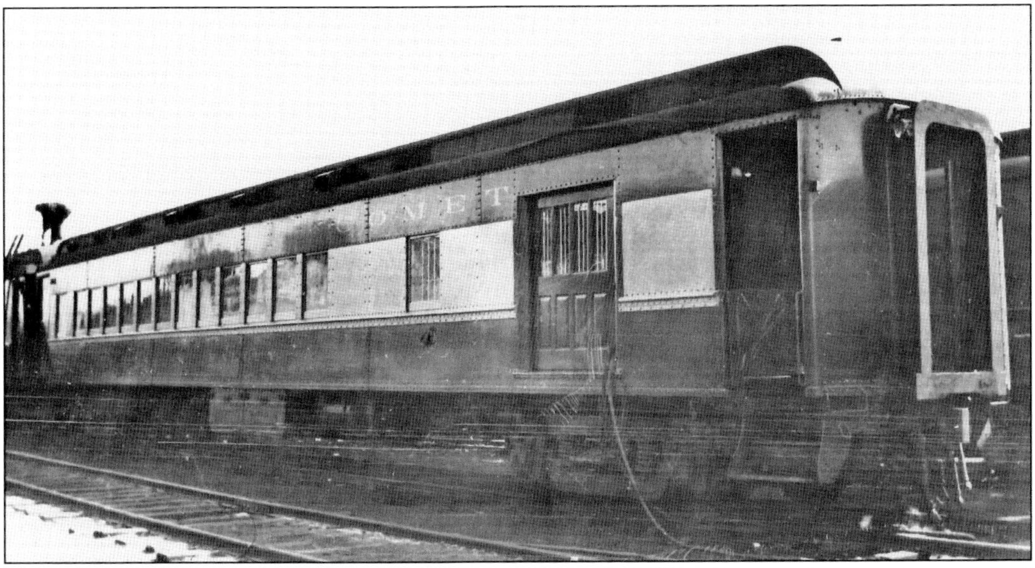

The Blue Comet combine-smoker *Halley* was No. 300 in the NJC rolling stock roster. It was named after Halley's Comet or Comet Halley, which has become one of the most famous comets. Halley is the only known short-period comet that is clearly visible to the naked eye from Earth, seen every 75–76 years. It has been observed and recorded by astronomers since at least 240 BC. It was named after Edmond Halley, who first observed it in 1682 and accurately predicted its return in 1758–1759. Halley last appeared in the inner Solar System in 1986 and will return in mid-2061. (Courtesy Joel Rosenbaum and Tom Gallo.)

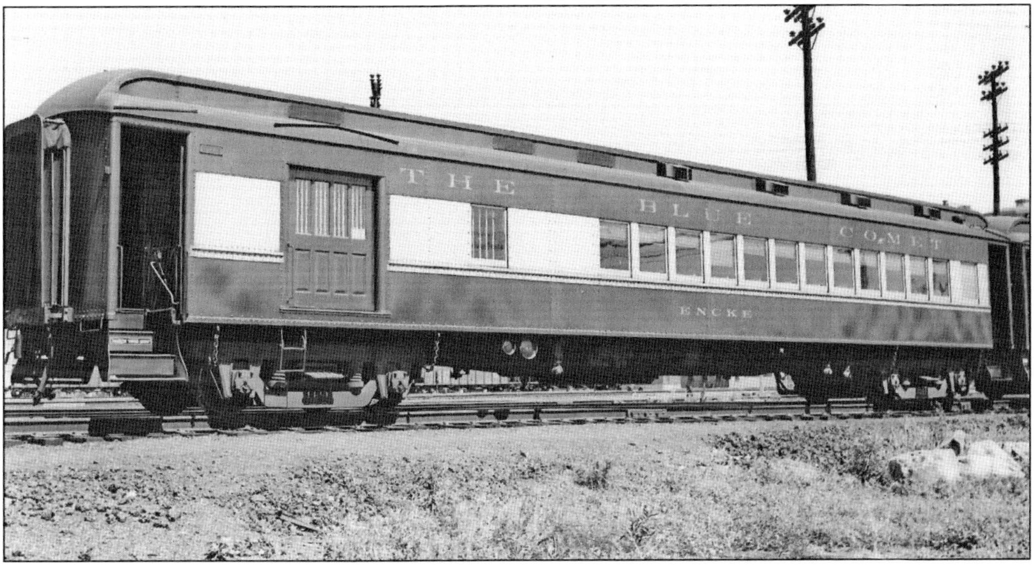

The Blue Comet combine *Enke* was one of two combines assigned to the service, the other being *Halley*. It was No. 302 in the NJC rolling stock roster. It is seen at Atlantic City on August 30, 1936. It was built by Bethehem Shipbuilding in 1928. It seated 48 passengers in individual bucket-type leather chairs. Each smoker car was furnished with 22 nickel-plated cuspidors. The combine was named after Comet Encke or Encke's Comet, which completes an orbit of the Sun every 3.3 years. Encke was last seen in March 2017. (Photograph by George Votava, courtesy Joel Rosenbaum and Tom Gallo.)

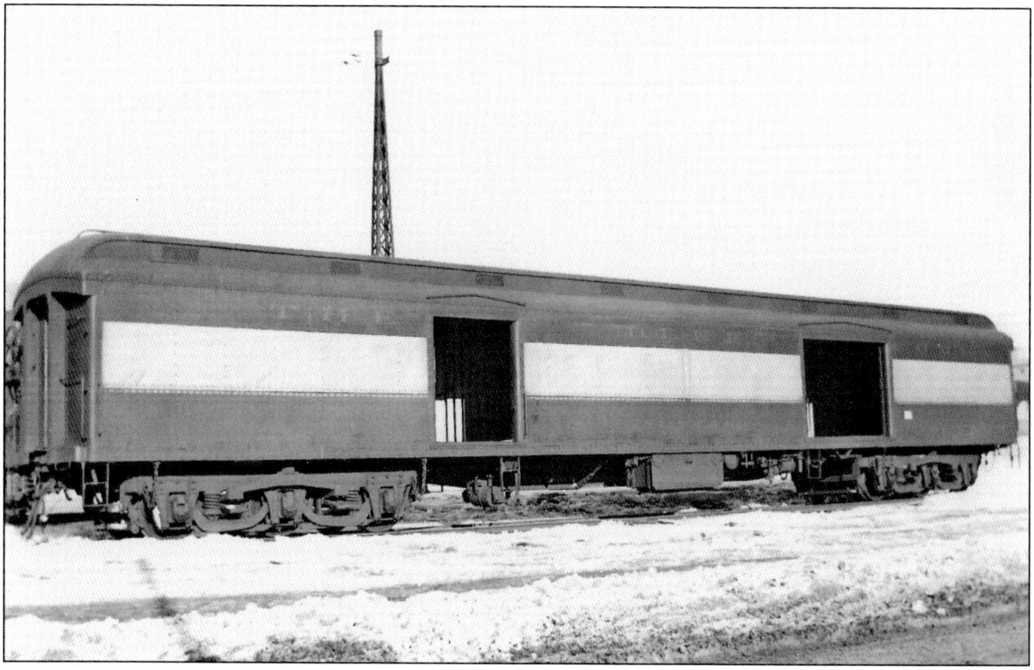

The Blue Comet 70-foot baggage car *Olbers* was one of two and was assigned No. 391 in the NJC rolling stock roster. The other baggage car assigned to the Blue Comet was the *Barnard*. The *Olbers* is seen here at Newark on January 25, 1935. The baggage car was named after Comet Olbers, with an orbit of 69 years. Heinrich Olbers discovered the comet on March 6, 1815. It was last seen in 1956 and is scheduled to reappear in June 2024. (Photograph by George Votava, courtesy Joel Rosenbaum and Tom Gallo.)

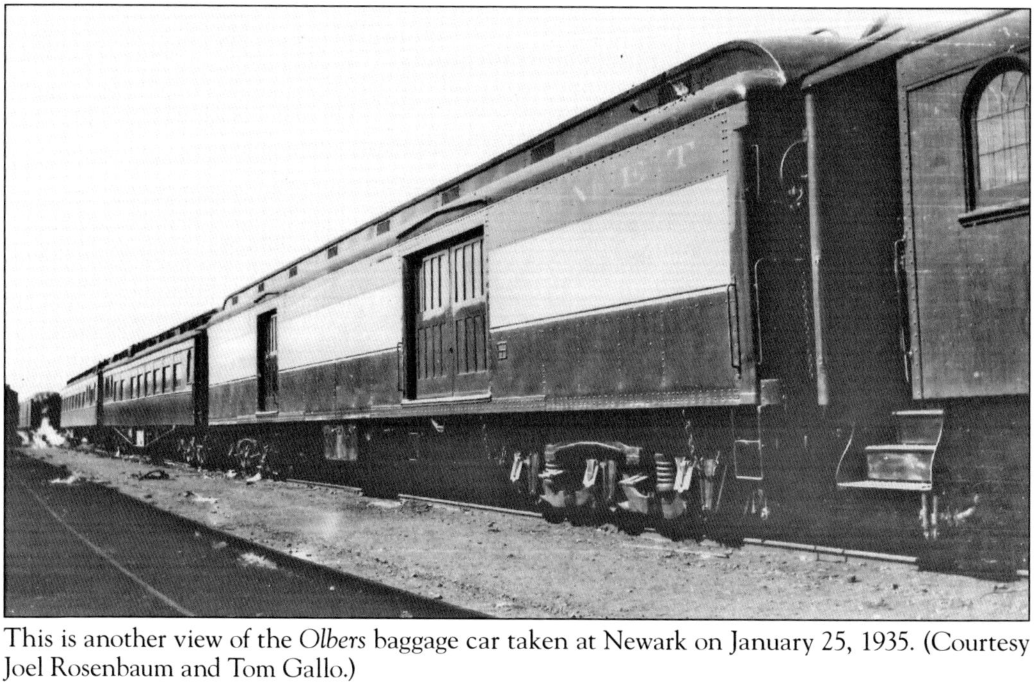

This is another view of the *Olbers* baggage car taken at Newark on January 25, 1935. (Courtesy Joel Rosenbaum and Tom Gallo.)

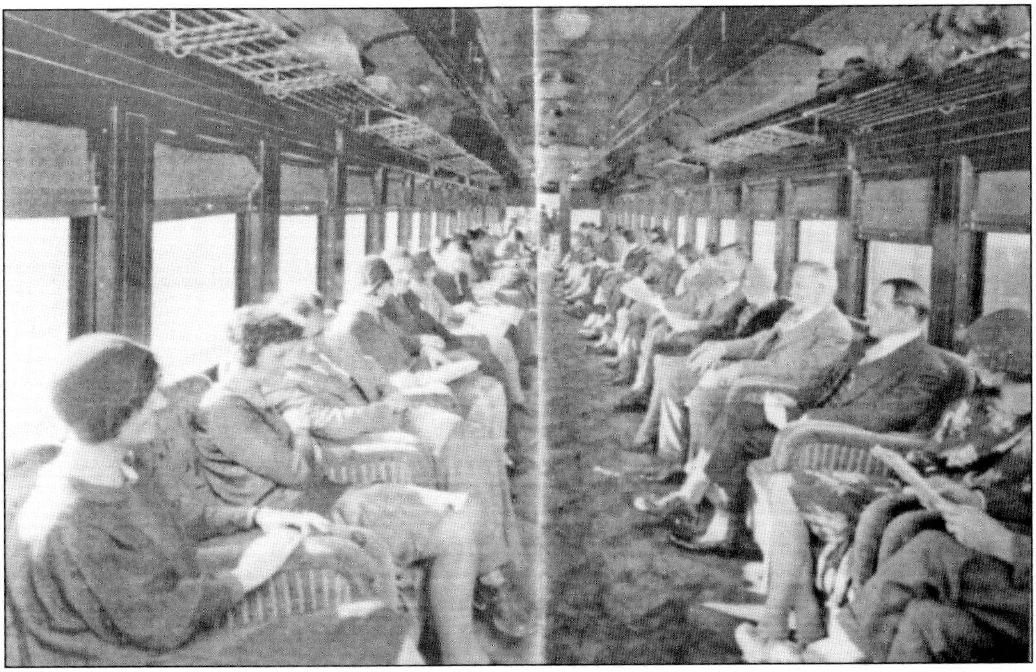

Passengers are relaxing in one of the Blue Comet observation cars. The observation cars had 48 silver-blue reed arm chairs upholstered in Persian blue Aralon plush. Prior to air-conditioning of the Blue Comet, the observation cars had four nickel-plated 12-inch fans, two at each end of the car. The window shades of the observation cars were made of blue Spanish pantasote material. The observation platform had six folding chairs. (Courtesy Robert A. Emmons.)

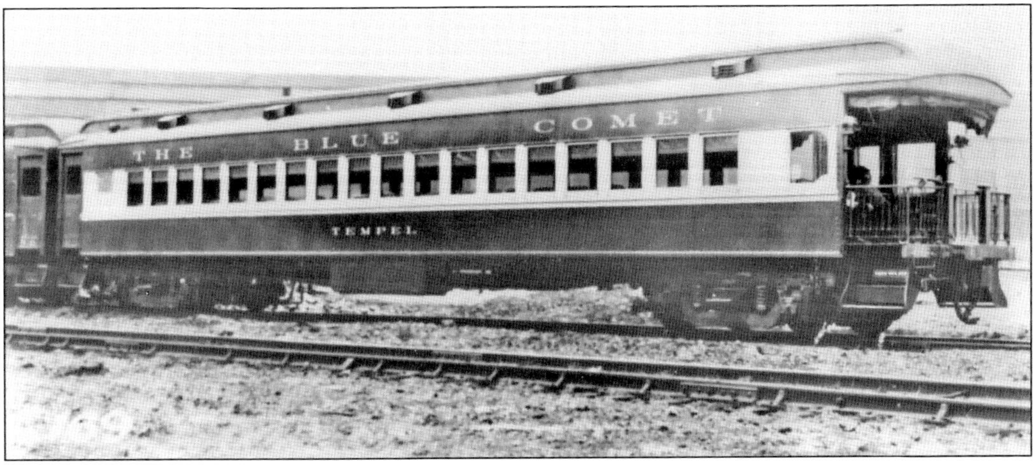

The Blue Comet observation car *Tempel* was designated No. 1169 in the NJC rolling stock roster. It was the only one of the three observation cars that was never air-conditioned. The NJC utilized the *Tempel* in a variety of purposes after its Blue Comet service, including as a temporary tower to control Lincoln interlocking, a temporary Point Pleasant Beach passenger station, and as a yard office at Bay Head Junction. The observation car was named after Tempel 1, discovered by Wilhelm Tempel in 1867. It completes an orbit of the Sun every 5.5 years. It last appeared in August 2016 and will be seen again in February 2021. (Courtesy Joel Rosenbaum and Tom Gallo.)

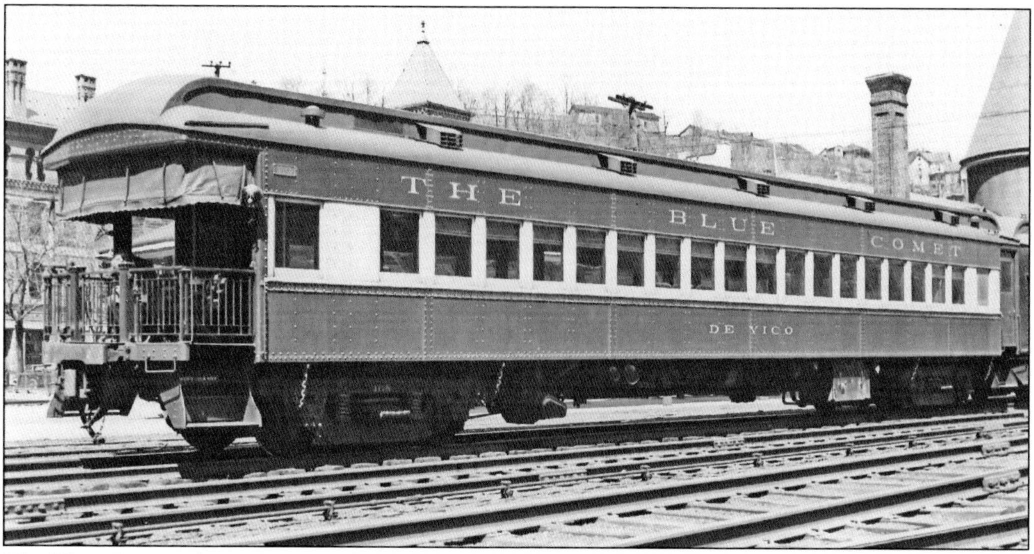

The Blue Comet observation car *De Vico* was designated No. 1178 in the NJC rolling stock roster. It made its last revenue service run on September 27, 1941. After that date, the observation car was used for a number of different purposes, lastly as a New Jersey Transit inspection car (NJT-1), from which it was retired in 1993. The *De Vico* is pictured on a fan trip in Mauch Chunk (Jim Thorpe), Pennsylvania, on April 10, 1938. It was named after the Comet De Vico, which has an orbital period of 74 years. It was discovered by Francesco de Vico in Rome on February 20, 1846, and is scheduled to reappear in October 2069. (Photograph by George Votava, courtesy Joel Rosenbaum and Tom Gallo.)

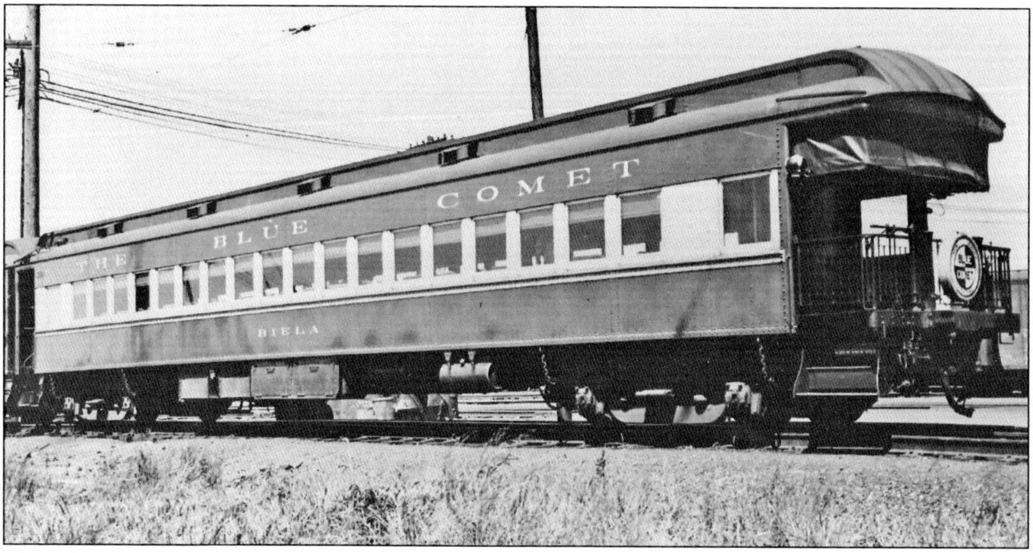

The Blue Comet observation car *Biela* was designated No. 1179 in the NJC rolling stock roster. It is seen here in Atlantic City on August 30, 1936. It was one of three observation cars converted from a coach for service on the train. In the early 1970s, it became part of a restaurant in Clinton, New Jersey. It was named after Comet Biela or Biela's Comet, identified as a periodic comet in 1826 by Wilhelm von Biela. It was subsequently observed to split into two pieces in February 1846 and has not been seen since 1852. As a result, it is currently considered to have been destroyed. (Photograph by George Votava, courtesy Joel Rosenbaum and Tom Gallo.)

The luxurious seats in the Blue Comet coaches were made by the Hale & Kilburn Company of Philadelphia. This advertisement expounds the comfort and restfulness of riding in the soft deep cushions of their seats while being transported on the new Blue Comet train to Atlantic City. Seats were assigned in the coaches in advance, and special tickets were printed on blue stock, which carried a number and a letter to designate the particular coach in which the seat had been assigned. The coach floors were covered with thick carpet laid on ozite. (Courtesy Robert A. Emmons.)

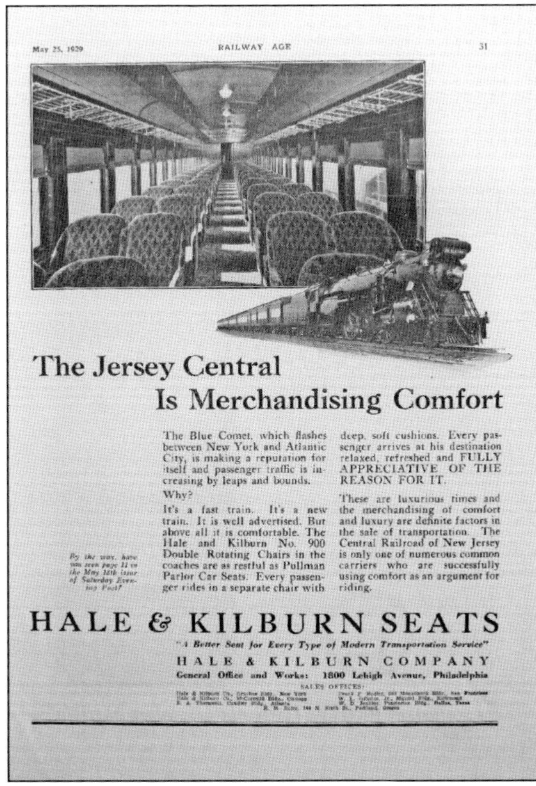

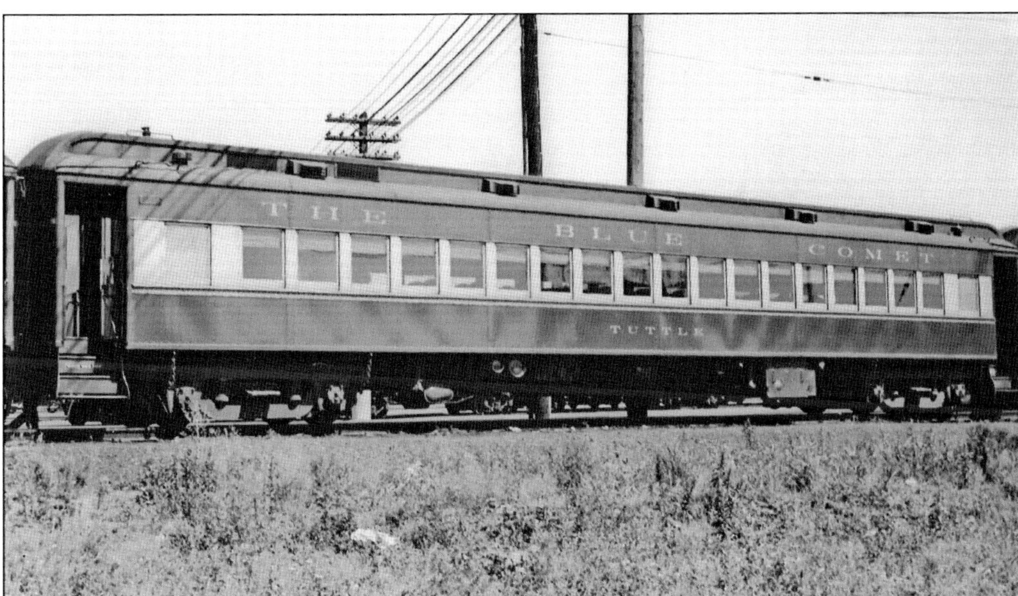

The Blue Comet coach *Tuttle* was built in 1926. It was designated No. 1170 in the NJC rolling stock roster. It is seen here in Atlantic City on August 30, 1936. It was named after Comet Tuttle, also known as Tuttle's Comet), with an orbital period of 13.8 years. It was discovered by Horace Tuttle on January 5, 1858, and was last seen in January 2008. It is scheduled to reappear in August 2021. (Photograph by George Votava, courtesy Joel Rosenbaum and Tom Gallo.)

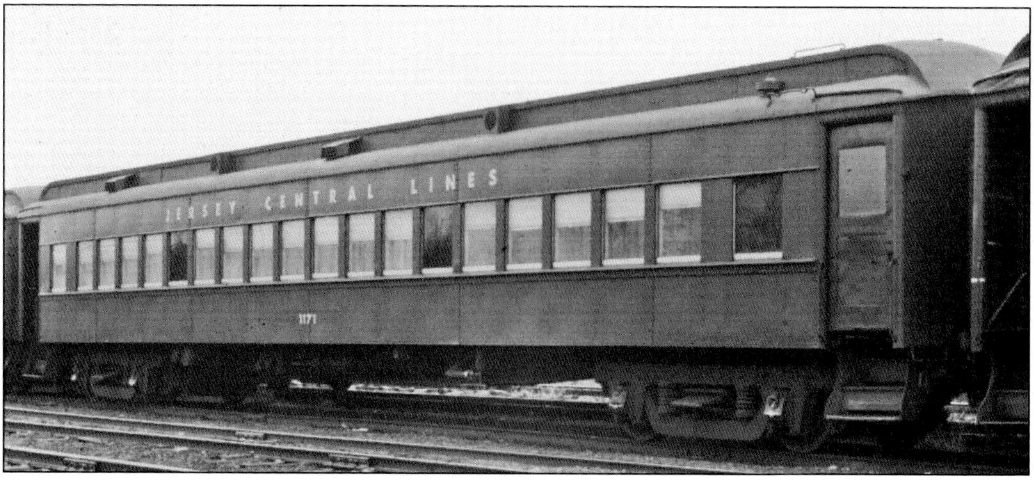

The Blue Comet coach *Holmes* was designated No. 1171 in the NJC rolling stock roster. It is shown here not in the traditional Blue Comet livery. (Courtesy Robert A. Emmons,)

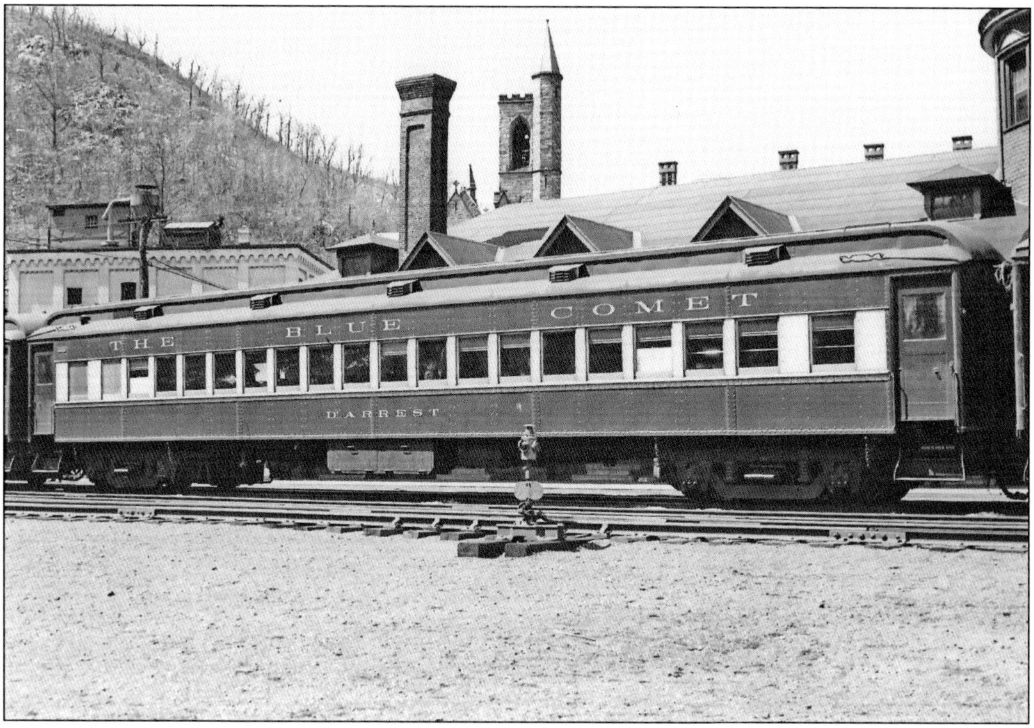

The Blue Comet coach *D'Arrest* was designated No. 1173 in the NJC rolling stock roster. It is seen here at Mauch Chunk, Pennsylvania, on a fan trip on April 10, 1938. It was painted green in April 1940 and became the commuter club car *Beachcomer* in 1956 in service for the CRNJ between Jersey City and Bay Head Junction. The coach was named after the Comet d'Arrest, also known as d'Arrest's Comet, with an orbital period of 6.5 years. It was first observed by Heinrich Ludwig d'Arrest in Leipzig, Germany, in June 1851. The comet last approached the Sun on March 2, 2015, and is scheduled to reappear in August 2021. (Photograph by George Votava, courtesy Joel Rosenbaum and Tom Gallo.)

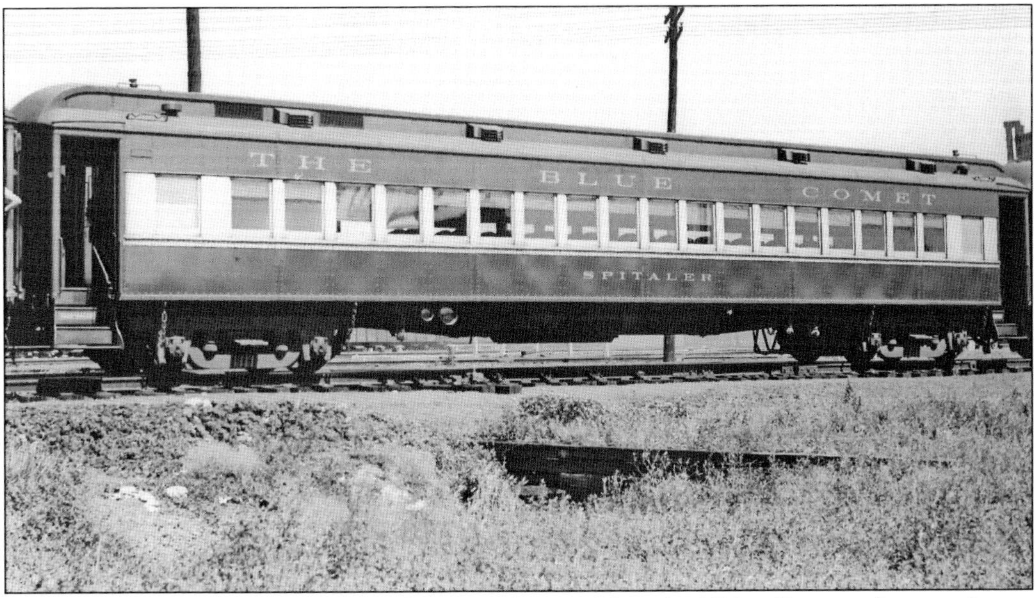

The Blue Comet coach *Spitaler* was designated No. 1175 in the NJC rolling stock roster. It was built by Bethehem Shipbuilding in 1928. It is seen here in Atlantic City on August 30, 1936. It was repainted green in 1940 and converted to the commuter car *Wekearny* on the CRNJ run between Plainfield and Kearny, New Jersey, from 1954 to 1967. The coach was named after Comet Spitaler, a faint comet discovered by Rudolf Spitaler on November 17, 1890. It has an orbital period of 7.1 years and is scheduled to reappear in May 2022. (Photograph by George Votava, courtesy Joel Rosenbaum and Tom Gallo.)

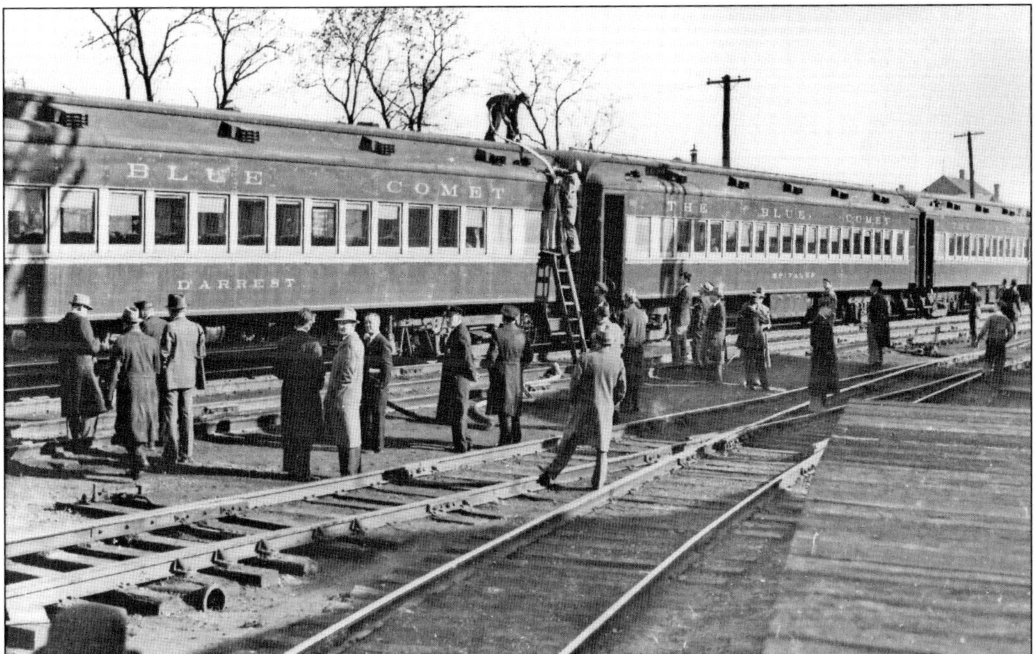

The Blue Comet coaches *D'Arrest* and *Spitaler* and the observation car *De Vico* are pictured on a fan trip. (Courtesy Joel Rosenbaum and Tom Gallo.)

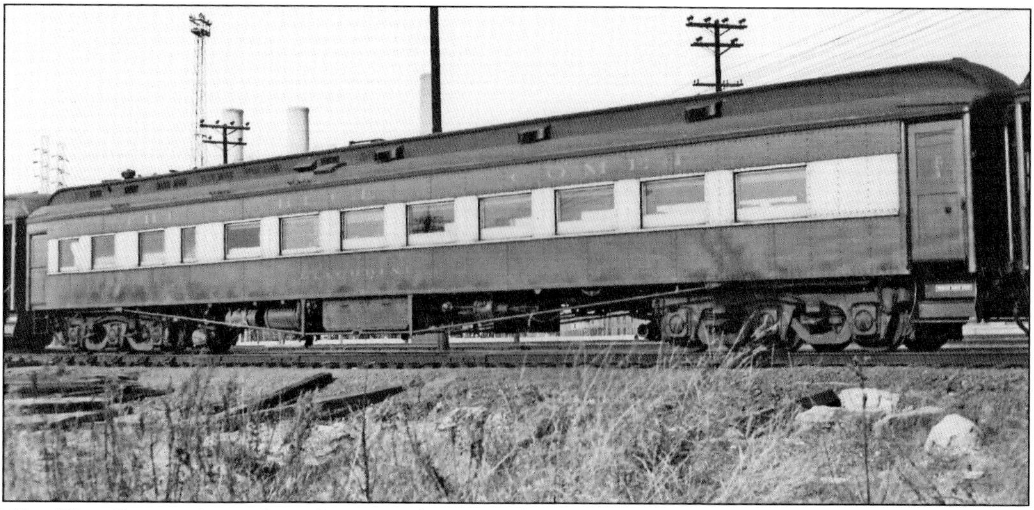

The Blue Comet diner *Giacobini* was designated No. 81 in the NJC rolling stock roster. It was originally built by the Pullman Company as a dining club car in 1905 but was rebuilt by the NJC as a 36-seat full diner for the Blue Comet. When two round trips were made daily by the Blue Comet in its first four years of operation, the diner was assigned only to the morning departure south from Jersey City and the late afternoon departure north from Atlantic City. The *Giacobini* was taken out of service after the wreck at Chatsworth on August 19, 1939. This photograph was taken at Atlantic City on January 26, 1936. The diner was named after the Comet Giacobini, which was discovered on December 20, 1900, by Michel Giacobini and Ernst Zinner. It has an orbital period of 6.6 years and is scheduled to reappear in September 2018. (Photograph by George Votava, courtesy Joel Rosenbaum and Tom Gallo.)

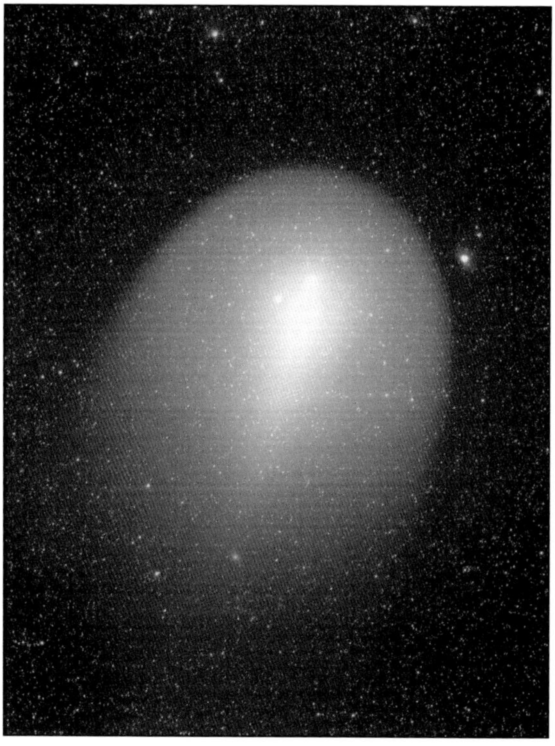

According to Hopi Indian lore, if the human race became too iniquitous, a giant blue comet (or star) would streak across the sky as a last warning from the heavens prior to Armageddon. The Blue Comet train streaked through New Jersey from February 21, 1929, to September 27, 1941. Some have speculated that the comet Holmes might be the blue comet, since it made appearances on March 26, 1928, July 16, 1935, and November 5, 1942, close to the actual service years of the Blue Comet train. The comet was discovered by Edwin Holmes on November 6, 1892, and has an orbital period of 6.88 years. Although usually a very faint object in the night sky, Holmes became notable in October 2007 when its coma unexpectedly expanded to a diameter greater than the Sun, temporarily becoming the largest object in the Solar System. The comet is expected to reappear in February 2021. (Courtesy spaceweather.com.)

Four

Joshua Lionel Cowen's Tribute to the Blue Comet

A frequent passenger aboard the Blue Comet was Joshua Lionel Cowen, who was head of the Lionel train company. He enjoyed the seaside resort city that was Atlantic City. It was surely because of his patronage that the Blue Comet would become immortalized by Lionel. Cowen was so impressed with the real Blue Comet that, in 1930, Lionel came out with a model train set in standard gauge. After the Lionel Transcontinental Limited (State Set), the Blue Comet was the most elaborate passenger train Lionel ever produced in standard gauge. In 1930, Lionel introduced the Blue Comet set No. 396E, which included the No. 390E, a two-tone blue-and-cream-striped steam locomotive, and the No. 390T tender, which were produced for only one year. The set also included three standard-gauge passenger cars, the No. 420 Pullman *Faye*, the No. 421 Pullman *Westphal*, and the No. 422 Observation *Tempel*. From 1931 to 1934, the 390E set included the larger No. 400E locomotive with its No. 400T tender and the same consist of cars. During the years 1935–1939, Lionel produced the No. 396W with the same consist, but this time with a tender containing a whistle. In order to promote the massive No. 400E, Cowen hired Robert E. Butterfield, one of the actual engineers on the 20th Century Limited train. During the era of the actual Blue Comet service, Lionel also produced Blue Comet train sets in O-gauge. The Lionel Blue Comet set No. 283W is headed by the very popular No. 263E steam locomotive. The cars were not named after comets, as were the standard-gauge Blue Comet sets that Lionel produced during the 1930s. Despite the best efforts of Lionel to promote these trains, the economic realities of the Depression hampered any hope of monetary success. The cost of these sets was financially prohibitive for the majority of typical working-class Americans at the time. Not many people were going to buy toys when they cost as much as a bedroom set or an automobile. Lionel suffered its first losing year in 1931, going into the red by $207,000. The effects of the Depression and a financial scandal caused a series of economic challenges for the company during the 1930s.

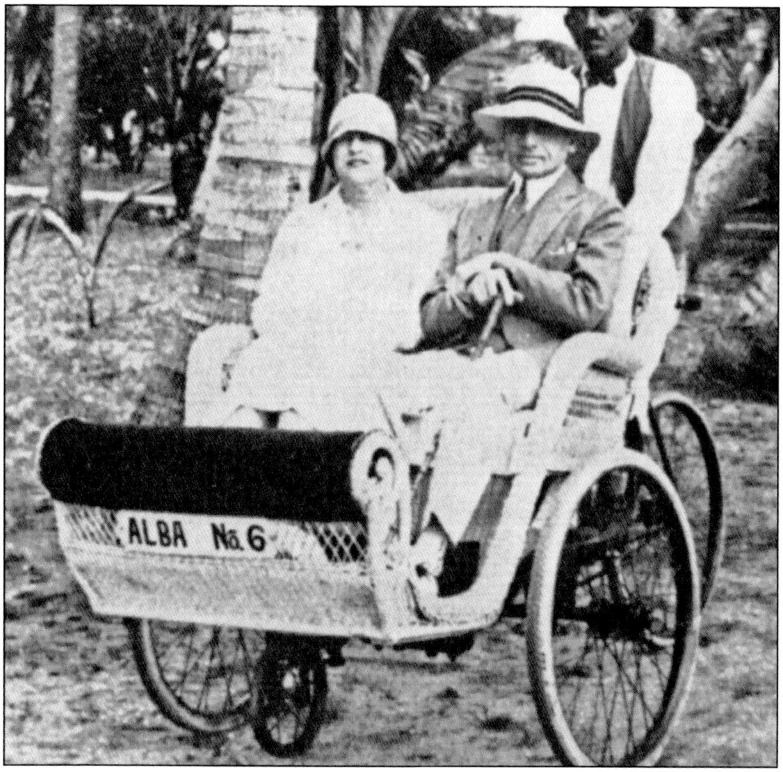

Although this photograph was actually taken in Florida, one can easily envision Joshua Lionel Cowen and his wife taking a leisurely ride in one of the wicker rolling chairs along the Atlantic City Boardwalk. He could have just arrived in the city via the morning Blue Comet train from Jersey City sometimes during the fall of 1929. (Courtesy Robert A. Emmons.)

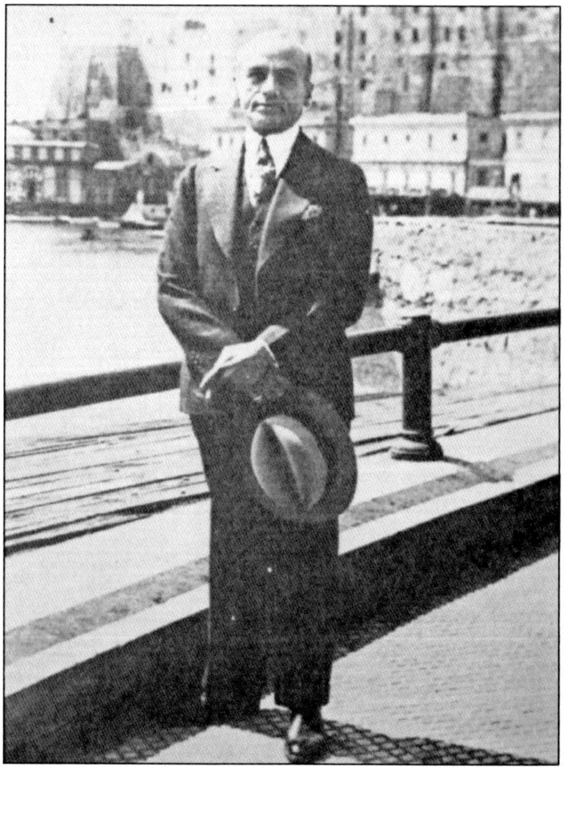

This photograph was taken in Naples, Italy, another of Cowen's favorite places to vacation. (Courtesy Robert A. Emmons.)

When the Lionel Corporation began making the standard-gauge Blue Comet train in 1930, it went all-out. In the booklet that accompanied each train, it appealed "to the young engineer" to take pride in their recent possession of "the greatest achievement in model railroading—beauty, speed and service that has never been surpassed." (Courtesy Joel Rosenbaum and Tom Gallo.)

TO THE YOUNG ENGINEER

WE HOPE you will be as proud of your BLUE COMET train as are the train crew who operate its famous original, and that you will keep it as clean and smooth-running as the big BLUE COMET. If you care to write us and tell us how you like your BLUE COMET train or if you wish any further information about its namesake, we will be glad to hear from you.

A REPRINT
COMPLIMENTS OF
TREASURE HOUSE

THE LIONEL CORPORATION
NEW YORK, N. Y.

THE BLUE COMET
by
Lionel

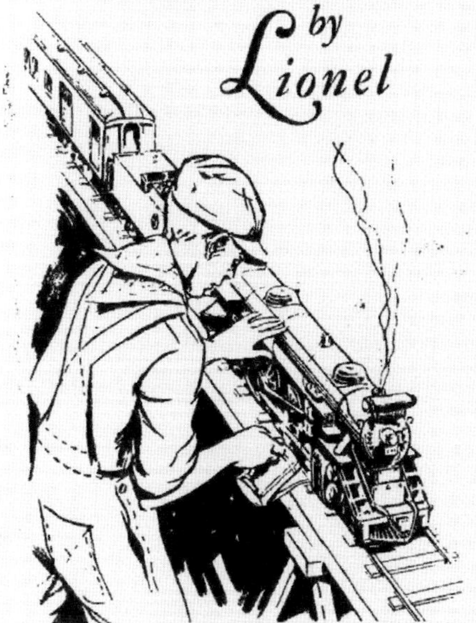

THE LATEST ADDITION TO LIONEL'S FLEET OF FAMOUS TRAINS
THE NEW JERSEY CENTRAL—THE BLUE COMET

WHEN you show your new Lionel train to your friends, you can tell them it isn't just an ordinary toy train. It's an exact reproduction of THE BLUE COMET, the famous fast train of the Central Railroad of New Jersey that makes its daily run between New York and Atlantic City in three hours.

Like a blue streak, THE BLUE COMET wings its way across the beautiful state of New Jersey, passing through many interesting places known the world over, among them Red Bank, where the boat races are held. At Lakehurst we see the great airport, with its immense hangårs and the giant mooring mast to which have been fastened the Graf Zeppelin, the Los Angeles and other world-famous dirigibles.

At the end of the run is Atlantic City, America's greatest playground, with its crowds of carefree pleasure seekers bathing in the surf or strolling on the Boardwalk that stretches in front of the great luxurious hotels along the beach.

Your BLUE COMET shows the luxurious chair coaches, each named after a famous comet, as well as the roomy, comfortable observation car, where passengers get a wonderful view of the beautiful country through which THE BLUE COMET flashes in its speedy flight.

You will be proud to know that this replica of THE BLUE COMET is authorized by the officials of the New Jersey Central Railroad who have worked closely with the Lionel Corporation to be sure that the reproduction is as faithful as their experts can make it.

While not an "exact reproduction" of the actual Blue Comet train in every detail, as claimed in the booklet, the Lionel Blue Comet trains were a wonderful and exciting introduction to the happiness and joy of being transported to Atlantic City, America's Favorite Playground, by such luxurious means of transportation. (Courtesy Joel Rosenbaum and Tom Gallo.)

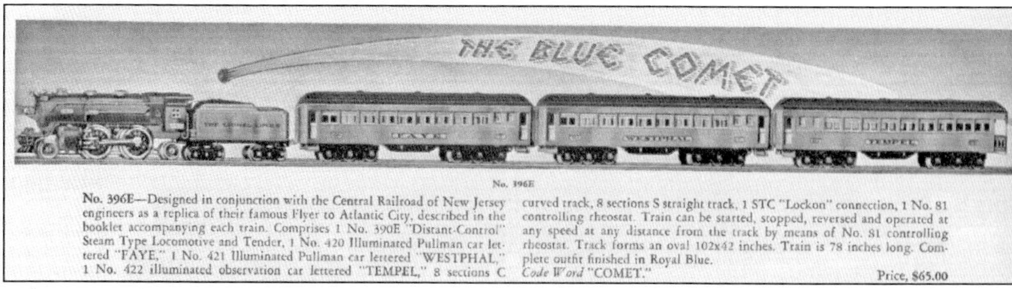
THE BLUE COMET

No. 396E

No. 396E—Designed in conjunction with the Central Railroad of New Jersey engineers as a replica of their famous Flyer to Atlantic City, described in the booklet accompanying each train. Comprises 1 No. 390E "Distant-Control" Steam Type Locomotive and Tender, 1 No. 420 Illuminated Pullman car lettered "FAYE," 1 No. 421 Illuminated Pullman car lettered "WESTPHAL," 1 No. 422 illuminated observation car lettered "TEMPEL," 8 sections C curved track, 8 sections S straight track, 1 STC "Lockon" connection, 1 No. 81 controlling rheostat. Train can be started, stopped, reversed and operated at any speed at any distance from the track by means of No. 81 controlling rheostat. Track forms an oval 102x42 inches. Train is 78 inches long. Complete outfit finished in Royal Blue.
Code Word "COMET."

Price, $65.00

When Lionel introduced the No. 396E in its 1930 catalogue, it retailed for $65, about the average monthly earnings for most American workers that year. The set came with a powerful Bild-A-Loco Motor engine installed in the two-tone blue No. 390E (Type IV) locomotive. The sides of its running boards were painted cream, as were the beads on the tenders' side. The three cars, with removable roofs, featured full interiors, including seats, bathrooms, and interior lighting. The cars were appointed with lavish six-wheel trucks and air tanks and finished in royal blue. (Courtesy Robert A. Emmons.)

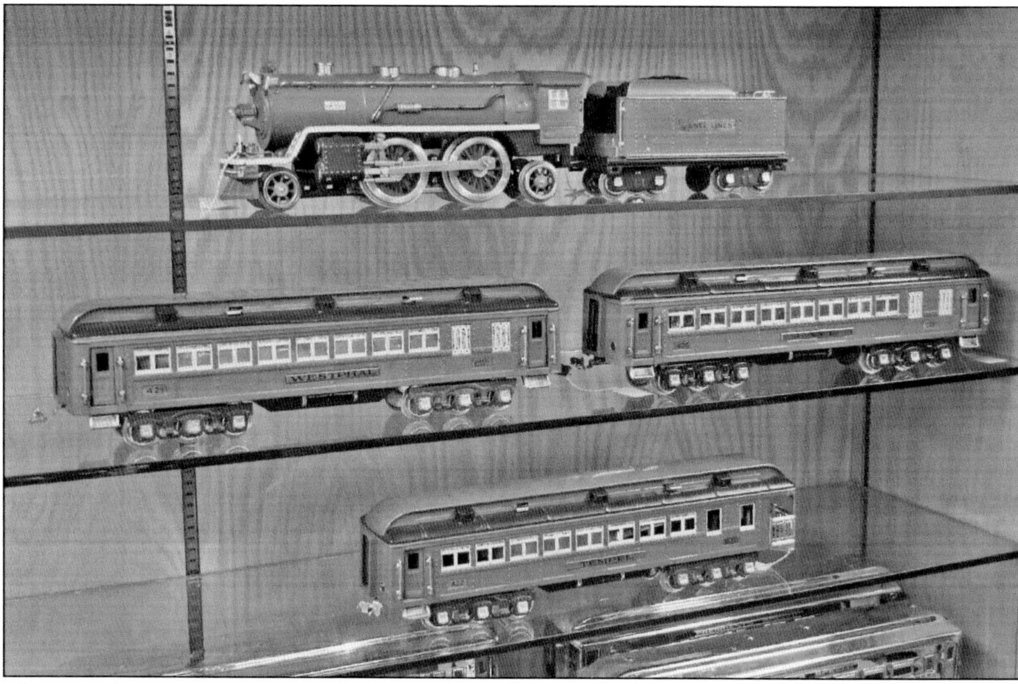
The Lionel No. 396E set is remembered as the very first standard-gauge model train to be marketed and probably the most treasured as a collector's item. It was first introduced in the 1930 Lionel catalog, beginning a long line of Lionel Blue Comet trains that would be produced in standard gauge, O-gauge, and S-gauge in the years to come. (Author's collection.)

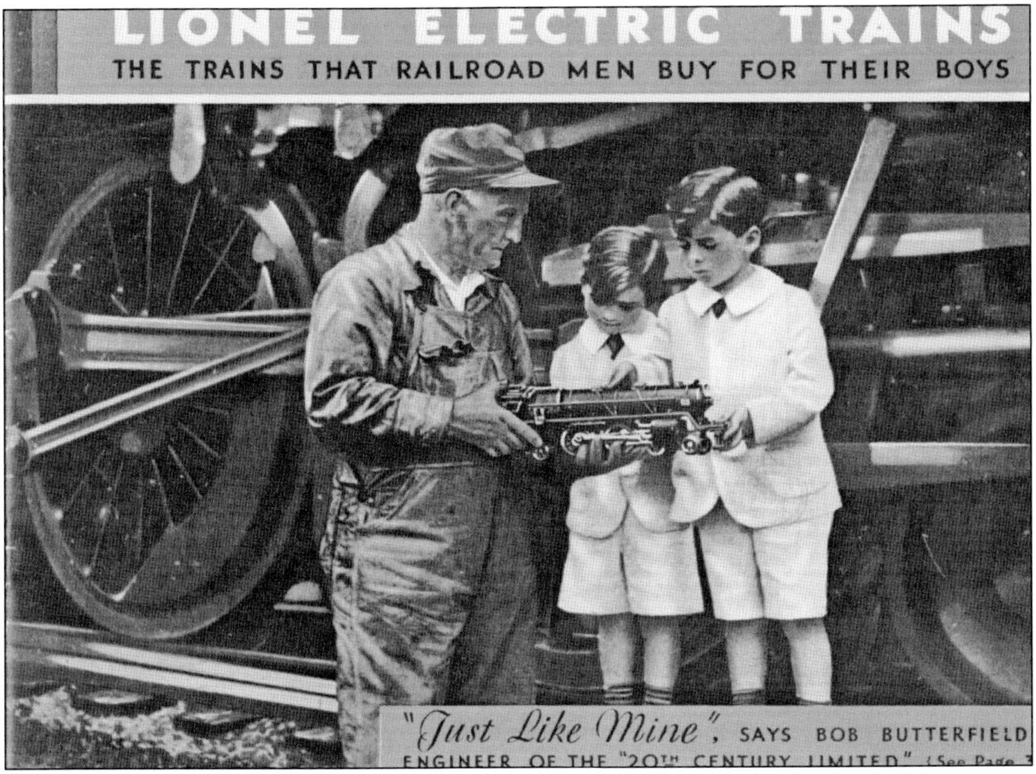

Robert Butterfield is seen on the cover of the 1931 Lionel catalog, standing in front of the massive six-foot driving wheels of his own Hudson locomotive, which pulled the 20th Century Limited. His two grandsons, Richard and Robert III, stand beside him as they hold the No. 400E, the largest and most powerful locomotive ever manufactured by Lionel. According to the byline, Lionel manufactures "the trains that railroad men buy for their boys." (Courtesy Robert A. Emmons.)

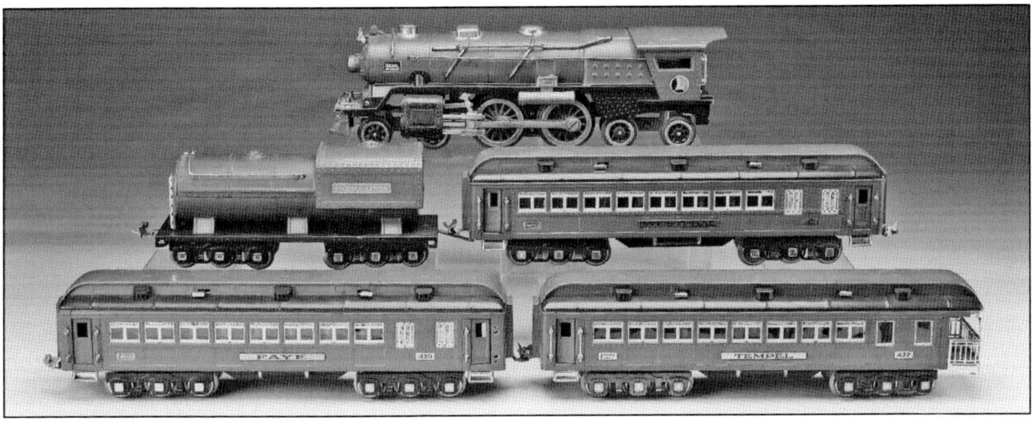

The Lionel Blue Comet set No. 396W was first advertised in the 1935 Lionel catalog. This is probably the most striking train set Lionel ever produced in standard gauge. It is headed by the infamous No. 400E locomotive, the largest standard-gauge engine ever produced by Lionel. The No. 400W oil tender is equipped with a whistle. The passenger cars are probably what make this set so special. Like the No. 396E set, the roofs are all removable and reveal their opulent interiors. This set originally retailed for $70 in 1931. Today, a set in mint condition is valued at around $20,000. (Courtesy Robert A. Emmons.)

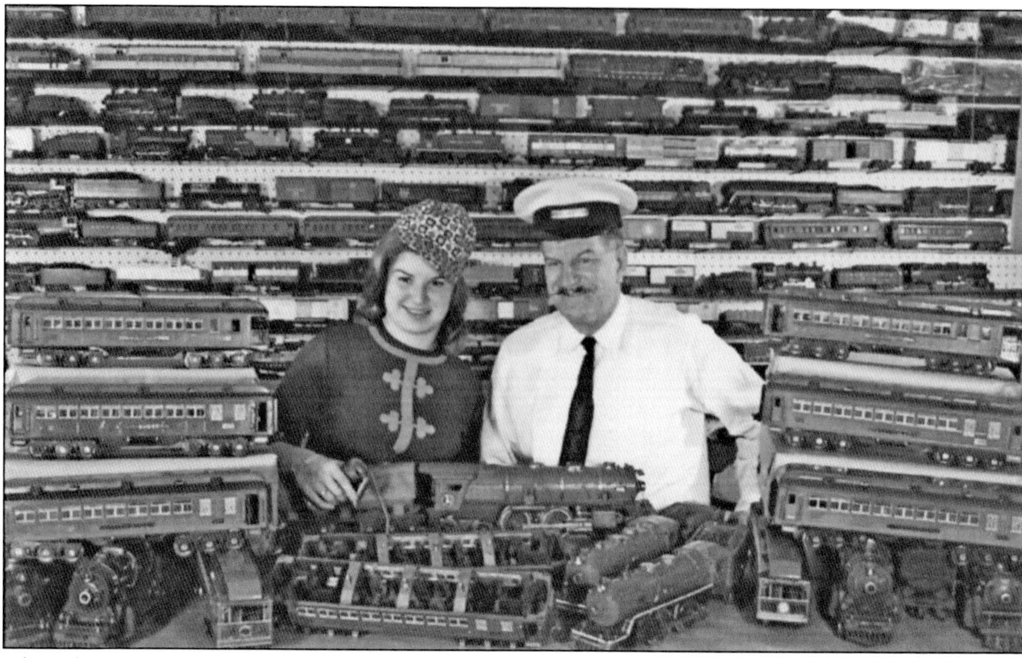

This photograph, probably taken in the 1950s, shows an array of standard-gauge Blue Comet trains on display at a Lionel train store called Red Wheels, located at 330 Hackensack Street in Carlstadt, New Jersey. The happy faces belong to Muriel Rochat and her yardmaster dad, Frank. (Author's collection.)

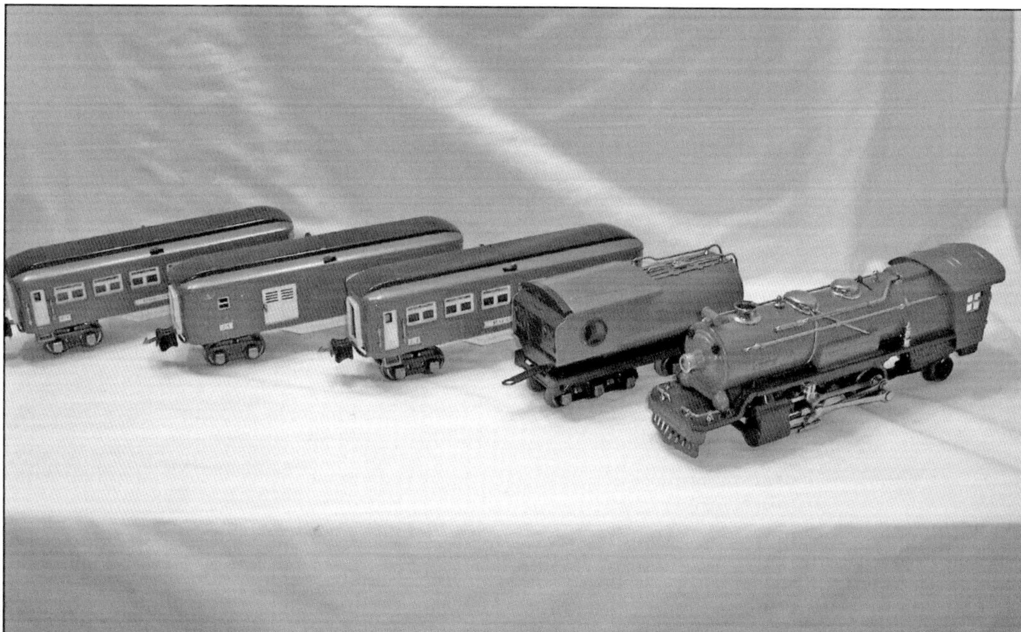

This is the pre-war O-gauge Lionel Blue Comet Set No. 283W. It includes the No. 263E steam locomotive, No. 263W whistle tender, No. 613 Pullman car, No. 614 observation car, and the No. 615 baggage car. The No. 283W appeared in both the 1936 and 1937 Lionel catalogues. (Author's collection.)

Five

Keeping the Memory of the Blue Comet Alive

The only remaining NJC locomotive that was used to haul the Blue Comet train is the Atlantic Camelback 4-4-2 No. 592. It is preserved in the roundhouse at the Baltimore & Ohio Railroad Museum in Baltimore. The combine *Halley* (NJC No. 300) was reconfigured and repainted, and is still in service on the Santa Fe Southern Railway. In Tuckahoe, New Jersey, the Tri-State Railway Historical Society has the former Blue Comet observation car *Tempel* (NJC No. 1169) parked and awaiting restoration. The United Railroad Historical Society (URHS) owns two coaches, the *Westphal* (NJC No. 1172) and *D'Arrest* (NJC 1173). Restoration is currently underway on both coaches. Various pieces of the coach *Winnecke* (NJC No. 1176) were donated by the URHS to the Black River & Western Railroad's restoration of NJC coach No. 1009. The historical society would like to restore the car and use it in passenger service along the Cape May Seashore Lines. The *De Vico* (NJC No. 1178) is currently located at the URHS yard in Boonton, New Jersey, where it is awaiting restoration. The Blue Comet observation car *Biela* (NJC No. 1179) was moved to Clinton, New Jersey, in the 1970s and continues to serve as part of the Clinton Station Diner. In the northeast corner of Liberty State Park, which opened in 1976, is the NJC terminal, which served the Blue Comet train. The terminal was restored after being heavily damaged by Superstorm Sandy in October 2012 and has only recently been reopened to the public. In December 1975, a special Blue Comet Nostalgia Train was operated from Raritan to Bay Head along the former New York & Long Branch Railroad. In 2007, during season six of the HBO series *The Sopranos*, one episode was called "The Blue Comet." Documentary filmmaker Robert A. Emmons Jr. detailed the history of the Blue Comet in his 2009 feature length film *De Luxe: The Tale of the Blue Comet*. In addition, Lionel and other toy train manufacturers continue to produce operating scale models of the Blue Comet locomotives and trains. The renowned artist Angela Trotta Thomas has captured and sustained the fond memory of the Blue Comet in a number of her works for Lionel. Also, there are many historical societies and libraries that maintain archival photographs and memorabilia associated with the Blue Comet, including the Jersey Central Railway Historical Society, the Ocean County Historical Society, and the Hagley Museum and Library. The original Blue Comet train may be history, but thanks to these and many other purveyors of the train's physical legacies and remembrances, it will not be forgotten.

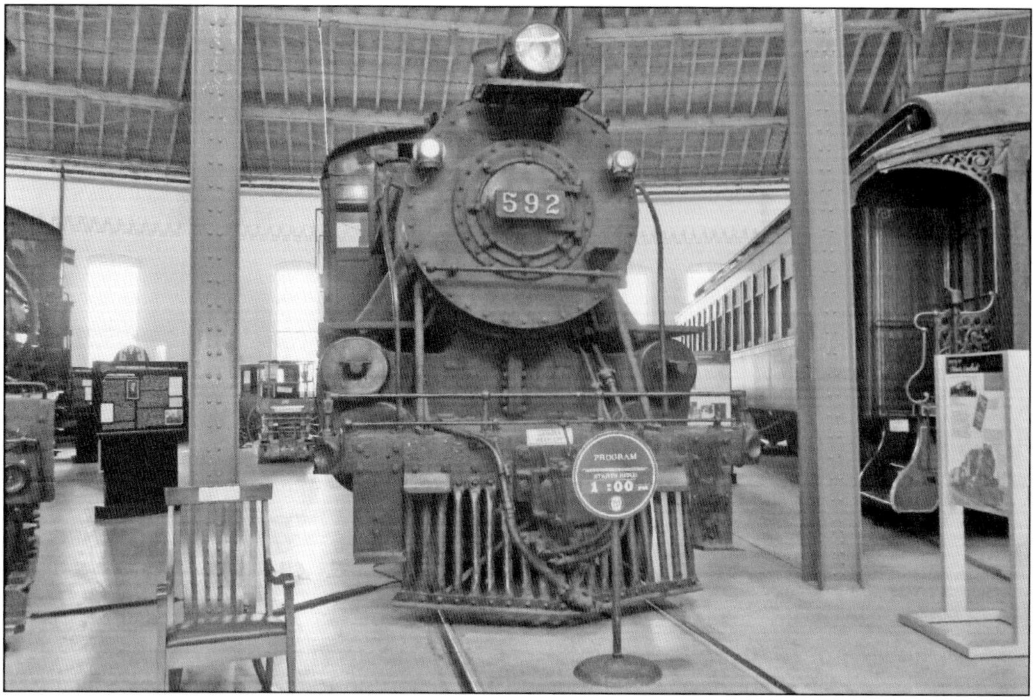

The NJC 4-4-2 Atlantic Camelback No. 592 saw service on the Reading Railroad's Philadelphia to Atlantic City express route, the B&O's Royal Blue Line and, in later years, hauling the Blue Comet train to Atlantic City for the NJC as a substitute for the traditional Pacific class G-3s. A few years after the No. 592 was retired from service, it was donated to the Baltimore & Ohio Railroad Museum, where it remains today on static display in the roundhouse. (Author's collection.)

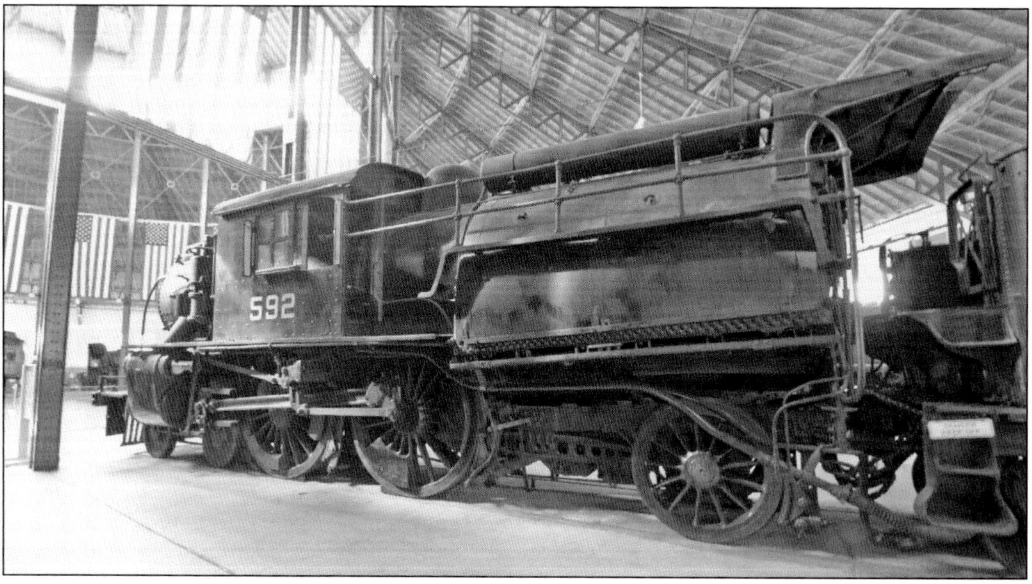

A side view of the No. 592 is seen at the Baltimore & Ohio Railroad Museum. It sits right next to the B&O's Royal Blue Line railcar No. 445, which it most likely hauled on many trips to Atlantic City and other destinations. The Royal Blue Line was in operation from 1890 to 1958. (Courtesy Baltimore and Ohio Railroad Museum.)

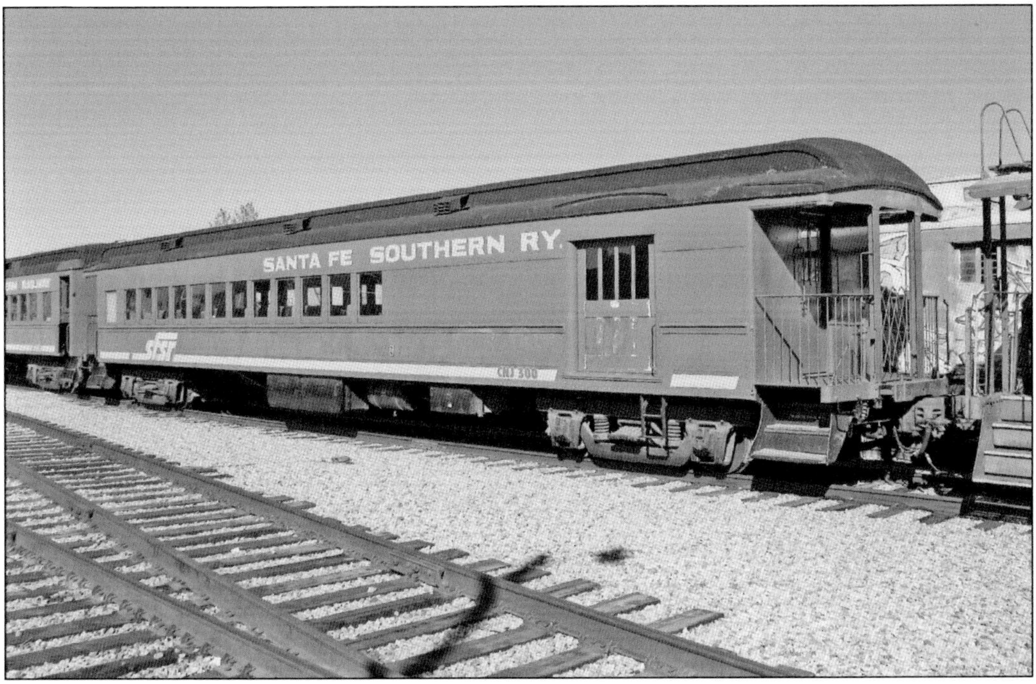

The combine *Halley* is used in service on the Santa Fe Southern Railway after being modified with the removal of the vestibules and the baggage area window being blanked out. Of course, it was repainted in Santa Fe Southern Railway livery. This photograph was taken in the railroad's yard on May 6, 2009, in Santa Fe, New Mexico. (Courtesy Scott Barr.)

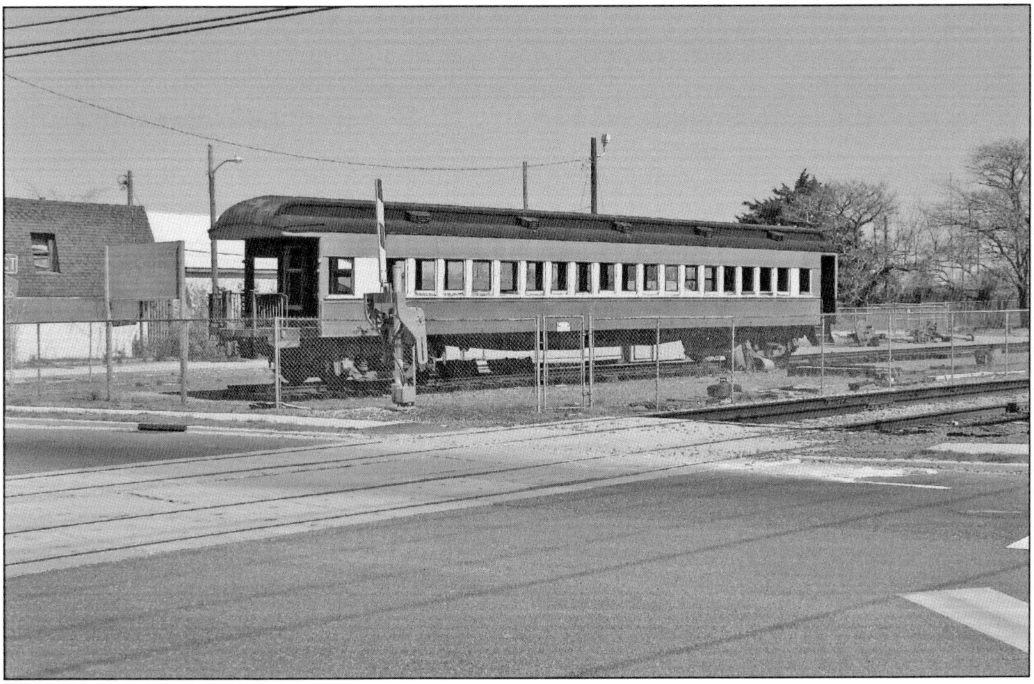

The Blue Comet observation coach *Tempel* is pictured on April 17, 2008, on static display in Tuckahoe, New Jersey. (Courtesy Bob Vogel.)

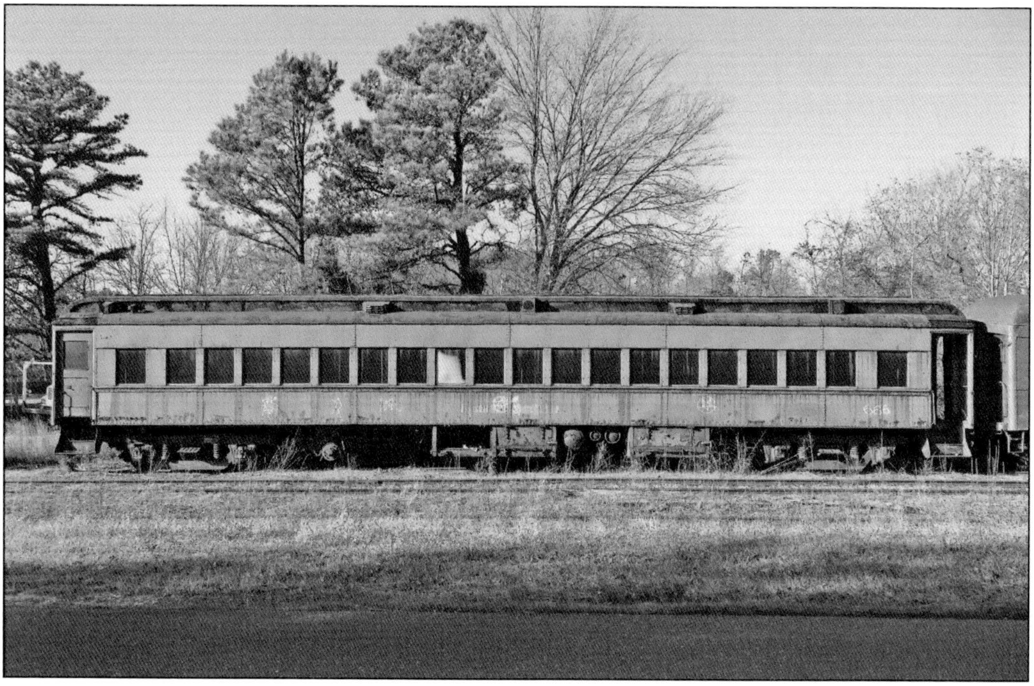

The United Railroad Historical Society owns the coaches *Westphal* (above) and *D'Arrest* (below), pictured at Winslow Junction, New Jersey, on December 18, 2014. The URHS restoration plan calls for these two coaches to be moved by truck from the Winslow Junction location to Lakehurst, where they will be painted. Lakehurst was a scheduled stop for the Blue Comet. (Both, courtesy Ben Kranefeld.)

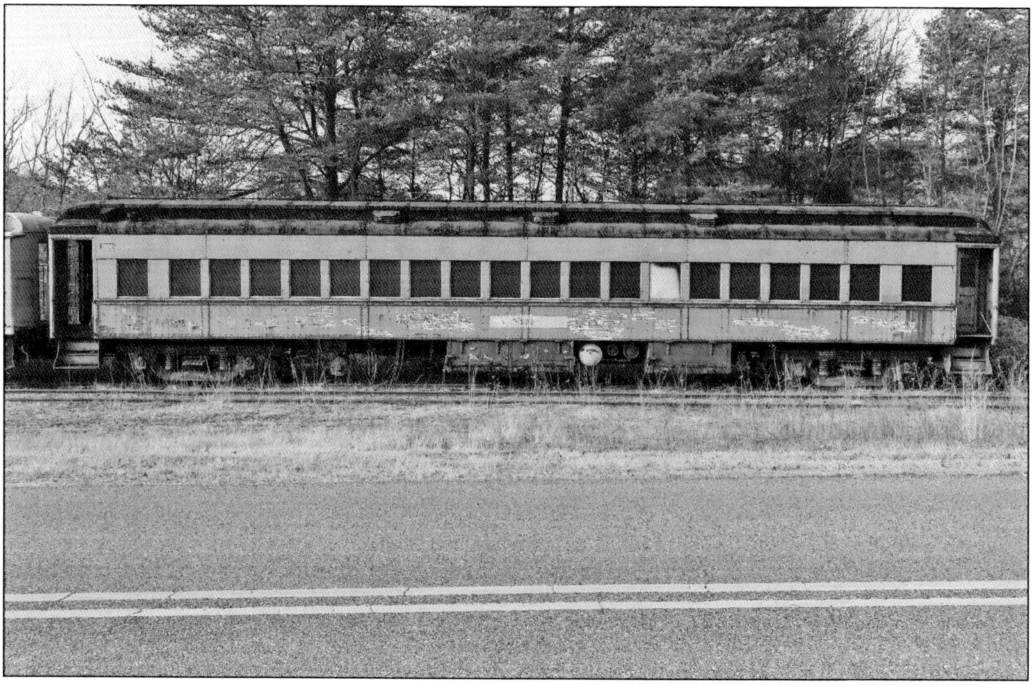

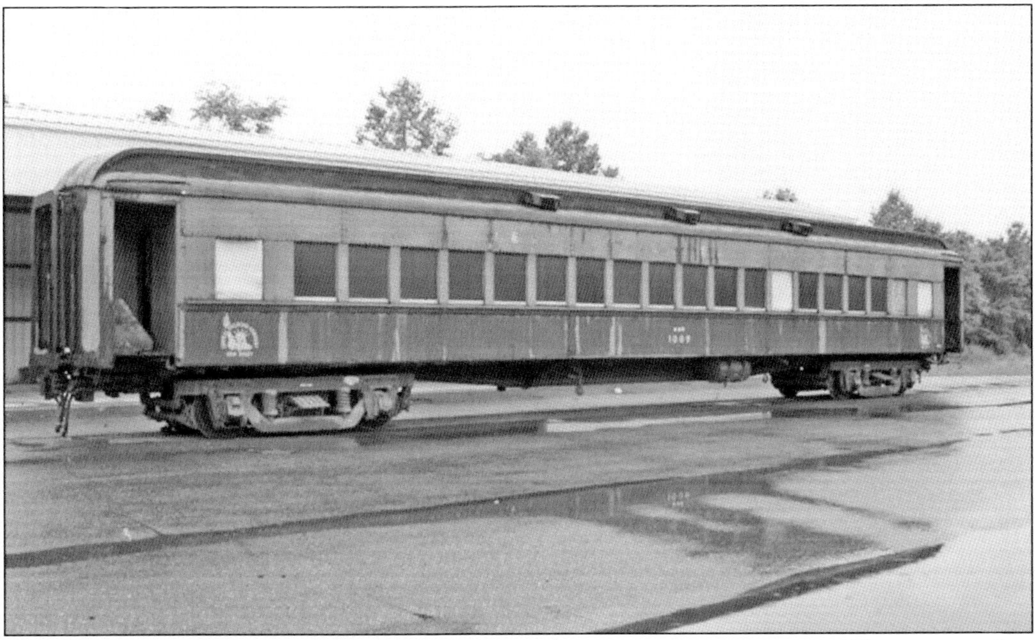

Coach No. 1009 was built for the NJC and served in commuter service until being retired in the 1960s. The coach found its way into the collection at the Steamtown National Historic Site in Scranton, Pennsylvania. Steamtown subsequently donated the coach to the Black River & Western Railroad Historical Trust. In addition, various pieces and parts of the NJC Blue Comet coach *Winnecke* were salvaged and eventually donated by the URHS to the Black River & Western (BR&W) Railroad, and used in the restoration of coach No. 1009. The photograph above shows coach No. 1009 awaiting transport in Phillipsburg, New Jersey. Below is the fully restored coach No. 1009 in Flemington, New Jersey, where it will be used on most BR&W passenger trains and events. (Both, courtesy Black River & Western Railroad.)

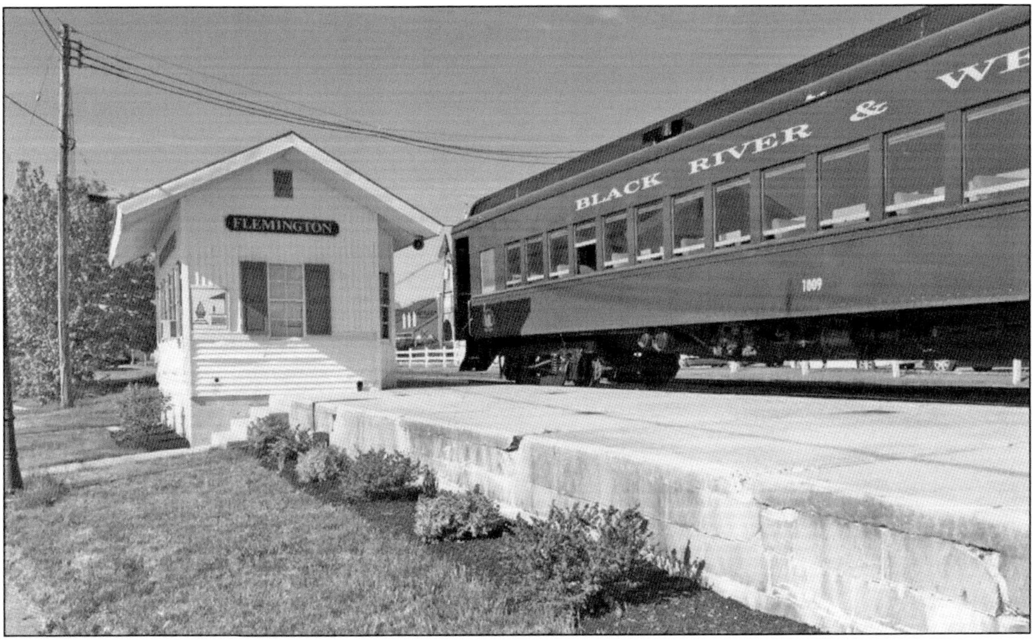

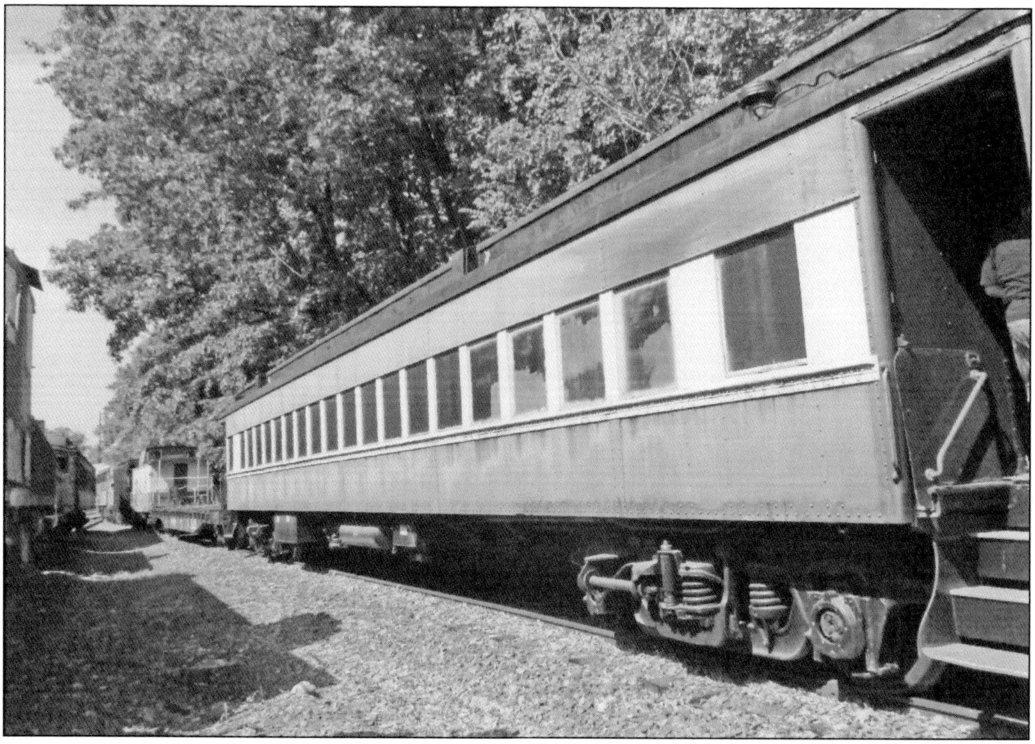

The *De Vico* (above) is seen in a recent photograph taken at the URHS yard in Boonton, New Jersey. It was repainted in the Blue Comet livery in 2009, but its exposure to the weather has faded its colors to the point where its name is no longer visible. The interior of the *De Vico* (below) still shows the seats that were installed when the car was used by New Jersey Transit as a commuter car, denoted NJT-1. (Both, author's collection.)

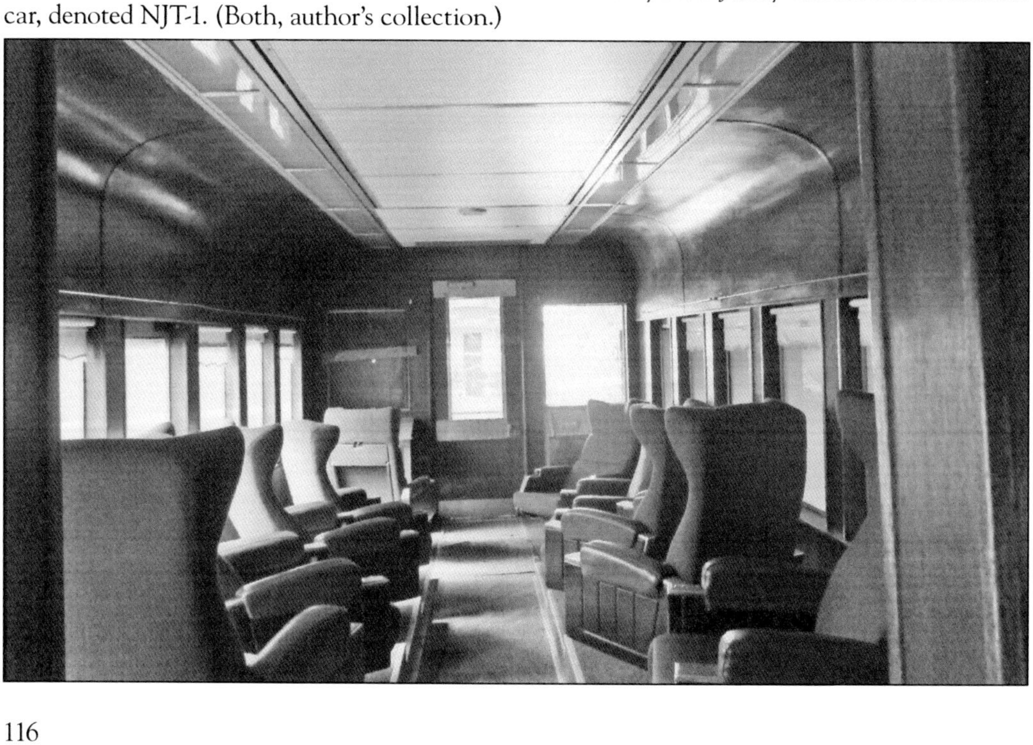

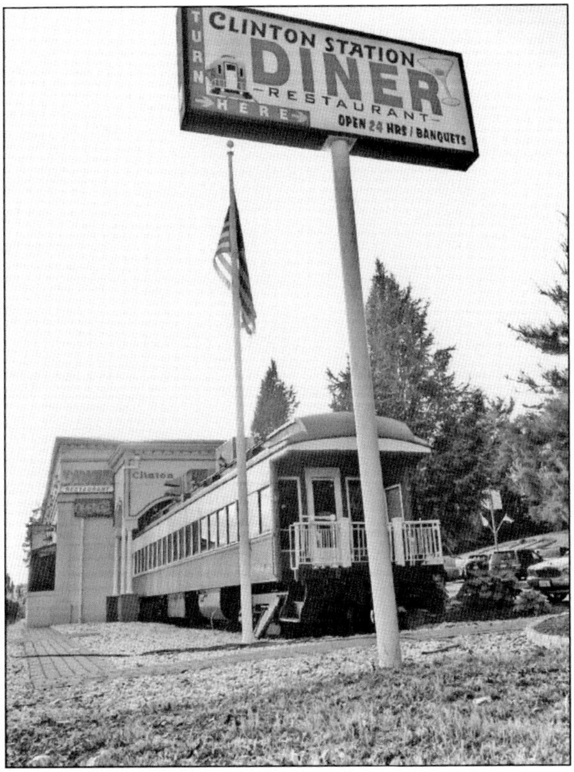

The former NJC Blue Comet observation car *Biela* became part of the former Union Gap Restaurant, then the renamed Clinton Station Diner (right). The diner is located at Exit 13 just west of Clinton. The main dining room includes an operating O scale NJC Blue Comet passenger train suspended from the ceiling. The photograph below shows the interior of the dining room decorated for Christmas. (Both, courtesy tinplate times.com.)

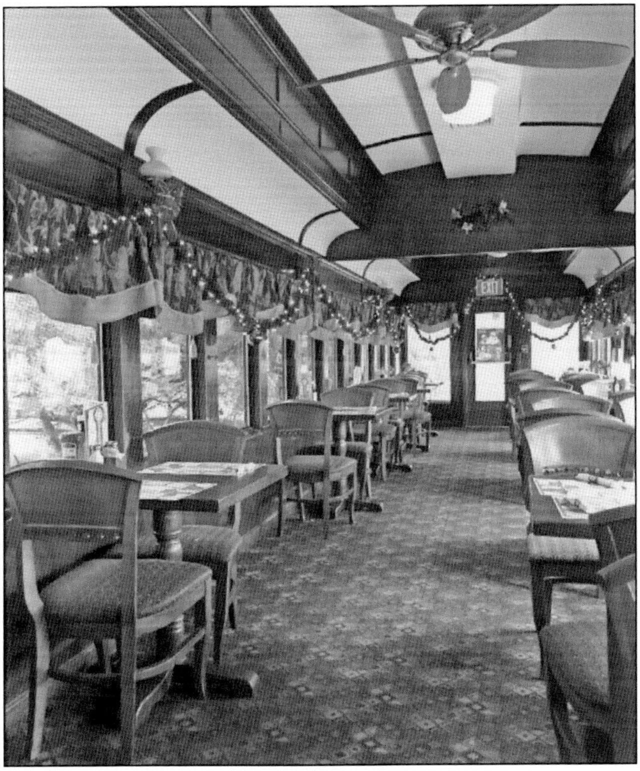

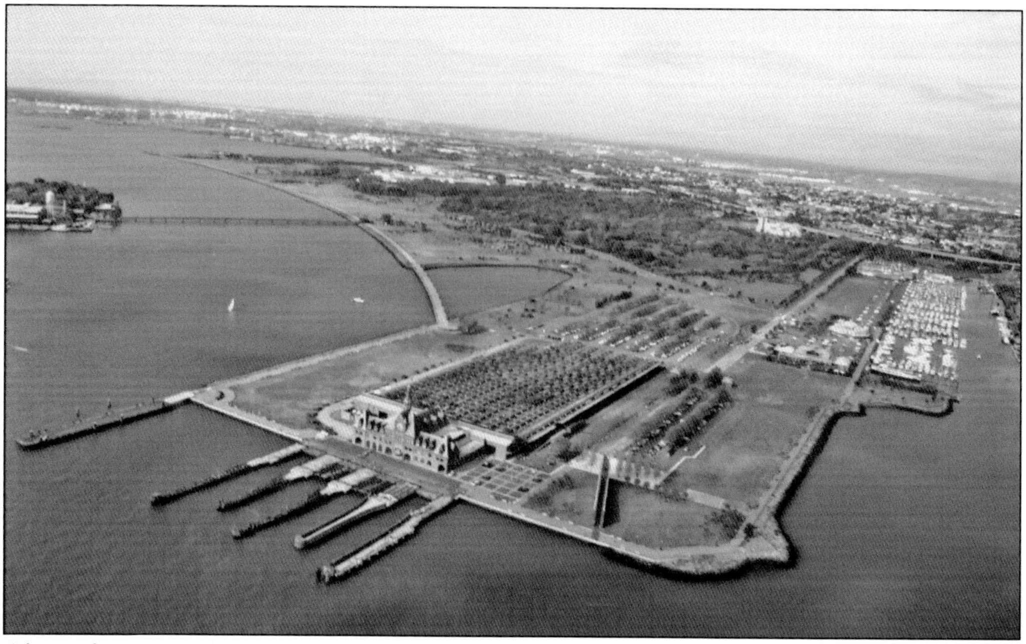

Almost four years after Superstorm Sandy (2012) caused extensive water, electrical, and structural damage to the NJC Terminal at Liberty State Park, New Jersey celebrated the reopening on Wednesday, June 22, 2016, of the historic building on the shore of the Hudson River in Jersey City. The photograph above shows an aerial view of the terminal. From 1892 to 1954, the terminal served as the largest rail hub in the New York metropolitan area. Below is a side view of the terminal showing the sign directing tourists to ferry tickets to the Statute of Liberty and Ellis Island. Of the 12 million to 17 million immigrants who passed through Ellis Island during those years, approximately two-thirds embarked on their new lives on trains departing from the terminal. (Both, courtesy Library of Congress.)

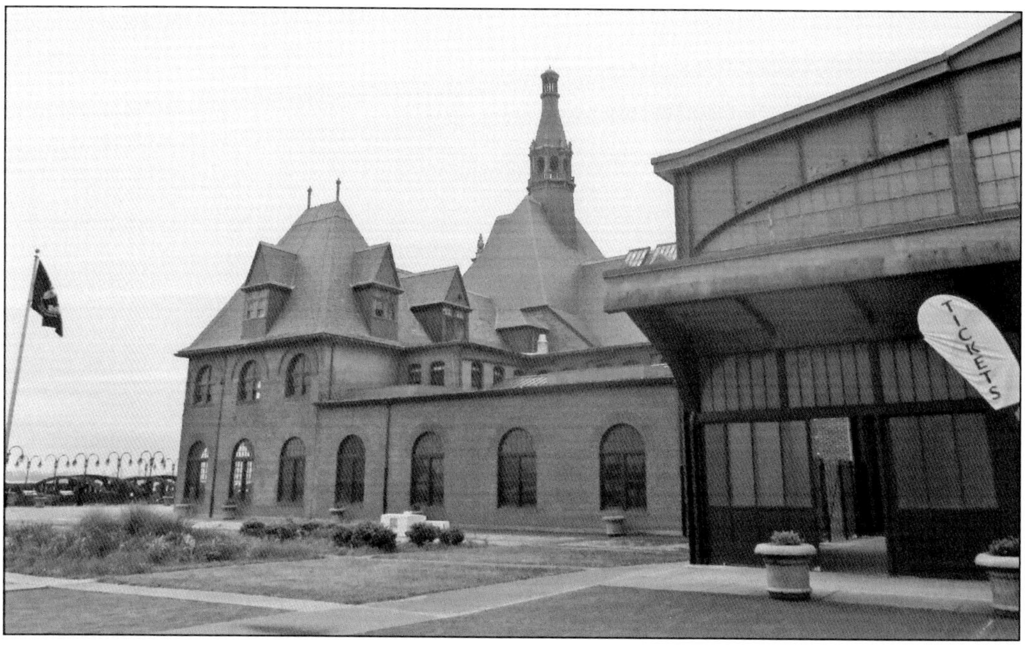

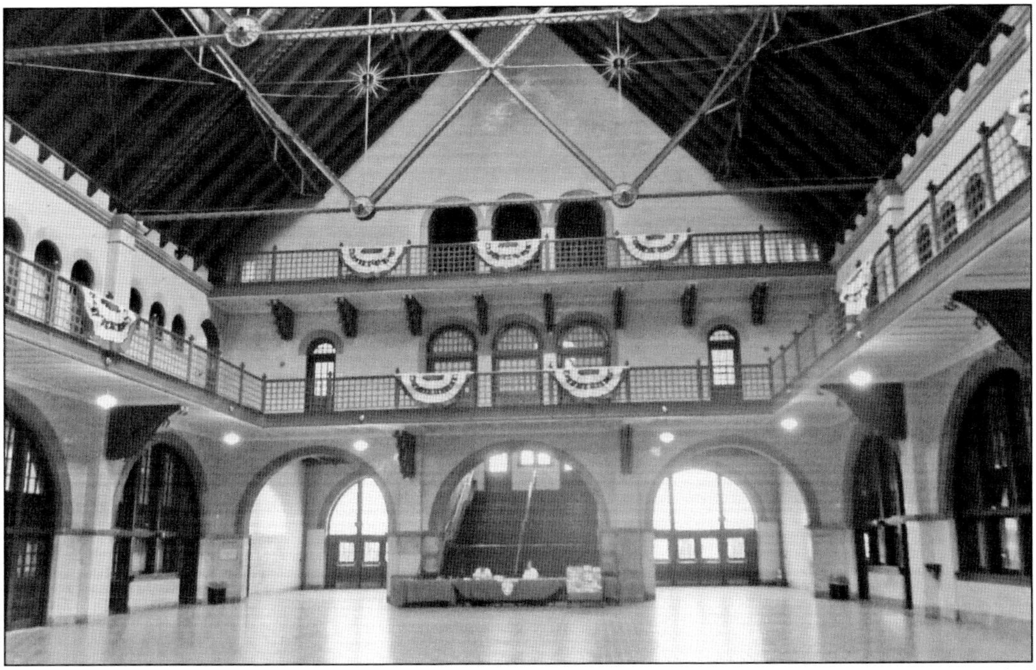

The interior of the NJC terminal (above) is seen with its characteristic "star clusters" suspended from the ceiling. Only a small ticket sales office, selling ferry tickets, is seen on the Romanesque-style main floor. It is easy to imagine the crowds that filled this area when the Blue Comet reigned. In the rear of the terminal (below), some vintage NJC rolling stock is visible, along with a portion of the track platforms that stretched well behind the terminal, which once transported passengers to and from various destinations in Southern New Jersey, including Atlantic City. (Both, author's collection.)

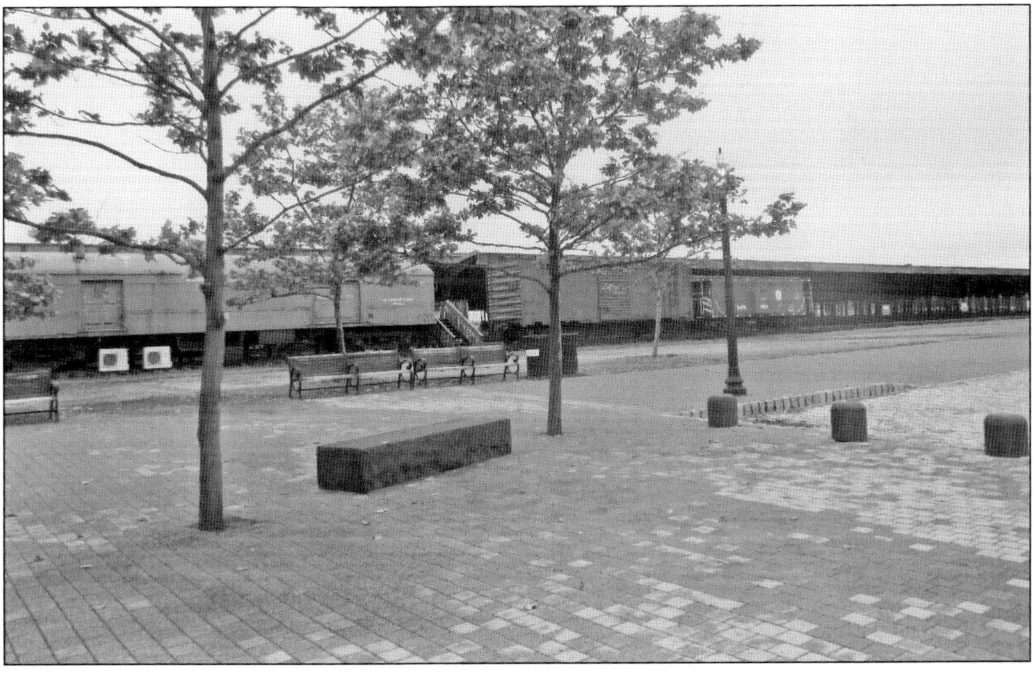

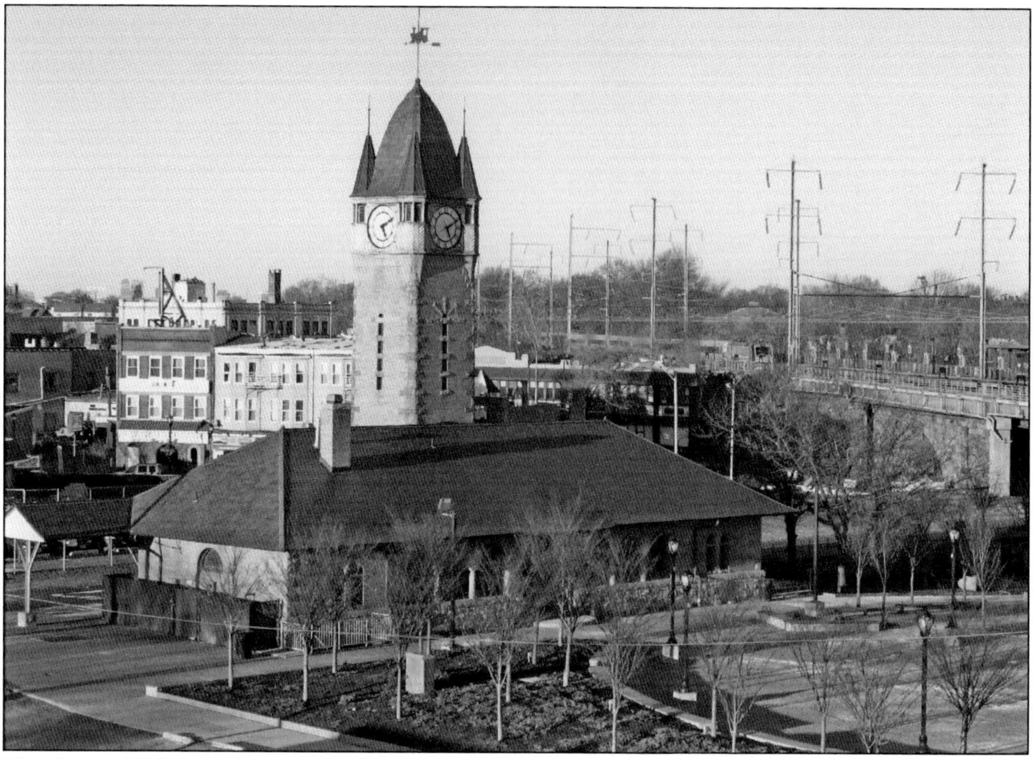

The former NJC Broad Street Elizabeth Station (above) has been listed in the National Register of Historic Places since 1984. Passenger trains stopped using this station in 1978 when the Cranford-Bayonne Scoot was eliminated. Its stately clock tower dominates the view north toward the station. The photograph below shows a NJC Budd Rail diesel car at the station during the period when the station was a passenger stop. (Both, courtesy Railroad Station Historical Society.)

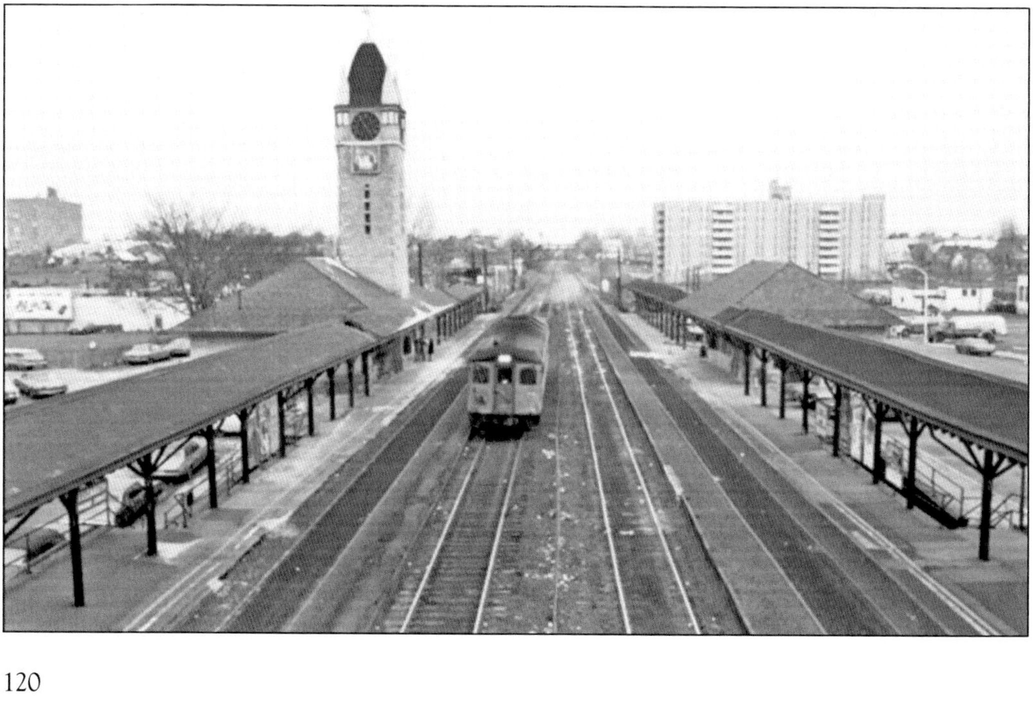

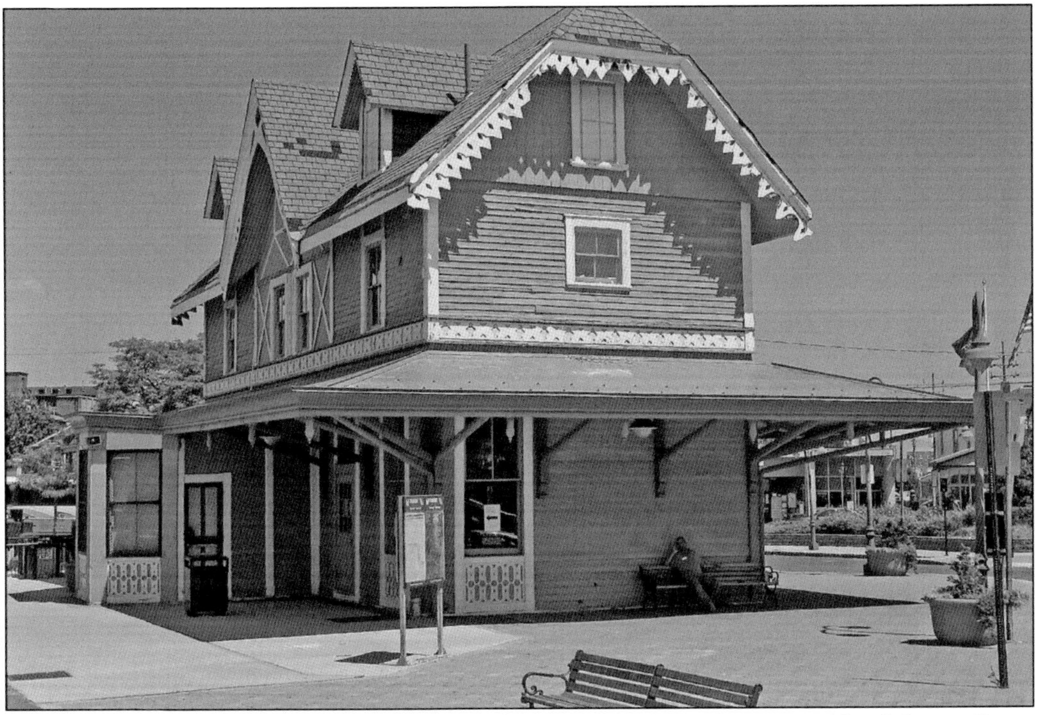

The former NY&LB Red Bank Station (above) is now an NJT station on its North Jersey Coast Line. Red Bank Station has been listed in the National Register of Historic Places since 1976. It is located at 175 Monmouth Street in Red Bank. The station began operations in 1876. In 2014, it was renovated using historically correct material and its original color scheme. The photograph below shows the station platforms after high-level platforms were installed. (Both, courtesy Railroad Station Historical Society.)

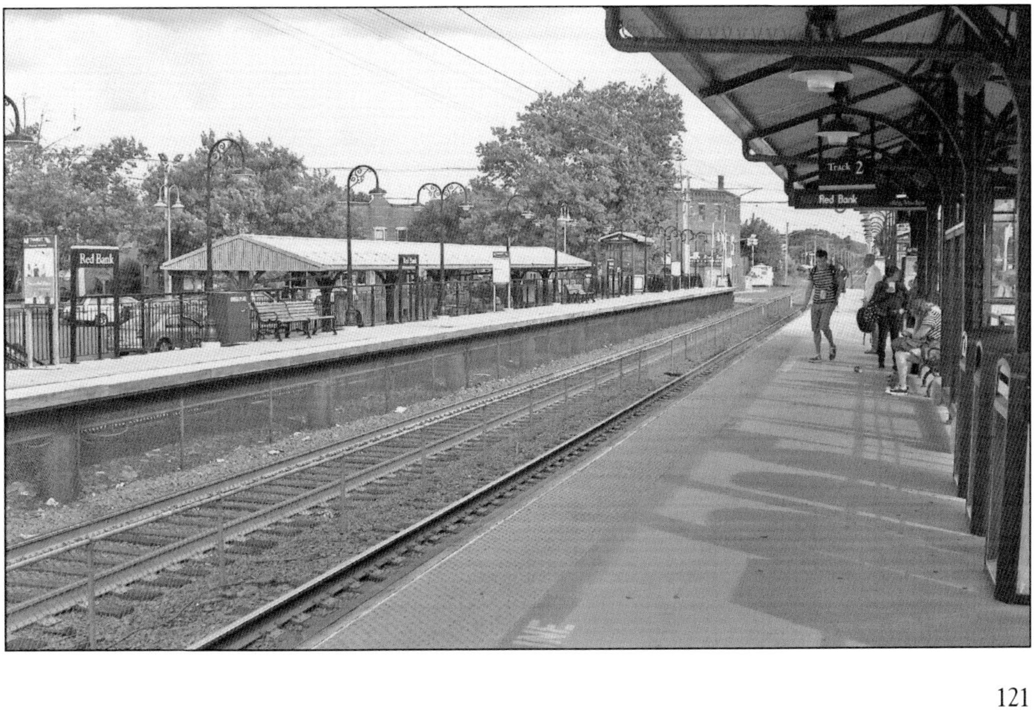

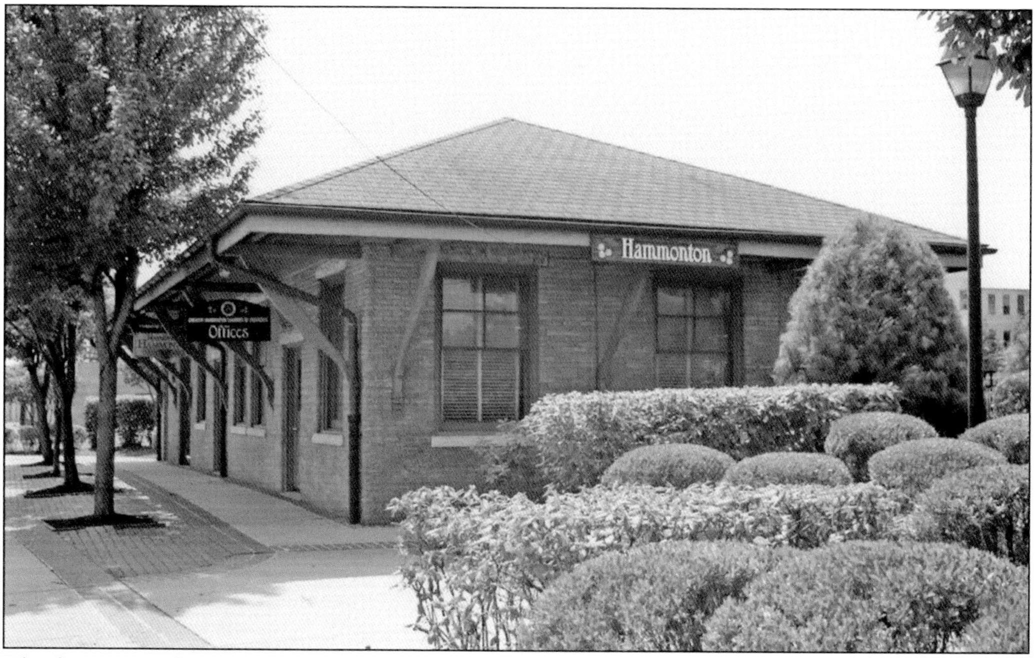

The former Reading station in Hammonton, once a stop for the Blue Comet, is now owned by the town of Hammonton and is used as a welcome center and a place for bus connections. (Courtesy Greater Hammonton Chamber of Commerce.)

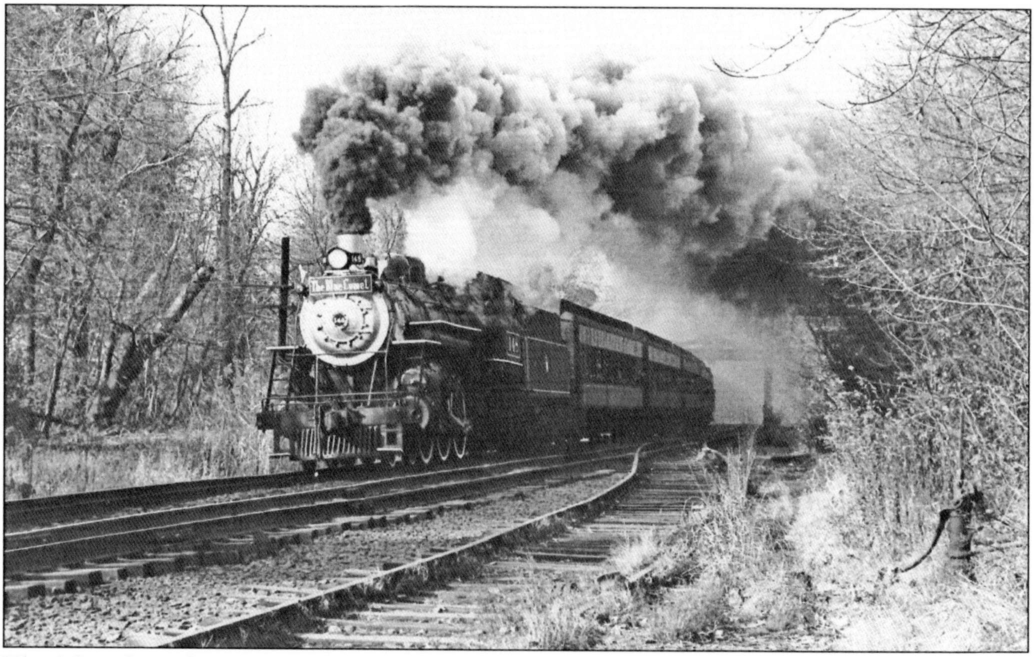

The Main Line Steam Foundation–sponsored Blue Comet Nostalgia Special roars through Middletown on a run from Raritan to Bay Head Junction on December 6, 1975. The train consisted of eight matched Central Railroad of New Jersey coaches and the observation car No. 1178, the *De Vico*. Tom Snyder and his *Tomorrow* show staff rode in the No. 1178, filming for a segment. (Photograph by Myron Silverman, courtesy Joel Rosenbaum and Tom Gallo.)

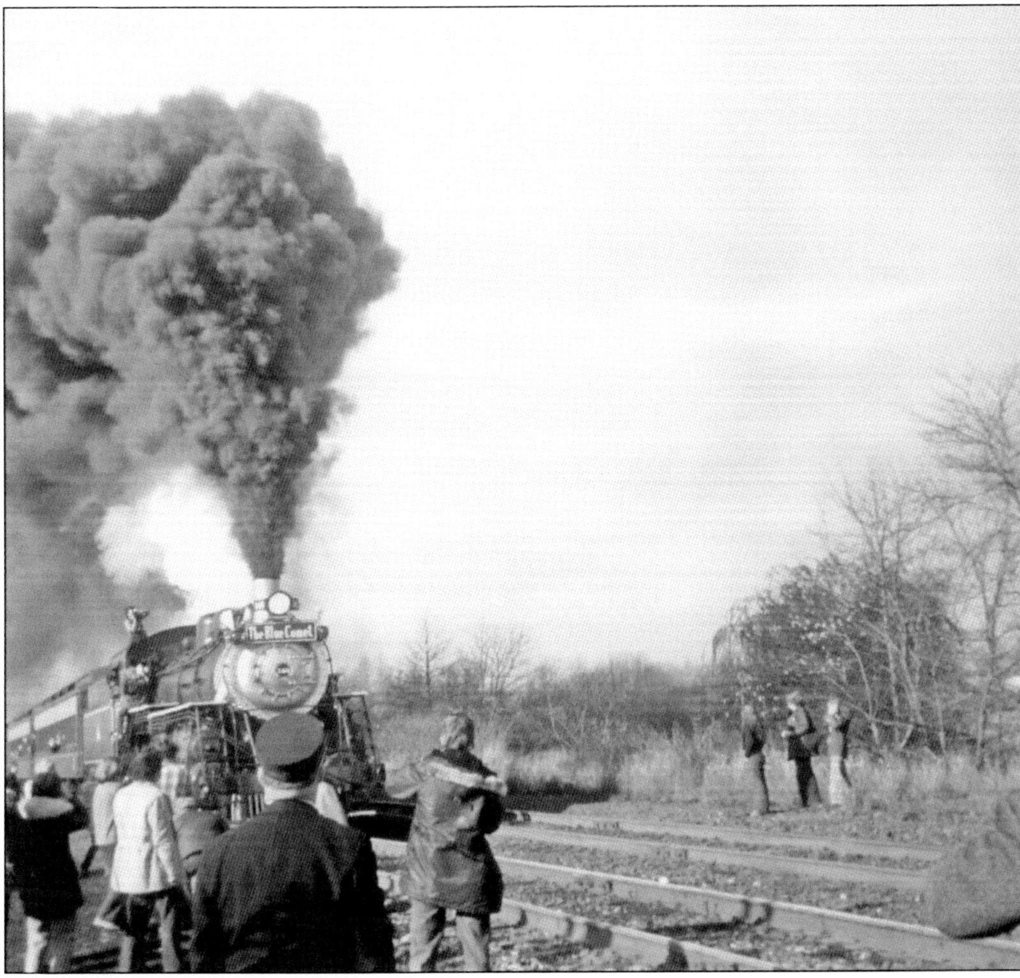

The Blue Comet Nostalgia Special, headed by the American Locomotive Company's Pacific (4-6-2) No. 148 engine, is seen at Monmouth Park, New Jersey, during a run-by with an NBC cameraman situated precariously on the running board of the steam engine. (Courtesy Joel Rosenbaum and Tom Gallo.)

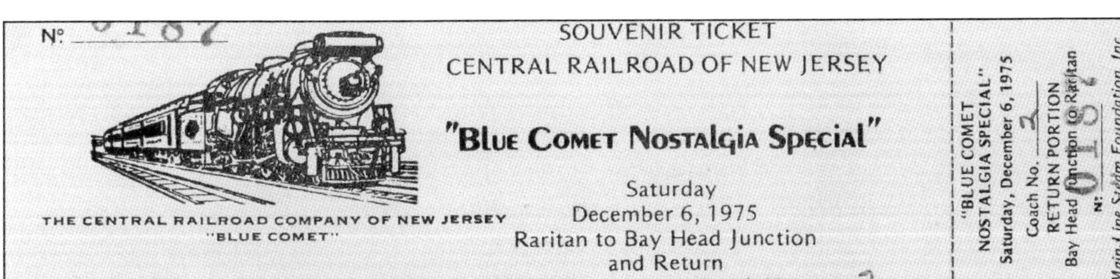

A souvenir ticket for the Blue Comet Nostalgia Special of the NJC is shown here. (Courtesy Joel Rosenbaum and Tom Gallo.)

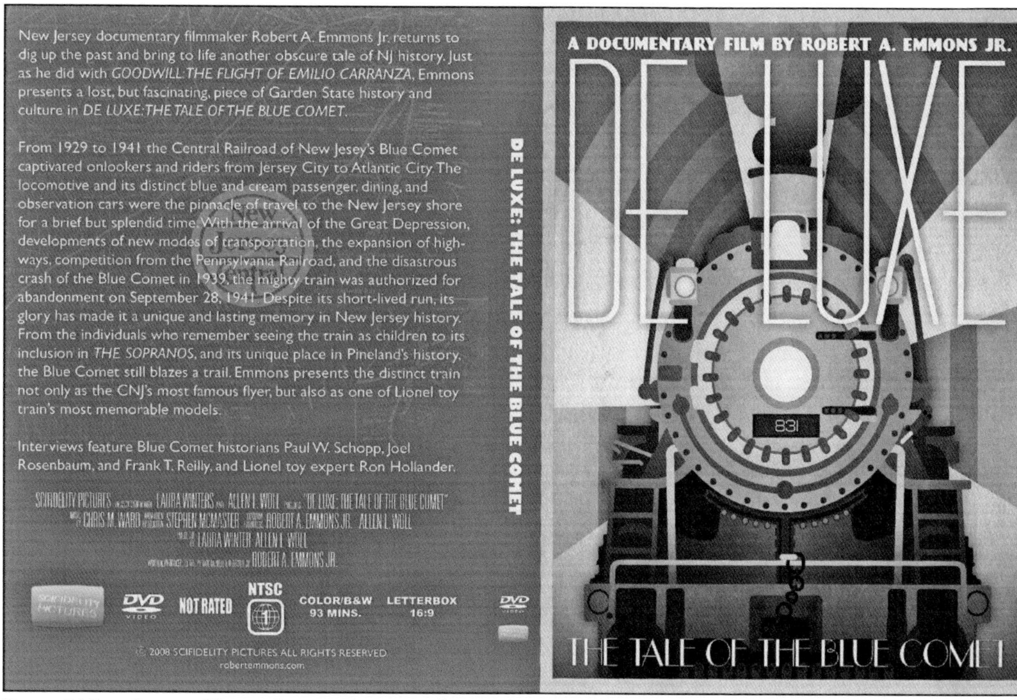

Famed New Jersey filmmaker and storyteller Robert A. Emmons Jr. spent a year and a half in the production of his documentary *De Luxe: The Tale of the Blue Comet*. The film was released in 2009 on DVD. Emmons's goal in producing this documentary was to tell the uniquely New Jersey story of the Blue Comet in the hope of preserving the memory of the iconic train for generations to come. (Author's collection.)

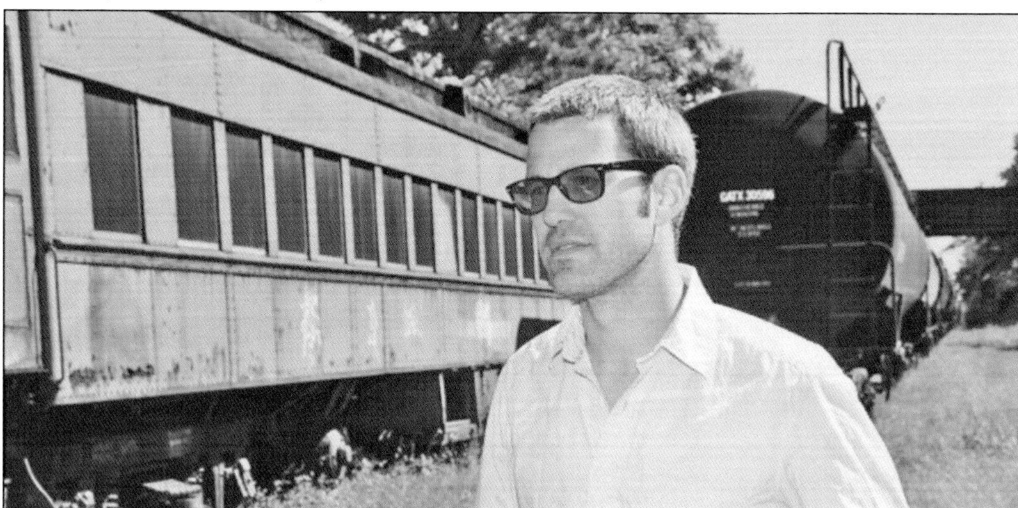

During the production of his documentary on the Blue Comet, Emmons visited a number of sites where some of the former NJC coaches are stored, including Winslow Junction. Besides gathering background material for his documentary, Emmons hoped to draw public awareness to these sites and the blight of the deteriorating passenger cars through these visits and through the film itself. His hope was to save them from being scrapped, despite the inordinate cost of rehabilitating them, so that they can be functional once again. (Courtesy the Press of Atlantic City.)

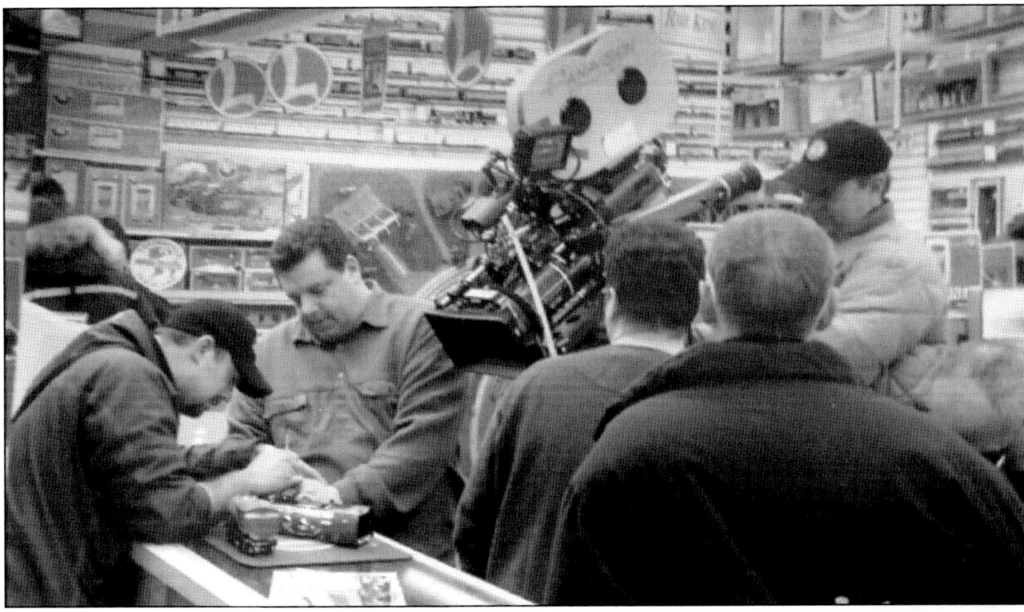

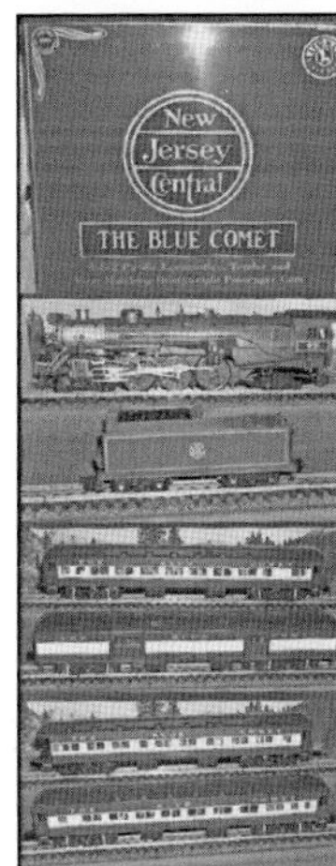

"The Blue Comet" was the 85th episode of the HBO series *The Sopranos* and the next-to-last episode of the final season, airing on June 3, 2007. In one scene, which takes place in a train store, mobster Bobby "Bacala" Baccalieri is brutally murdered by two hitmen as he examines and bargains for a Lionel Blue Comet train set. The scene was filmed on a frosty Valentine's Day, February 14, 2007, at Trainland located at 293 Sunrise Highway in Lynbrook, New York. This pre-production photograph was personally taken by Ken Bianco, one of the owners of Trainland. The actor Steven R. Schirrippa, who plays Bobby Baccalieri, is seen along with a Blue Comet train set in front of him on the counter. The specific Blue Comet train set is never identified in the show, but it was the Lionel Classics 6-51004 O-gauge set first produced in 1991. (Courtesy Ken Bianco.)

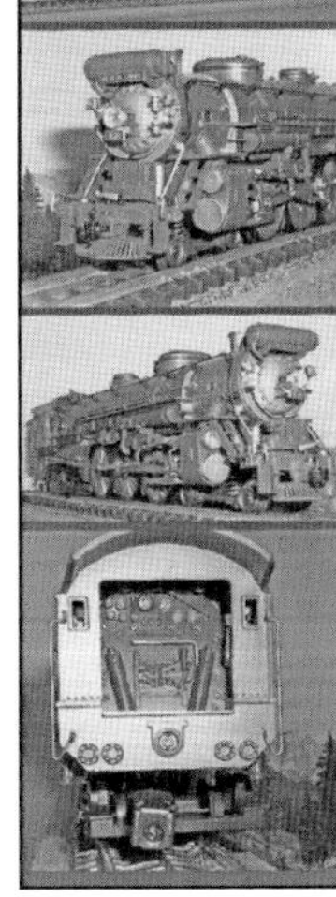

The O-gauge Lionel New Jersey Central Blue Comet Passenger set (No. 6-21787) was first produced in 2002. According to Lionel, its research staff pored over photographs and historical documents in order to produce as near a replica of the actual Blue Comet train as they possibly could, down to colors, floor plans, lettering styles, and the sound of the whistle on the locomotive itself. The set is led by the G-3 Pacific No. 831 and includes a tender, as well as the cars *Barnard*, *Faye*, *Westphal*, and *Tempel*. The wheel configuration of the locomotive and the baggage car *Barnard* did accurately reflect the actual configurations used on the original Blue Comet train. (Courtesy lionel.com.)

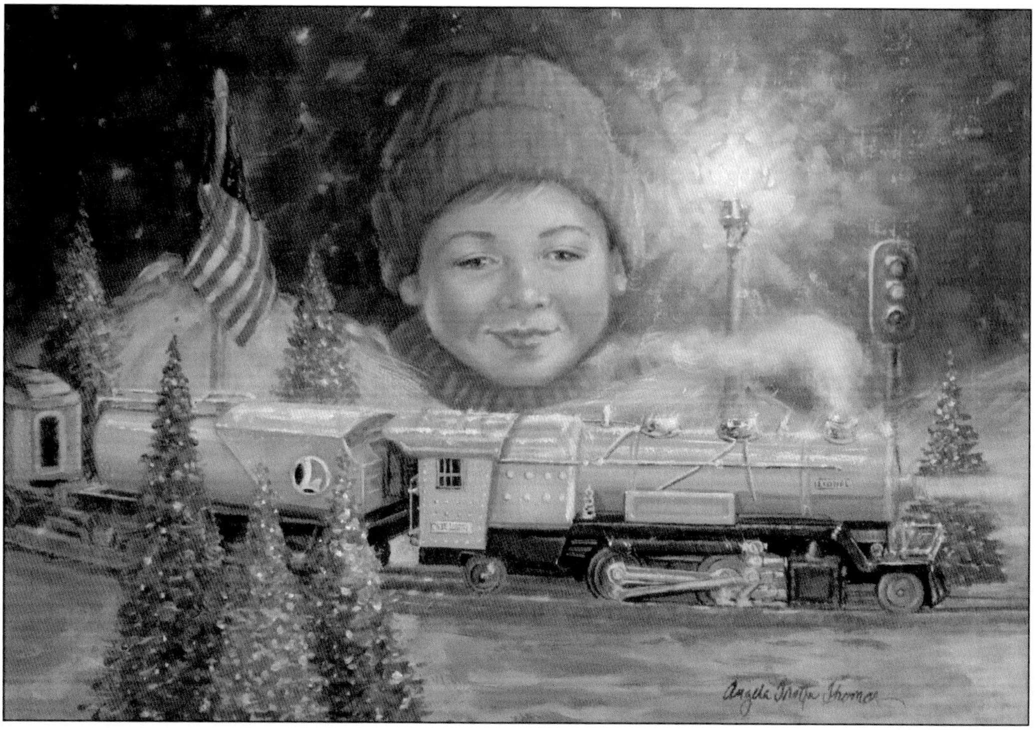

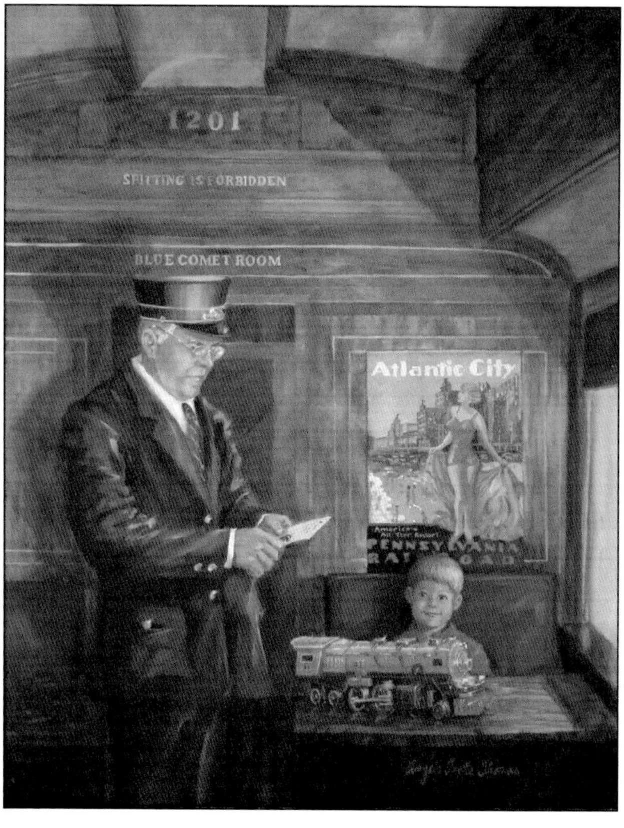

Angela Trotta Thomas has captured the enduring emotion and legacy of the Blue Comet in her depictions of Lionel trains and toys. "All I want for Christmas is a Blue Comet" (above) shows a child marveling over a Blue Comet train. "The Blue Comet Room" (left) shows a conductor punching the ticket of a young traveler who has brought his own Blue Comet locomotive along for the trip. More of Thomas's Blue Comet–themed artwork can be found at www.angelatrottathomas.com. (Both, courtesy Angela Trotta Thomas.)

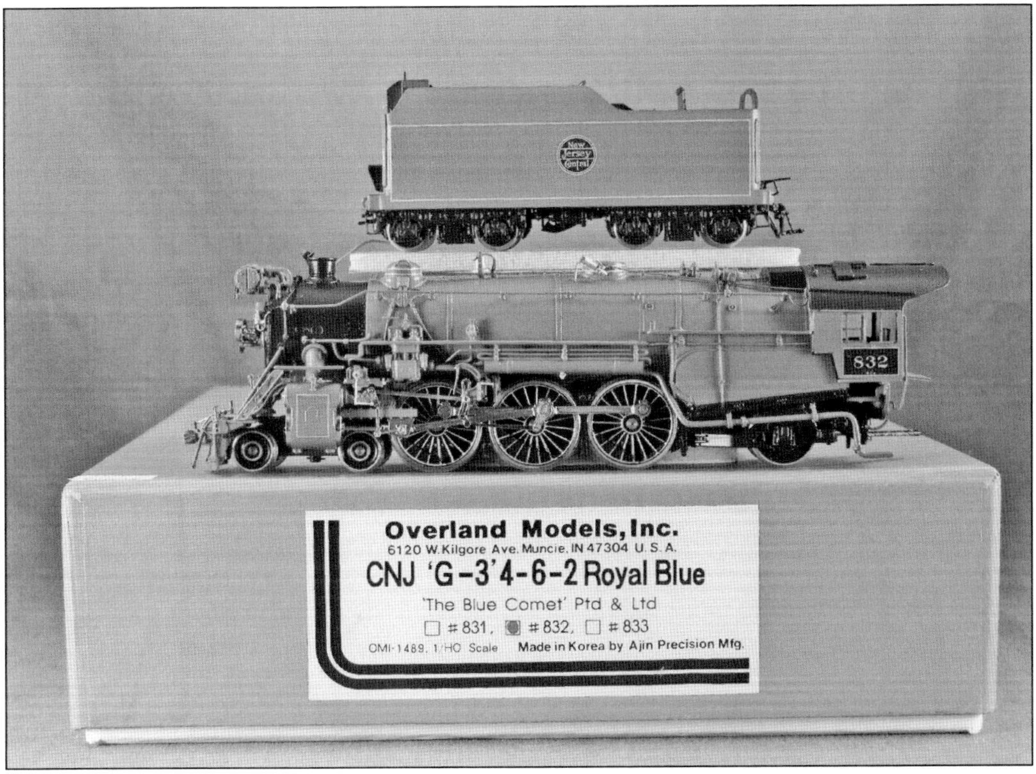

Overland Models Inc. made an HO-scale version limited edition of the Central of New Jersey's Blue Comet G-3 4-6-2 Pacific type locomotives Nos. 831–833. These models are very accurately detailed and are representative of the actual Blue Comet locomotives. They are painted cobalt blue with dark blue and black trim and gold stripping. The retail price for each locomotive is $1,495. (Author's collection.)

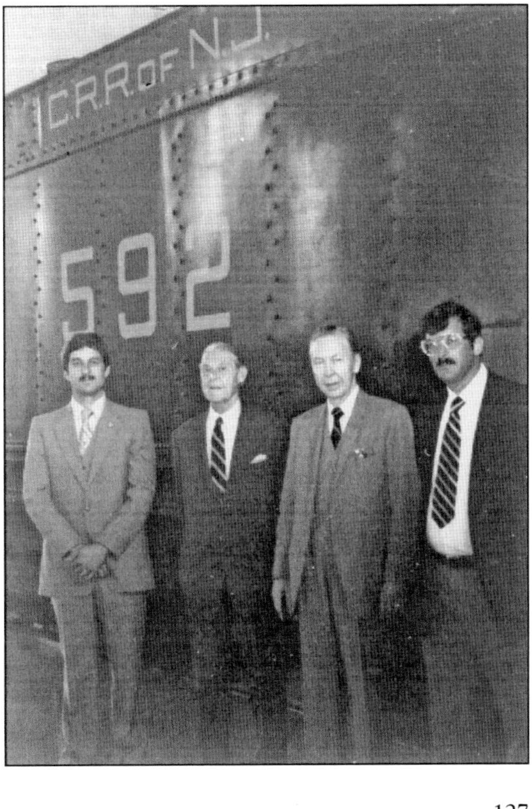

Joel Rosenbaum arranged to meet Howard E. Simpson at the Baltimore & Ohio Railroad Museum in Baltimore through E. Lewis Pardee. Pardee knew Simpson, who enthusiastically agreed to meet to discuss details of the very secretive creation of the Blue Comet. From left to right are Tom Gallo, Howard E. Simpson, E. Lewis Pardee, and Joel Rosenbaum with the NJC No. 592 in July 1983. Through the efforts of these gentlemen, the legacy of the Blue Comet will be sustained as long as its memory remains in the minds of children of all ages. (Courtesy Joel Rosenbaum and Tom Gallo.)